T0323673

GOVERNING COMPLEXITY

There has been a rapid expansion of academic interest and publications on polycentricity. In the contemporary world, nearly all governance situations are polycentric, but people are not necessarily used to thinking about them in this way. *Governing Complexity* provides an updated explanation of the concept of polycentric governance. The authors provide examples of the concept in contemporary settings, involving complex natural resource systems, as well as a critical evaluation of the utility of the concept. With contributions from leading scholars in the field, this book makes the case that polycentric governance arrangements exist and it is possible for polycentric arrangements to perform well, persist for long periods, and adapt. Whether they actually do function well, persist, or adapt depends on multiple factors that are reviewed and discussed, both theoretically and with examples from case studies.

Andreas Thiel is Professor of International Agricultural Policy and Environmental Governance at the Faculty of Organic Agricultural Sciences at Universität Kassel, Germany. He is an Affiliated Faculty Member of the Ostrom Workshop in Political Theory and Policy Analysis and Senior Fellow at the Centre for Global Cooperation Research at the University of Duisburg-Essen. His research addresses the institutional dimension of social-ecological systems with specific focus on governance in the water, agriculture and biodiversity sectors.

William A. Blomquist is Professor of Political Science at Indiana University-Purdue University, Indianapolis, and is an Affiliated Faculty Member of the Ostrom Workshop in Political Theory and Policy Analysis. He is the author of *Dividing the Waters* (1992), co-author of *Embracing Watershed Politics* (2008) and *Common Waters, Diverging Streams* (2004), and co-editor of *Integrated River Basin Management through Decentralization* (2007).

Dustin E. Garrick is Associate Professor of Environmental Management at the University of Oxford. His research on polycentric governance focuses on water allocation and markets as responses to climate change, urbanization and sustainable development challenges. His book, *Water Allocation in Rivers under Pressure* (2015), assesses the evolution and performance of water markets and polycentric river basin governance in Australia and the USA.

CAMBRIDGE STUDIES IN ECONOMICS, CHOICE, AND SOCIETY

Founding Editors

Timur Kuran, *Duke University*
Peter J. Boettke, *George Mason University*

This interdisciplinary series promotes original theoretical and empirical research as well as integrative syntheses involving links between individual choice, institutions, and social outcomes. Contributions are welcome from across the social sciences, particularly in the areas where economic analysis is joined with other disciplines such as comparative political economy, new institutional economics, and behavioural economics.

Books in the Series:

BENJAMIN POWELL *Out of Poverty: Sweatshops in the Global Economy*

MORRIS B. HOFFMAN *The Punisher's Brain: The Evolution of Judge and Jury*

PETER T. LEESON *Anarchy Unbound: Why Self-Governance Works Better Than You Think*

TERRY L. ANDERSON and GARY D. LIBECAP *Environmental Markets: A Property Rights Approach*

CASS R. SUNSTEIN *The Ethics of Influence: Government in the Age of Behavioral Science*

JARED RUBIN *Rulers, Religion, and Riches: Why the West Got Rich and the Middle East Did Not*

JEAN-PHILIPPE PLATTEAU *Islam Instrumentalized: Religion and Politics in Historical Perspective*

TAIZU ZHANG *The Laws and Economics of Confucianism: Kinship and Property in Preindustrial China and England*

ROGER KOPPL *Expert Failure*

MICHAEL C. MUNGER *Tomorrow 3.0: Transaction Costs and the Sharing Economy*

CAROLYN M. WARNER, RAMAZAN KILINÇ, CHRISTOPHER W. HALE, and ADAM B. COHEN *Generating Generosity in Catholicism and Islam: Beliefs, Institutions, and Public Goods Provision*

PAUL DRAGOS ALICIA *Public Entrepreneurship, Citizenship, and Self-Governance*

RANDALL G. HOLCOMBE *Political Capitalism: How Political Influence is Made and Maintained*

NOEL D. JOHNSON *Persecution and Toleration: The Long Road to Religious Freedom*

VERNON L. SMITH and BART J. WILSON *Humanomics: Moral Sentiments and the Wealth of Nations for the Twenty-First Century*

ANDREAS THIEL, WILLIAM A. BLOMQUIST and DUSTIN E. GARRICK *Governing Complexity: Analyzing and Applying Polycentricity*

Governing Complexity

Analyzing and Applying Polycentricity

Edited by

ANDREAS THIEL

University of Kassel

WILLIAM A. BLOMQUIST

Indiana University–Purdue University Indianapolis

DUSTIN E. GARRICK

University of Oxford

CAMBRIDGE
UNIVERSITY PRESS

University Printing House, Cambridge CB2 8BS, United Kingdom

One Liberty Plaza, 20th Floor, New York, NY 10006, USA

477 Williamstown Road, Port Melbourne, VIC 3207, Australia

314–321, 3rd Floor, Plot 3, Splendor Forum, Jasola District Centre, New Delhi – 110025, India

79 Anson Road, #06–04/06, Singapore 079906

Cambridge University Press is part of the University of Cambridge.

It furthers the University's mission by disseminating knowledge in the pursuit of education, learning, and research at the highest international levels of excellence.

www.cambridge.org
Information on this title: www.cambridge.org/9781108419987
DOI: 10.1017/9781108325721

© Cambridge University Press 2019

First published 2019

Printed in the United Kingdom by TJ International Ltd, Padstow Cornwall

A catalogue record for this publication is available from the British Library.

Library of Congress Cataloging-in-Publication Data
Names: Thiel, Andreas, editor. | Garrick, Dustin, editor. | Blomquist, William A. (William Andrew), 1957- editor.
Title: Governing complexity : analyzing and applying polycentricity / edited by Andreas Thiel, University of Kassel, Germany; Dustin E. Garrick, University of Oxford; William A. Blomquist, Indiana University-Purdue University, Indianapolis.
Description: Cambridge, United Kingdom ; New York, NY, USA : Cambridge University Press, [2019] | Series: Cambridge studies in economics, choice, and society | Includes bibliographical references and index.
Identifiers: LCCN 2019011354 | ISBN 9781108419987 (hardback : alk. paper) | ISBN 9781108411011 (pbk. : alk. paper)
Subjects: LCSH: Social structure. | Pluralism. | Complexity (Philosophy) | Organization.
Classification: LCC HM706 .G68 2019 | DDC 117–dc23
LC record available at https://lccn.loc.gov/2019011354

ISBN 978-1-108-41998-7 Hardback

Contents

Figures

Tables

Boxes

Contributors

Elizabeth Baldwin is an assistant professor at the University of Arizona. Her research focuses on environmental governance and natural resource policy, with a focus on understanding how institutions shape interactions between governmental and non-governmental actors.

William A. Blomquist is a professor of political science at Indiana University in Indianapolis (IUPUI). His research focuses primarily on institutional arrangements for governing and managing water resources.

Bryan Randolph Bruns is a consulting sociologist, specializing in improving stakeholder engagement in irrigation and water resources governance. His research and applied interests include facilitating polycentric problem-solving, developing groundwater governance institutions, and transforming social dilemmas.

Dustin E. Garrick is an associate professor of environmental management at the Smith School of Enterprise and the Environment, University of Oxford. His research examines environmental governance with a focus on the institutional underpinnings of natural resource allocation and markets.

Tanya Heikkila is a professor and Associate Dean at the University of Colorado Denver's School of Public Affairs. Her research focuses on collaboration and conflict in the governance of natural resources.

Tomas M. Koontz is a professor of environmental policy at the University of Washington Tacoma, USA. His research examines collaborative environmental governance, institutional analysis, and the science-policy nexus.

Mark Lutter is Founder and Executive Director of the Center for Innovative Governance Research, a nonprofit creating the ecosystem for charter cities. Prior to launching the Centre for Innovative Governance Research, he was Lead Economist for NeWAY Capital, an asset management firm which made early stage investments in charter cities. During graduate school, he consulted on several new city projects and special economic zones.

Anas Malik is professor of political science at Xavier University in Cincinnati, Ohio. His research interests are in collective action, self-governance, and polycentricity in Islamic and multicultural contexts, with an emphasis on Pakistan and the Middle East, as well as communities in North America.

Michael D. McGinnis is a professor of political science and Associate Dean for Social & Historical Sciences and Graduate Education in the College of Arts and Sciences at Indiana University. He has published research on arms races, game theory, international conflict, religion policy, institutional analysis and social-ecological frameworks. His current research focuses on US health policy.

Graham R. Marshall is a principal research fellow at the University of New England, Australia. His research focuses on understanding interactions between governance and collective action in environmental management, particularly from an institutional economics perspective.

Christine Moser is a PhD candidate at the Leuphana University in Lüneburg, Germany, the Centre for Sustainability Management. She studies hybrid transnational governance for sustainable biofuel production through the lens of polycentricity.

Edella Schlager is a professor in the School of Government and Public Policy at the University of Arizona. Her research centres on comparative institutional analyses of different forms of watershed governance with an emphasis on adaptation.

Nadine Jenny Shirin Schröder is a PhD candidate at Leuphana University Lüneburg, Research Group Governance, Participation and Sustainability. Her research covers polycentricity in the implementation of the EU Water Framework Directive in Germany, with a primary focus on very local governance structures and their influence on the implementation progress.

Mark Stephan is an associate professor of political science at Washington State University Vancouver, USA. His research focuses on environmental governance, climate change policies, and environmental justice in US states.

Vlad Tarko is Assistant Professor in the Department of Political Economy and Moral Science at the University of Arizona. He studies the institutional diversity of capitalist systems, and the application of polycentricity to more areas, such as the scientific community, the resilience of financial and banking systems, democratic politics, and the operation of regulatory agencies.

Andreas Thiel is a professor of international agricultural policy and environmental governance at the Faculty of Organic Agricultural Sciences, University of Kassel, Germany. His research focuses on the institutional analysis of natural resource and agri-environmental governance in the EU and Africa.

Sergio Villamayor-Tomás is Ramon y Cajal Research Fellow at the Environmental Science and Technology Institute (ICTA), Autonomous University of Barcelona. His research covers climate change adaptation, the water-energy nexus and agro-environmental schemes in the context of community-based natural resource management regimes.

Raúl Pacheco-Vega is an assistant professor in the Public Administration Division of the Centro de Investigacion y Docencia Economicas (CIDE). His research in comparative public policy focuses on the governance of unorthodox commons (wastewater, garbage and bottled water), polycentricity and institutional theories, and the human dimensions of public service delivery.

Acknowledgements

This book developed over a period of five years, with the helpful assistance and support of several people and organizations – and Skype. We are glad to have this opportunity to recognize and thank them.

Conferences organized and hosted by professional societies gave our group of authors and editors valuable opportunities to meet, spend time discussing and developing our interests in polycentricity, and make progress on this book. We thank the organizers of the 2015 biennial conference of the International Association for the Study of the Commons (IASC) in Edmonton, Canada; the 2015 biennial conference of the International Public Policy Association in Milan, Italy; and the 2017 biennial conference of the IASC in Utrecht, the Netherlands. Special thanks to Frank van Laerhoven at Utrecht University, who arranged a meeting space on the Utrecht campus the day before the 2017 IASC conference, so that our group could spend a valuable day together refining the structure and contents of the book, its parts and chapters.

We are grateful also to the Ostrom Workshop at Indiana University – Bloomington, especially the workshop's Director, Lee Alston, and Facilities and Technology Coordinator David Price. At the close of the 2014 Workshop on the Ostrom Workshop conference, a brainstorming session with several colleagues about polycentricity started us down this path. The Ostrom Workshop then donated space for a four-day meeting of our group in December 2015, when we were still working through whether to try to develop a book about polycentric governance and what it could and should contain. That time spent together was instrumental in incubating this project.

Along the way, colleagues, whose names do not appear as authors or editors in this book, have contributed helpful thoughts and advice to our project, by joining our discussions at some of the meetings mentioned above. We thank Troy Abel, Xavier Basurto, Keith Carlisle, Elizabeth Clark, Dan Cole, Maria Esposito, Rebecca Gruby, Claudia Pahl-Wostl, Insa Theesfeld, Jitske van Popering-Verkirk, and Antje Witting for the time and care they devoted to our conversations and our thinking at those various gatherings.

Funding support for some of our meetings and manuscript preparation came from the Einstein Foundation Berlin, the German Research Council DFG, and the Centre for Global Cooperation Research of Kate Hamburger Kolleg at the University of Duisburg-Essen, Germany.

As the book developed, we benefited greatly from the assistance of Arvind Lakshmi Sha and Hussam Hussein at the University of Kassel, who helped with formatting the manuscript and references. Joanna Broderick provided exceptionally skilful and timely indexing. We thank Peter Boettke and Timur Kuran for their encouragement and support in placing this book within the Cambridge Series on Economics, Choice, and Society. We are indebted to Karen Maloney, Rachel Blaifeder and Matt Sweeney at Cambridge University Press for seeing the project through from proposal to publication.

Of course, the essential contributors to this book have been our colleagues who have authored chapters and co-edited the parts of the book with us. All of them have been a joy to work with. This has been a polycentric project from its inception, and we are truly grateful for the collaboration.

Andreas Thiel, William A. Blomquist, and Dustin E. Garrick

Introduction

Andreas Thiel, William A. Blomquist, and Dustin E. Garrick

> [T]he new world is a polycentric, multi-nodal, multi-sector, multi-level, multi-actor, multi-logic, multi-media, multi-practice place characterized by complexity, dynamism, uncertainty and ambiguity in which a wide range of actors are engaged in public value creation and do so in shifting configurations.
>
> (Bryson et al. 2017: 641)

Almost all governing arrangements are polycentric, and all of us as citizens, scholars or policymakers can benefit from better understanding polycentricity. A community of authors has collaborated on this book, and on other related work,[1] to contribute towards meeting that need. *Governing Complexity* provides an updated explanation of the concept of polycentric governance, examples of it in contemporary settings involving complex natural resource systems, and critical evaluation of the utility of the concept.

PRESENT TIME AND MOTIVATION FOR THIS BOOK

Trends and transformations in social organization, economic activity, and the environment have led to the prevalence of and need for polycentric organizational structures. These trends sharpen the need to understand, characterize, and evaluate polycentricity. Examples include networked communications, globalization, and climate change. Rethinking social organization and reimagining human interaction with the environment have raised and focused attention on conceptions of complex adaptive

---

[1] See especially the special issue of the journal *Environmental Policy and Governance* – 28 (4) (2018) – edited by Tanya Heikkila, Sergio Villamayor-Tomás, and Dustin Garrick and with contributions from several other authors of chapters in this volume.

systems, diversity (biological and social), and resilience (Adger, Brown and Tompkins 2005). These social and economic, as well as intellectual changes, are generating a more polycentric world and growing interest in better means of comprehending it and working effectively in it.

On the governance front alone, consider the following: calls for 'global governance' to deal with interrelated phenomena that affect people everywhere and yet do not confine themselves to the boundaries of nation-states or even continents, such as climate change, migration and the global economy; the presence of both unconventional 'de facto states' asserting control over various territories and 'stateless elites' with influence that is not territorially bound (Myint 2012, 199). Non-governmental organizations and private philanthropists operate locally and globally as founders, funders, and implementers of a wide variety of initiatives, projects, and programmes. Last but far from least, our information, communication, and actions in these and all other realms are now mediated through an Internet that operates without a central authority, yet has become essential everywhere and connects people in networks from household to international levels (Axelrod and Cohen 2000, 30; Folke et al. 2005, 447).[2]

It is not enough to observe and comment upon these changes. We need ways to make sense of them – concepts and a language by which to organize and share our thoughts, theorize about causes and effects and the linkages among them, gather and analyze information about the world around us, build knowledge, and make it more nearly possible for people everywhere to cope at the very least and, far better, to develop and thrive in fruitful and sustainable relationships with each other and our environment. 'Until we have a language that is appropriate to an understanding of what it is that is constitutive of democratic societies, people cannot learn how to maintain such societies in a world of increasing complexity and interdependence' (E. Ostrom 1990, 261).

We have witnessed growing attention to polycentric governance. There has been a proliferation of recent publications discussing polycentricity, and applying and critiquing polycentric systems in various settings. A search on Google Scholar returns 1,900 articles and books mentioning 'polycentricity' or 'polycentric' published in the five-year period 1990–4, followed by 3,445 during 1995–9, and 20,298 in 2010–14. Between 6,700 and 7,600 such articles and books appeared each year in 2015, 2016, and 2017. Although 'polycentric' and 'polycentricity' have usages across many

---

[2] For a specific and thought-provoking application of polycentric governance to the Internet itself, see Shackelford (2014).

fields, those terms have appeared with increasing frequency in political economy, public administration, political science, urban studies, environmental studies, sociology, law, and more. In this context, we organized and created *Governing Complexity* with the intent and hope that it can play a useful role at this moment of heightened interest and relevance.

STATEMENT OF PURPOSE

There are many important prior publications about polycentricity and polycentric governance – see especially Ostrom, Tiebout, and Warren (1961), McGinnis (1999a, 1999b, 2000), E. Ostrom (2010), Aligica and Tarko (2012, 2013), Aligica (2014), Cole and McGinnis (2014), and Aligica and Sabetti (2014b). These works offer eloquent and, in some cases, empirically supported arguments in favour of polycentric governance. We strongly recommend any of these contributions to the reader who is looking for a persuasive case that polycentricity is a good idea.

There have been somewhat fewer treatments of the concept that take an analytic stance towards it – moving beyond the normative proposition that polycentric governance is automatically 'good' to examine how and how well polycentric governance arrangements and systems work . Especially in light of the current moment, there are vital analytic questions of what polycentricity is, how to identify and understand polycentric governance arrangements, and how to compare and assess them. *Governing Complexity* was conceived and designed for that purpose. Our goal is to articulate and demonstrate what polycentric governance is, how to recognize it, how to make use of it, and how to evaluate it. We wish to go beyond making a case *for* polycentricity, and engage instead in an analysis *of* polycentricity – one that addresses its perils as well as its possibilities.

Altogether, the book therefore sets out to explain and illustrate what we want to call 'thinking polycentrically'. The topics covered include what makes polycentric governance come into being, how it may perform in relation to a multitude of normative criteria, and why. Thinking polycentrically implies not accepting simple blueprints, but digging into details of institutional design and human behaviour. It means pursuing empirical work using research strategies and designs that warrant tentative recommendations, which themselves require deeper scrutiny when evaluated for diverse social-ecological contexts. In other words, thinking polycentrically accepts that multiple, contingent multi-scalar arrangements involving public, private, civil society or other actors are ubiquitous and may be suitable for particular purposes. Second, thinking polycentrically accepts the notion that governance arrangements result from context-specific factors and have context-specific effects. Third, thinking polycentrically accepts the possibility of iterative theory development following inductive–deductive research designs and multimethod research. Fourth, thinking polycentrically implies that virtues of particular governance arrangements usually come at a cost, whose distribution is negotiated in political processes and which require study and respect by analysts. Fifth, despite its extraordinary openness for extensions and its versatility in regard to objects of research, thinking polycentrically subscribes to a relatively clear set of assumptions concerning actors, their capacities and orientations and their relation to the role of institutions.

In this work, we build upon and identify with 'the Bloomington School of Political Economy' founded by and associated with Elinor and Vincent Ostrom, and readers will find them cited and quoted throughout this book. Polycentricity was a concept that was common and fundamental to Vincent Ostrom's work on public administration and the problems of democratic government, and to Elinor Ostrom's work on collective action and the performance of institutions. In pursuing research on polycentric governance, we clearly draw upon the Ostroms' work and the conceptual tools of the Bloomington school, while also working to advance this thinking and analysis in a rapidly changing world.

By making the foundational elements of polycentricity explicit, and by illustrating the way polycentric governance changes and operates in concrete cases, we want to describe the challenges that lie ahead of institutional scholars in engaging with this research agenda. We want to make headway regarding how institutional analysis can confront the growth of research on self-organization and multi-scalar systems, in order to encourage further and even more fruitful research on polycentric governance. Thus, even as we acknowledge and honour their intellectual legacy, *Governing Complexity* is not a homage to the Ostroms. Many well-deserved tributes to them and their scholarly impact exist, including Aligica and Sabetti (2014a), Sabetti, Allen, and Sproule-Jones (2009), Sabetti and Castiglione (2017), Sproule-Jones et al. (2008), and Tarko (2017a), as well as others who did not know them. Throughout the book, we engage with the Ostroms' work but also that of many other scholars. We hope that our efforts bring renewed attention to the Ostroms' contributions, but also highlight new scholarship on polycentric governance and encourage further research and practice.

SELECTIVE REVIEW OF RECENT WORK REFERRING TO POLYCENTRIC GOVERNANCE

Polycentricity has been used either explicitly or implicitly in many prior studies. We have already highlighted that in recent years, an increasing number of scholars has used the concept of polycentric governance. However, in many cases, this implied a metaphorical use of the concept. In these kinds of publications, an introduction references polycentric governance – broadly understood as diversity of governance arrangements and multitude of actors involved – as a description of the context in which research took place (see, Abe et al. 2016). Such use of the concept is certainly legitimate; we have already noted that the concept has a multidisciplinary genealogy, but for the purposes of this book, we want to draw attention mainly to authors whose work has contributed substantially to our thinking about polycentric governance from empirical, conceptual, or methodological perspectives.

We cannot cover comprehensively anything near to all of the relevant publications that have appeared in recent years, given the incredible dynamism of the field and the remarkable versatility of the concept and its theorization. Indeed, several contributions to the literature that do not even mention the term polycentric governance in their manuscripts would also need to be included in such a review. This includes work that focuses on institutions and that engages in iterative, inductive–deductive theory development, with strong reference to the alluded assumptions underlying the work of the Bloomington School of Political Economy. Additional work on the study of public and political economy, industrial organization and environmental, behavioural, and New Institutional Economics would need to be included as well. Therefore, in what follows we selectively review what we considered to be some of the most instructive recent contributions that have referred explicitly to polycentric governance, its understanding or research.

First, an important part of the literature tends to perceive polycentric governance as a solution to a multitude of governance failures and challenges. Claims are made about the positive role of polycentric governance for adaptive management, resilience and robustness (Anderies, Janssen, and E. Ostrom 2004; Garmestani and Benson 2013; Gupta et al. 2010; Pahl-Wostl 2015), or its capacities to keep opportunistic behaviour in check (Nagendra and Ostrom 2012). Elinor Ostrom became more explicit about the virtues of polycentric governance when she discussed climate change mitigation. She stated that polycentric governance 'tend[s] to enhance innovation, learning, adaptation, trustworthiness, levels of cooperation of participants and the achievement of more effective, equitable, and sustainable outcomes at multiple scales. . .' (E. Ostrom 2010, 511; see also Rayner and Jordan 2013; Sovacool 2011). It helps to overcome opportunistic behaviour, enhances face-to-face communication, and matching of ecosystem, institutional, and social scales. Spreng and colleagues develop similarly normative work on polycentric climate change insurance (Spreng, Sovacool and Spreng 2016).

Second, we have learned from recent work on polycentric governance that has brought the concept into new empirical fields and more scales of analysis. Consonant with the origins of Bloomington School work on polycentricity, research on water governance has remained productive and prominent (cf. Garrick 2015; Koontz 2004; Marshall 2005; Schlager and Blomquist 2008; Thiel 2012). Most remarkable in this regard is work on analysing the determinants of successful coordination in polycentric governance (Knieper and Pahl-Wostl 2016), on collaborative governance (Koontz 2004; Lubell and McCoy 2010), on the role of transaction costs in water governance (Challen 2000; Garrick et al. 2013), on institutional change and performance of polycentric water governance (Baldwin et al. 2016; Boelens, Hoogesteger, and Baud 2015; Kerr 2007b; McCord et al. 2016; Newig, Schulz, and Jager 2016; Thiel 2014; Woodhouse and Muller 2017), and the comprehensive review of water governance provided by Pahl-Wostl (2015). Also prominent among these recent contributions were the works of Boelens and colleagues (Boelens, Hoogesteger and Baud 2015) and da Silveira and Richards (2013), who have raised questions about the way polycentric governance is embedded, and Buytaert and colleagues (2016) who specifically address the polycentric organization of monitoring activities in water management. From this review, it emerges that many decades of work on polycentric water governance naturally lead us to an increasingly differentiated understanding of processes and factors relating to polycentric governance, something we would like to promote in other fields.

The early Bloomington School work on polycentricity focused also on metropolitan governance, although this topic has received less attention in recent decades compared with the amount of attention to water resources (for exceptions, see Giffinger and Suitner 2014; Oakerson and Parks 2011; Parks and Oakerson 2000). Another traditional field of application on which insightful work is carried out addresses forestry, where similar advances can be observed (Andersson and E. Ostrom 2008; Nagendra and E. Ostrom 2012).

Recently, work on polycentric governance inspired by the Bloomington perspective has addressed new fields. Work on environmental issues at the global or regional scales is noteworthy, e.g. research on marine and marine protected area governance (Ban et al. 2011; Galaz et al. 2012; Gruby and Basurto 2014; Kerber and Heide 2017). A large field of application for empirical scrutiny of the concept and theory of polycentric governance has emerged in regard to climate change. Some of this work praises the benefits of polycentric governance and laments climate change governance as we can observe it (Cole 2015). Others take a more analytical stance (Abbott 2012; Dorsch and Flachsland 2017; Jordan and Huitema 2014). The extension of research on polycentric governance to this field nicely shows the versatility and inspirational, but also empirical value that this perspective holds.

Most remarkable in this context is the recently published edited volume by Jordan and colleagues (Jordan et al. 2018). It examines whether climate governance is polycentric, or becoming more polycentric, how it has been operating and what its implications have been. In an insightful first chapter, the authors derive a set of propositions about polycentric govern-ance that they examine throughout the book. Similar to the understandings conveyed in *Governing Complexity*, they show great sensitivity to the descriptive, explanatory and normative dimensions of writings on poly-centric governance. There can be no doubt that this application of poly-centricity thinking is ground-breaking, not only in relation to our understanding of climate change, but also in relation to our understanding of polycentric governance in general, across multiple scales including the global. Nonetheless, a more stringent identification of the object of research may help going beyond this book in building our understanding and theory of polycentric governance. Further, much needs to be resolved, particularly with regard to assessing the performance of polycentric gov-ernance, as Jordan and colleagues also indicate, and we further elaborate.

Of comparable significance with the work of Jordan and colleagues is the simultaneous appearance of a special issue of the journal *Environmental Policy and Governance* devoted to empirical analyses of polycentric gov-ernance arrangements. The contributions to that issue make advancements in analytic approaches, methodological techniques, and empirical applica-tions in the study of polycentric governance. Readers will note a consider-able degree of overlap with this book, not only in the roster of contributors but in the emphasis on careful and empirically grounded consideration of the development, configuration, and effects of polycentric governance arrangements across a variety of settings.

We found additional fields of application, some of which very well illustrate fruitfulness of the concept. For example, Marshall and colleagues address co-management of invasive species (Marshall et al. 2016), Salter and Tarko address the banking sector from a polycentric governance perspective (Salter and Tarko 2017) and Liebermann addresses infectious disease governance (Lieberman 2011).

Third, understanding of polycentric governance has been deepened through recent development of a set of frameworks, many of which we also mention and discuss throughout this book. Some focus on the conceptualization of interdependence of collective actors (Feiock 2013; Lubell 2013; Lubell, Henry, and McCoy 2010; McGinnis 2011b; Thiel and Moser 2018). Others address the role that polycentric governance can play in social-ecological systems governance (Biggs, Schlüter, and Schoon 2015; Folke et al. 2005), or what conditions promote polycentric governance (DeCaro et al. 2017; Koontz et al. 2015). Further, some studies have zeroed in on particular relations within polycentric governance arrangements. For example, Andersson and Ostrom (2008) analyzed vertical interlinkages between actors through the attributes of frequency of interaction between local resource users and local governments, financial transfers between central and local governments, and upward political pressure for explaining commitments by local actors to invest in the governance of natural resources. Heikkila and colleagues (2011) address the role of specific types of cross-scale or cross-level linkages between two or more actors in transboundary river management. Marshall (2009) couches his analysis of conservation within the notion of polycentricity when he analyzes relations between communities of farmers and public agencies at lower levels. Basurto (2013) studies how multi-level institutional linkages (for example employment, membership, or different kinds of partnership) affect processes of local institutional change while Galaz and colleagues (2012) (see also Vousden 2016) specifically conceptualize polycentric governance in the international realm.

Fourth, beyond these empirical and conceptual contributions, a number of scholars have specifically advanced methods for the analysis of polycentric governance. The benchmark overview of the tools available and way to combine them has no doubt been provided by Poteete et al. (2010). A particular advance that makes explicit reference to the analysis of polycentric governance is social network analysis. It has been applied to polycentric governance in different fields and related to the way types of relations and configurations shape governance processes (Berardo and Scholz 2010; Smaldino and Lubell 2011) – see also Chapter 11. The use of exponential random graphic methods for network analysis has been an important contribution as well (see especially Berardo and Lubell 2016). Chaffin and colleagues (2016) have developed another method for identifying and assessing adaptive governance networks of organizations, which they call institutional Social Network Analysis. Heikkila and Weible (2018) review the application of semi-automated methods to the study of polycentric governance. Standing out in relation to these new tools of analysis of polycentric systems are methods that connect what we call social-problem characteristics and institutions in the form of legal rules or relations connecting actors. The corresponding approach, Social-Ecological Network Analysis (SENA) is a way to analyze the spatial fit of institutions (Folke et al. 2007) and has provided impressive illustrations of relational dimensions of social-ecological systems governance (Sayles and Baggio 2017).

Among others, these recent contributions have inspired and informed the work on polycentric governance by the authors in this book. Throughout *Governing Complexity,* we aim to deepen, apply, and extend the understanding of polycentric governance that others have pioneered and developed.

NATURAL RESOURCES – ESPECIALLY WATER – AS A SETTING FOR ANALYSING POLYCENTRIC GOVERNANCE

We noted that a great deal of prior work on polycentric governance has employed the concept in relation to the governance and management of water resources. This book follows that pattern. To illustrate the analysis of polycentric governance in actual settings, we have chosen to ground our analysis and arguments in examples and findings concerning natural resource management, most often with water resource examples. In addition to the fact that many of our authors have experience in water-resources research, our reliance on water and other natural resource examples derives from our sense as editors that having some commonalities among the cases presented in the book is beneficial to the reader. As should be clear from the prior discussion, however, the concept of polycentric governance is not limited to this context and can be applied in myriad other ways.

Studies of natural resource governance have been important to the development and application of theorizing about polycentric governance. Research on natural resources and the environment – including common-pool resources – from the 1960s brought further awareness of the importance of scale and cross-scale linkages (Berkes 2006). Attention to the diversity of scales of common-pool resources highlights the mismatch between those resources and most established jurisdictions for public decision-making. Thus the matter of scale directly ties to the question of governance – how collective decisions are made regarding the use and protection of resources, and how should they be made, when resource boundaries typically do not align with traditional jurisdictional boundaries.

Furthermore, current thinking about natural resource management emphasizes adaptive management. In practice, adaptive management often requires co-management, which 'relies on the collaboration of a diverse set of stakeholders, operating at different levels, often through networks from local users to municipalities, to regional and national organizations, and also to international bodies' (Folke C. et al. 2005, 448). Through this focus, we are to a certain extent putting to the test the broader observation made by Tun Myint (2012: 219):

> The theory of polycentricity has robust power to explaining transforming phenomena of world politics, especially in the area of environmental governance where a state-centric approach alone will not provide solutions to problems associated with human-environment interactions. In environmental governance, we are dealing with multiple actors and their sources of power, legitimacy and influence in addition to the dynamics of ecosystems.

Natural resource governance, involving multiple decision-centres engaged in adaptive co-management, brings the concept of polycentricity squarely into relevance.

PREVIEW

Polycentricity is a phenomenon to be identified and studied in the social world, but it is also a way of thinking about the social world – an analytical lens through which situations involving multiple organizations may be perceived and understood. Part I addresses polycentricity as a concept that people use to identify and understand phenomena and as a lens for viewing the social world; this part grounds the idea of polycentric governance in terms of its intellectual development, its central features and underlying concepts, and how it may be understood and evaluated. Our approach to understanding polycentric governance is based upon institutional analysis, with an emphasis on how people develop and use institutional arrangements to try to order their interactions with one another and address social problems. Throughout Part I, the authors focus on how and why people create multiple decision-centres – a defining characteristic of polycentric governance – and how those centres interact and evolve in relation to the social-problem context and other aspects of the broader institutional environment.

In Chapter 1, Mark Stephan, Graham Marshall, and Michael McGinnis review early uses of the idea of polycentricity by Polanyi (1951) and Ostrom,

Tiebout, and Warren (1961). In their analysis of the delivery of public services in metropolitan areas, Ostrom, Tiebout, and Warren introduced polycentricity as a way of thinking about governing complexity. From there, Stephan, Marshall, and McGinnis trace the development of theorizing about polycentric governance and its importance to the Ostroms' research programme and the emergence of the Bloomington School. They offer and discuss definitions of governance, and of polycentric governance arrangements and polycentric governance systems (the latter being a subset of the former). The chapter identifies the potential bases of order in polycentric arrangements, connects polycentric governance with the provision and production of collective goods, and distinguishes polycentric governance from monocentric governance and unitary political systems. Chapter 1 introduces several concepts and categories for the analysis of polycentric governance arrangements: central and common aspects of polycentric governance, and a set of dimensions along which polycentric governance arrangements can be studied, differentiated, and assessed.

William Blomquist and Nadine Schröeder continue the discussion of polycentric governance in Chapter 2. Their chapter presents an inquiry-based approach to identifying and comprehending polycentric governance arrangements. Chapter 2 imagines an unspecified analyst – a citizen, a student, a scholar – who encounters a situation where multiple decision-centres are present and active in relation to some collective good or resource. As a threshold matter, how could the analyst determine whether he or she is observing some kind of polycentric governance arrangement or just an incoherent jumble, and if it does appear to be a case of polycentric governance, how could the analyst develop an understanding of its structure and operation? The chapter emphasizes our overall perspective in this book that polycentric governance arrangements are inherently neither good nor bad; rather, the goal of inquiry is to gain a degree of understanding of a polycentric governance structure at a given time and place that would be sufficient to allow for evaluation of its operation and effects. Such a context-dependent assessment involves several concepts that recur throughout the book such as scale, institutional diversity, autonomy, and coordination.

In Chapter 3, Andreas Thiel and Christine Moser take a deeper look at three of those essential foundational concepts. First, the chapter focuses on how polycentric governance arrangements operate within and are shaped by an overarching set of rules – a constitutional context that establishes the framework within which people create and alter institutions. Second, the chapter examines the ways in which perceived similarities and differences in the characteristics of social problems affect the governing structures and policy approaches that people develop and implement. Third, Chapter 3 explores how heterogeneity of communities influence the choices people make when organizing governance arrangements. Discussions of water governance institutions in Germany and Spain, and the organization of biomass processing, provide points of comparison and illustration for these three foundational concepts and their relationships to polycentric governance arrangements. Throughout the chapter, Thiel and Moser direct the reader's attention to the ways in which knowledge is still developing about these concepts and relationships, with a view towards promising areas for further research.

Change in polycentric governance arrangements is a recurring theme in this book, making it essential to theorize about how institutional change takes place. Chapter 4 by Andreas Thiel, Raúl Pacheco-Vega, and Elizabeth Baldwin brings important elements of the literature on institutional change to bear upon the dynamics of polycentric governance. Sources of institutional change in polycentric arrangements may be external to the arrangements themselves – changes in the overarching set of rules within which the centres operate and interact, economic or environmental shocks, etc. Change may also (and often does) come from within. Such endogenous drivers of change include alterations in people's perceptions of problems and changes in people's preferences and information that result from learning. Changes may originate within one of the centres in a polycentric arrangement and then through interactions initiate ripple effects across the other centres. The authors emphasize the influence of path dependence in any analysis of institutional change, since what happens at one time will affect perceptions of what is feasible, preferable, or undesirable at subsequent moments – therefore the trajectory of change in any polycentric governance arrangement will be shaped by prior occurrences. One trigger for changes can be perceptions of performance. Individuals may initiate efforts to alter the structure or operation of a centre, or a relationship among centres, in the hope of attaining better outcomes. Assessing the performance of complex institutional structures always raises questions of spatial and temporal scale, i.e. over what range of space and time is performance to be assessed, and how does the choice of scale affect performance perceptions and therefore feed back into the prospects and processes of change.

After Part I has laid the groundwork for understanding what we see as crucial dimensions of polycentric governance and what determines its shape, performance and change, Part II addresses what one could call the operation of polycentric governance, i.e. the specific interactions of competition, cooperation, conflict and conflict resolution and their effects. These interactions among centres are present in any polycentric situation, but particular cases help to highlight how they occur and with what effects. Part II presents, compares, and analyses empirical cases of natural resource governance and management as instances of polycentric governance. A concluding chapter of the section draws together those lessons for the understanding of polycentricity in action and how we can understand and evaluate its performance.

From the perspective of polycentric governance, cooperation, competition, and conflict and conflict resolution are mechanisms through which actors 'take each other into account', i.e. they intendedly or not generate and share information which leads to mutual adaptation. Therefore, in certain ways, the idea is that to different degrees these interactions influence the patterns of order and coordination among decision-making centres. Rather than simply present those cases serially and analyse them one by one, the authors of the chapters in Part II employ an organizing framework for analysing cooperation, competition, and conflict and its resolution across those cases. In each case, the governance arrangements shape the authority, information, resources, and incentives available to the participants. Differences across the cases provide an opportunity for comparative analysis of how the governance arrangements fostered or frustrated cooperation, competition, and conflict and its resolution by affecting the presence and distribution of authority, information, resources, and incentives.

In Chapter 5, Tomas Koontz addresses cooperation, and presents a case of collaborative water management in the Puget Sound, Northwestern USA. Here, the state legislature, in a context of multiple, overlapping jurisdictions addressing activities in the Puget Sound, created an entity, the Puget Sound Partnership, that had the authority to (a) found and finance Local Implementation Organizations that brought multiple interdependent entities together and (b) to steer a competitive bidding process for financial resources to plan and implement particular local collaborative action for which Local Implementation Organizations were to apply. However, neither the Partnership, nor any other actor was able to control affairs in the area in a way that it could command others in a hierarchical manner. Thus, polycentric provisioning and production of goods was a matter of necessity. Cooperation in this polycentric setting showed elevated transaction costs, but also increased adaptability, at least in relation to some kinds of problems. Nonetheless, the relatively loose way in which the government steered watershed management in the kind of collaborative case illustrated runs risks of lacking accountability.

Chapter 6, by Tanya Heikkila, addresses conflict and conflict resolution illustrated in the cases of hydraulic fracturing and shale development in New York State and Colorado. In both cases a multitude of actors at different jurisdictional levels hold authority over aspects of oil and gas development, land use, and environmental protection. Nonetheless, in Colorado two state-level authorities hold primary authority over licences; their counterparts are local authorities and NGOs, citizens and industry. Conflict predominantly addresses who holds authority over licensing shale gas development, no doubt it is an expression of diverging interests of actors at different levels in polycentric governance of hydraulic fracturing and shale gas development. In New York, governance of hydraulic fracturing and shale gas development is organized in similar ways as in Colorado. Nonetheless, a legally required review process led to the identification of health concerns that could additionally be taken up by local authorities that hold a constitutionally stronger position than in Colorado. Different leverage of local authorities in New York and Colorado was important for the policy outcomes that have emerged in those two states. Conflict resolution in both states has been relatively ineffective and inefficient, and accountability and representativeness have been compromised in certain respects by scalar stratification of authority. Nevertheless, some degree of adaptability is observed in both cases, but it has entailed, and to some extent been limited by, the expense of resources for creating venues and information.

Dustin Garrick and Sergio Villamayor-Tomás in Chapter 7 address competition among public authorities. It illustrates the interaction through a comparative case study of water allocation in the Ebro Basin in Spain and in the Columbia Basin in the United States of America. In Spain, redistribution of water among users and among water-use districts is analysed. In contrast, in the USA, competition on the one hand arises between water users and environmental conservation interests and on the other it arises in-between the organizations that implement projects to free water for allocation to environmental conservation purposes. In both cases, the distribution of authority is stratified across scales and creates tensions between local water users on the one hand and higher-level institutions to distribute water resources on the other.

In Chapter 8, the authors of Part II distil the comparison of cases from Chapters 5–7 into succinct assessments using multiple evaluation criteria that cover aspects of process as well as outcomes. The comparison highlights an important point: differences among polycentric governance arrangements do not make them more polycentric or less, but they do affect the ways in which those governance arrangements emerge, operate, and change, and the effects they have over time. Those processes and effects are also themes that run through Chapters 2–4.

The chapters in Part III address several dimensions of how polycentric governance arrangements work and may change over time. Polycentricity does not emerge in a void. Although sometimes neglected in current treatments of governance of this and other types, it needs to be viewed in the context of particular constitutional and metaconstitutional constellations. Chapters 9 and 10 concentrate on the reciprocal relationships between polycentric governance and certain cultural, constitutional, and legal foundations in communities. Chapter 11 more explicitly addresses the assessment of the performance of polycentric governance arrangements, and the prospects and practice of deliberate reform aimed at improving the performance of polycentric governance.

Experience in polycentric governance settings – including experience in the formation and reform of decision-centres and the relationships among them – may provide opportunities for learning and thus for the acquisition and development of skills of institutional artisanship and critique. With all of its complexity and diversity, polycentric governance may reinforce a social environment within which people become more accustomed to fashioning and refashioning governance arrangements. This is a central theme presented and discussed by Graham Marshall and Anas Malik in Chapter 9 as they consider the relationship between polycentric governance and the effective practice of citizenship. Polycentric governance arrangements can build upon a cultural and constitutional foundation that encourages individuals and communities to try to solve problems through institutional creation and reform. Conversely, such institutional experimentation may be discouraged by the cultural and constitutional context. At the same time, experience with polycentric governance can feed back into and alter that context. Marshall and Malik review Australia's attempted devolution of land and water protection to local communities, and discuss how the relative extent of polycentric practice and experience affected outcomes of that policy experiment.

In a related vein, in Chapter 10 Tarko, Schlager, and Lutter explore potential relationships between polycentric governance, limits on power, and the maintenance of the rule of law as an aspect of the overarching rules within which polycentric arrangements may operate. The legal and cultural environment may encourage, discourage, or simply allow the development of polycentric approaches to governance, as they illustrate with discussions of the emergence of institutional arrangements for protecting drinking-water quality in New York and the development of post-conflict political institutions in Somaliland and Puntland. Polycentric governance may promote contestation (and even conflict) among decision-centres in ways that facilitate the representation and articulation of differing interests, as well as agreements among centres for how to cooperate on common goals. Through these processes, people may develop and reinforce methods for the necessary exercise of governing power, while guarding against excesses that stifle dissenting voices or exacerbate ethnic, religious, or other dimensions of social difference. Whether and how those efforts work out in practice is contingent on numerous factors.

Scholars and students are not the only persons who may benefit from a fuller understanding of polycentric governance and how it works, particularly in regard to the sustainable use of natural resources. Bryan Bruns, in Chapter 11, draws lessons and offers advice, based on the theory and research described in the earlier chapters, for those engaged in directing natural resource management programmes, consulting in natural resource settings around the world, and reforming resource management in order to improve performance and sustainability. Bruns speaks directly of the challenges to the practice of polycentric governance and the opportunities for change and improvement. His chapter focuses on when and how governance outcomes may be improved in varied actual settings. He introduces 'principles for polycentric governance practice' as a basis from which actual polycentric governance arrangements may be examined with a view towards reform. Bruns provides recommendations for analysing the workings of polycentric arrangements through social network analysis, participatory rapid appraisal, and other techniques. The analytic approach is intended for practical purposes such as enhancing the performance of polycentric arrangements through the application of methods for inclusion, social learning, and shared power. He brings the discussion back to institutional artisanship – people's inherent and learned capabilities for engaging with one another for collaboration in addressing problems and pursuing opportunities – and offers advice for how to make those efforts more fruitful and sustainable.

Throughout the book, readers will find a combination of extended case studies (in some cases, chapter-length treatments as in Chapters 5–7), and shorter examples or vignettes, set apart in boxes. Our purpose has been to incorporate a wide variety of illustrations of polycentric governance arrangements while still leaving room for conceptual and theoretical discussion and development in most of the chapters.

Before we turn to Part I, we note that despite the variety of polycentric governance arrangements, the many factors that shape and influence them, and their myriad effects, the effort to understand, explain, and assess them is worthwhile. We have not shied away from defining polycentric governance and identifying its core attributes and common features, nor from applying and evaluating its effects in practice. While there is no ideal or defining type of polycentric governance, at a minimum 'polycentric connotes multiple centres of decision-making which are de jure independent or de facto autonomous of one another' (Chapter 1). Beyond that minimum, a host of considerations influence the multitude of polycentric arrangements in actual governance situations. Let's begin.

PART I

Foundations for Understanding and Researching
Polycentric Governance

Mark Stephan and William A. Blomquist

OVERVIEW

This part aims to lay the groundwork for understanding and theorizing polycentric governance. Chapter 1 maps the concept in the way it has historically been used and conceptualized. Also, it provides a stratified definition of polycentric governance arrangements and its potential dimensions. Chapter 2 addresses the core themes that are related to the study of polycentric governance: the study of centres of decision-making, the study of relation between these centres, the role of social problem characteristics, and their performance, among others. Most importantly, it proposes to consider polycentric governance as a mode of inquiry into the complexity of governance and as an inductive approach to its understanding. Chapter 3 starts from the opposite perspective, outlining the basic assumptions of the Bloomington School of Political Economy and how they shape theorizing about the way constitutional rules, social problem characteristics, and heterogeneity of groups induce polycentric governance. It illustrates the perspective relying on case examples of Spanish, German, and Chinese water governance and transnational biofuels' governance. Chapter 4 extends this perspective to understanding evolutionary institutional change in polycentric governance. It illustrates the approach with examples of Water Governance in Kenya and Mexico.

An Introduction to Polycentricity and Governance*

Mark Stephan, Graham Marshall, and Michael McGinnis

1.1 Polycentricity in Science, Local Politics, and Governance

Though our fundamental focus is on polycentric governance, in order to understand polycentric as an adjective that modifies the noun governance (defined below), we must start with the older term, polycentricity. According to Michael Polanyi, polycentricity had roots in the biological and chemical sciences and in the decentralized processes of decision-making within scientific communities (Polanyi 1964). The term had been used to describe the types of plants in botanical studies in the context of whether they have multiple reproductive cells (polycentric) or only a single reproductive cell (monocentric). The terms polycentric and monocentric are still used in this way in botany, and in other areas of scholarship and policy analysis. For example, many urban planning scholars and geographers use the term polycentric to refer to metropolitan regions which encompass both significant suburban centres and one major urban centre, in contrast to a monocentric metropolitan order centred about a single city that has greatly expanded over time.

Ostrom, Tiebout, and Warren (OTW) (1961) introduced the concept of polycentricity to the political science and public administration literatures as a way of making sense of the fact that most metropolitan areas in the United States lack a single dominant political leader, but instead include many local public authorities, each pursuing its own aims in a seemingly uncoordinated manner. Yet many such metropolises 'work', in the sense

* This material is based upon the work supported by the National Science Foundation under Grant Number 1431487. Any opinions, findings, and conclusions or recommendations expressed in this material are those of the authors and do not necessarily reflect the views of the National Science Foundation.

that economic growth, public safety, clean water, secure electrical power, and other local public goods are enjoyed by the residents.

Their basic point was that people living and working in densely populated communities want a wide range of local public goods, but different goods are most efficiently produced at different levels of spatial aggregation. Therefore, there is a certain logic to building political economic systems in which public jurisdictions and service delivery units of diverse sizes operate concurrently.

OTW (1961, 831) allude to the biological basis of the term in suggesting that a polycentric political system might instead be referred to as a 'multi-nucleated' political system, but since they were writing during the Cold War era, they had good reasons to bury that suggestion in a footnote. In any event, the conceptual leap from an organism with many reproductive centres to societal arrangements with 'many decision centres having limited and autonomous prerogatives and operating under an overarching set of rules' (Aligica and Tarko 2012) is a substantial move. Once this leap had been made by OTW, subsequent governance researchers rarely refer back to the chemical and biological basis of Polanyi's conceptualization, and instead focus on using it to better understand social, political, economic, and cultural systems where there is no hierarchy holding the whole system together.

It is worth noting that OTW never quoted nor cited Polanyi in their use of 'polycentric political system' as a concept. In an unpublished 1972 convention paper (subsequently reprinted in different forms in McGinnis 1999b; E. Ostrom 2012; V. Ostrom 1991), V. Ostrom admitted that he became aware of Polanyi's use of polycentricity only after the 1961 OTW article was published. But he also acknowledged that Polanyi's ideas connect well to the work on polycentricity by institutional scholars.

OTW (1961, 831) define polycentric (when referring to a political system) as follows: '[It] connotes many centres of decision-making[1] which are formally independent of each other.' Polanyi's (1951, 184) statement that a 'polycentric task can be socially managed only by a system of mutual adjustments' has some overlap with OTW's (1961) conceptualization. But it took later scholars (see Aligica and Tarko 2012; Boettke and Aligica

---

[1] In this chapter, we use the term 'decision centre' to refer to formal organizations or more informal groupings which have established (or informally follow) procedures which designate certain individuals (in defined roles or positions) as having the authority to make decisions binding on that group as a whole. Decision centres are the fundamental units of polycentricity in social settings.

2009; McGinnis 2005) to clarify the subtle links between the conceptualizations of Polanyi and Ostrom.

Despite the use by some scholars of polycentricity as equivalent to polycentric governance, we distinguish between polycentricity as it is understood in the social sciences (by both social science scholars broadly and by some in the subset of institutional scholars) and the particular use of polycentricity as it relates to governance alone. For example, when some, such as McGinnis (2011, 171), refer to polycentricity as a 'system of governance', we understand this in the context of the narrower term polycentric governance system rather than a statement that the wider term polycentricity applies only to structures and processes of decision-making. Polycentricity goes well beyond governance.

1.1.1 Expanded Understanding of Governance

As used by different scholars, the term polycentric governance may extend beyond the explicitly political activities engaged in by formal political units of government.[2] For example, Ostrom points out in the 1972 unpublished convention paper mentioned above that he and his colleagues in 1961 had been directly concerned only with the actions of government officials, but that he had since realized that this concept also applied to broader understandings of governance. By highlighting the critical roles placed by private firms and non-profit organizations in the production and delivery of local public services in metropolitan areas, OTW (1961) were way ahead of their time. Only later did scholars working in other traditions grant private firms and community organizations a full role in the process of governance, in studies of collaborative governance and governance networks involving public, private, and voluntary organizations. Ironically, the pioneering work of OTW had very little impact on this literature and is rarely cited by scholars of governance networks (McGinnis and Ostrom 2012).

---

[2] In this chapter, we use 'political' in a traditional way. That is, we define as political those organizations and processes primarily and explicitly focused on the allocation of valued resources towards alternative ends desired by different groups within a society. If this allocation requires some coercion, the general expectation is that most members of that society consider these efforts as legitimate, rather than being extra-legal in nature. For instance, OTW focused on local public agencies within a metropolitan area that were directly involved in the selection, financing, or evaluation of local public goods. Only some of the organizations responsible for the actual production of those goods would fit this definition of explicitly political organizations, since many local public goods are produced by firms or voluntary organizations, often operating under contracts with or regulations set by public agencies.

We define governance as a 'process by which the repertoire of rules, norms, and strategies that guide behaviour within a given realm of policy interactions are formed, applied, interpreted, and reformed' (McGinnis 2011, 171). It is important to understand governance as a process, in which both government officials and non-governmental actors can play critical roles. Some non-governmental actors are directly connected to explicitly political matters (parties, interest groups, etc.), but private corporations and voluntary organizations of diverse types are often critical to the delivery of public services and the formation of public policy.

According to V. Ostrom, the concept of polycentricity encompasses economic markets, legal orders, scientific disciplines, and multi-cultural societies. Within the political realm, federalism may be the most prominent example of polycentricity. Although many students of federalism focus on the complex relationships among public agencies operating at the local, state, or national levels, V. Ostrom emphasized the important contributions made by public agencies operating across these levels, as well as organizations that would not generally be considered explicitly political, such as neighbourhood associations, inter-state compacts, community councils, and special districts defined for particular policy needs, such as fire protection, schools, and water management. Water resource management often involves numerous governments at different levels in intricate processes of decision-making, service delivery, facilities operation, and usage regulation. Just as governance has become recognized as broader than just the actions of governmental organizations, polycentric governance needs to be understood as a richer concept than federalism.

1.1.2 Polycentric Systems and Arrangements

Polanyi focused on polycentricity as a form of emergent order, in the sense that a complex system of component parts may exhibit regularized patterns which are only apparent if one looks at the system as a whole. Emergence is the appropriate analytical term because it is typically impossible to directly attribute these system-level regularities to specific actions taken by the constituent units. Even so, these regularities need to be included in any comprehensive analysis. Exactly this kind of emergence is seen as a critical component of polycentricity in all its forms.

To talk about a polycentric order is to say that regularized patterns have emerged, but that these decision centres maintain independence. OTW initially used system and order in reference to polycentricity, but the distinction between system and order in OTW is not entirely clear. For our purposes we are primarily concerned with governance, and we require a governance system to exhibit a more coherent form of order that expresses a greater level of what OTW referred to as taking 'each other into account' between the multiple decision centres. Thus, order can be understood as a matter of degree or in terms of its dimensionality. Polycentric arrangements have some order and as the degree of order increases, the arrangements coalesce into a system.

We use the word system in relation to governance to denote the entirety of all the component decision centres that are interconnected beyond a mere formality. OTW said that decision-making centres constituted a system when a number of characteristics were fulfilled including options for competitive, contractual, or cooperative relationships. To call the decision centres significantly interconnected is our equivalent to OTW's taking each other into account. The term arrangement, when used with polycentric, is an attempt to account for all cases of polycentric governance regardless of whether they rise to the level of a polycentric governance system.[3] Thus, we use the phrase polycentric governance arrangements to capture all cases of polycentric governance including those that qualify as systems and those that do not.[4]

1.1.3 Monocentric and Unitary Governments

Monocentric governance is a phrase often used as the opposite of polycentric by scholars working in this tradition, but we consider its use somewhat problematic. The phrase is rarely used in the broader public administration or political science literatures on governance. The standard terminology instead is unitary government, to which federal systems are typically contrasted. We argue here that monocentric and polycentric forms of governance are related in more subtle ways than are federal and unitary forms of government.

For the purposes of this volume, we define monocentric governance as a governance arrangement in which a single decision centre has ultimate authority over all important decisions related to the governance of that group or community. Certain specific tasks may be delegated to other

---

[3] Our use of this expression parallels E. Ostrom's use of 'institutional arrangements' as an umbrella term for the wide variety of institutionalized practices and practices that may range from simple rules-in-use to complex formal organizations.

[4] Villamayor-Tomás (2018) treats polycentric governance arrangements and systems as distinct, citing Marshall (2015). Marshall actually understands all systems to be a subset of the wider set of arrangements.

decision units, but, ultimately, any decision by these delegated authorities can be overturned by the one uniquely designated ultimate centre for decision-making.[5] Conversely, polycentric systems of governance lack any uniquely designated final authority. Other aspects of polycentric governance are discussed below, but it is this lack of a single ultimate authority that distinguishes polycentric governance. To preview what is said below, the existence of overarching rules does not themselves mean a form of governance moves from polycentric to monocentric. Because overarching rules can be agreed upon and enforced by the decision centres themselves (without an ultimate centre for decision-making), they can be understood as part of polycentric arrangements.

A governance system that truly consisted of only one decision centre would be unambiguously monocentric, but that has generally proved impractical for any significantly sized social system. However, systems of highly concentrated authority have proven quite feasible at lower levels of aggregation. Some family or kinship units, for example, can be accurately described as monocentric, and the organizational charts of many private corporations uniquely identify a chief executive officer with authority over all aspects of that organization. Since many other, more complex or ambiguous forms of corporate and family governance also exist, whereas truly monocentric systems at the societal level remain rare, there may be a natural limit to the size of viable monocentric governance structures. To put it another way, the greater feasibility of monocentric governance at lower levels of aggregation of decision centres leads us to expect to find that the incidence of polycentric governance increases with the level of aggregation. Evidence of this relationship is nevertheless yet to be established.

Vincent Ostrom (1991, 1997) often used the Leninist organizational model to illustrate his understanding of a monocentric system of governance, and emphasized the practical limitations entailed by efforts to concentrate so much power in any single centre of authority. He realized that even totalitarian systems incorporate smaller organizations of diverse size and types, if only for the purposes of implementing central commands. A clever supreme leader may purposefully establish multiple organizations engaged in internal policing or the protection of state secrets and use each of them as a check on the potential power of the other. We are convinced that this more nuanced interpretation of monocentric governance fits his

---

[5] Polycentric governance can therefore be distinguished from certain 'decentralization' reforms where some implementation tasks are assigned to units but actual policymaking authority remains centralized.

meaning much better than using it as a simple foil for polycentric governance.

V. Ostrom similarly critiques the Hobbesian or Woodrow Wilsonian insistence of there being, somewhere in any viable system of societal governance, an ultimate source of authority, a single sovereign. For Wilson that role was played in the United States of America by Congress, for Hobbes by whatever actor satisfies his definition of a Leviathan (V. Ostrom 1991, 2008b). For OTW, advocates of a single consolidated government at the metropolitan level were pursuing the chimera of a Gargantua topped by a single centre of ultimate authority. In truly polycentric governance, there is no single decision centre with ultimate authority.[6]

Under Leninist, Hobbesian, or Wilsonian interpretations, a monocentric governance system may include many subordinate centres and may allow for diverse forms of communication and contacts among them. These complications do not undermine the core defining aspect of a monocentric system, not as long as one decision centre is unambiguously identified as the ultimate authority. Such a monocentric governance system might manage to generate a recognizable form of order and could be said to constitute a coherent and well-coordinated system of governance. But the nature of the resulting order would be fundamentally at odds with the concept of polycentricity.

1.1.4 Governance and Collective Goods

The polycentric governance arrangements in which we are primarily interested entail processes of selection, production, financing, and evaluation of collective goods, as well as the management of common-pool resources. Governance necessarily requires tough decisions involving trade-offs among alternative goods, many of which are high priority items for different parts of society. Since the benefits of enjoying collective goods or common-pool resources cannot be easily limited to the individuals who invest their time and resources in providing those goods, some kind of authority is critical for solving the problems of free riding typically associated with the production of collective goods (Olson 1965). Typically, these authorities need to be able to enforce at least a minimal level of legitimate

---

[6] Although the public as a whole might be referred to as sovereign, it cannot be understood as a single decision centre since the dominant coalition of interests within the general population shifts over time.

coercion to gather the resources needed to support public purposes, by requiring individuals to pay taxes or charging fees to individuals who seek access to more restricted goods.

V. Ostrom (2008b) observed that traditional principles of public administration imply that this collective action should be organized monocentrically by 'government' as the ultimate source of authority, with its decisions implemented by elaborate hierarchies of officials. OTW (1961) acknowledged that a centralized political system can be appropriate for providing goods that broadly benefit the public at a single, large (e.g. national) scale (cf. Chapter 4). For most collective goods, however, they argued that any economies of scale achieved by centralization would likely be outweighed by diseconomies arising from the complexity of the required bureaucratic and hierarchical structures as well as the diversity of preferences and priorities within and among constituencies. They observed that this complexity tends to make overly centralized arrangements unresponsive to localized public interests, and provided an example where two or three years may be required to secure improvements to a sidewalk even where local residents have undertaken to cover the costs. A polycentric political system was seen as alleviating such unresponsiveness by enabling closer matching of the level of decision-making for a particular action to the level of the public that would benefit from it.

In a series of empirical studies of police services in several US metropolitan areas in the 1970s, Elinor Ostrom and her colleagues demonstrated the partial advantages that polycentric arrangements had over unitary forms of governance (McGinnis 1999b). Similarly, positive findings were demonstrated in later research on community-based management of common-pool resources, the work for which Elinor Ostrom received the 2009 Nobel Memorial Prize in Economic Sciences (E. Ostrom 1990, 2010). In both areas of the work, the central focus on multiple decision centres was apparent. Whether making sense of local collective action or understanding systems built on self-organization (or doing both simultaneously), polycentric governance served as a conceptual base. It was not postulated that monocentric governance was always inferior, but rather that polycentric governance was superior in some cases.

In effect, these empirical research programs demonstrated the real-world relevance of the general concept of polycentric governance in a limited range of empirical settings. The current volume continues in this same tradition, while also being more self-consciously attentive to the need to clearly define and measure the extent of polycentric governance present in different policy settings.

1.1.5 Review of Concepts

We introduced several concepts in this section, which we can now summarize. The subject of our investigation is the general class of 'polycentric governance arrangements', each of which is a configuration of multiple 'decision centres' that maintain at least some formal or informal autonomy on matters within their respective jurisdictions. These governance arrangements are 'polycentric' in contrast to 'monocentric', since none of the decision centres has a uniquely powerful system-wide influence on the decisions of all other centres. The term 'governance' is appropriate because their outcomes help shape the processes through which the rules, norms, and strategies their participants deem relevant to making those decisions are (or will be) formed, applied, interpreted, and reformed.

Although all polycentric governance arrangements generate some degree of 'polycentric order' in their patterns of behaviour, interactions, and outcomes, we are particularly interested in evaluating the subset of 'polycentric governance systems', which we define by taking OTW's lead in requiring that decision centres take each other into account. Polycentric governance arrangements and systems come in many forms, and their varying characteristics can influence policy performance along several evaluative criteria. The remainder of this chapter elaborates on the potential effects of variation in these characteristics, to provide a general context for evaluations of real-world examples that appear in subsequent chapters.

1.2 Identifying the Characteristics of Polycentric Governance

Polycentric governance is a complex term that has been used in different ways by different scholars. In Box 1.1 we list examples of definitions or other statements that illustrate various meanings of polycentricity or polycentric governance as used in the institutional literature.

In order to begin making headway on a common understanding of the variety of concepts associated with polycentric governance, we highlight those aspects most commonly employed by scholars in the field, followed by a discussion of less common aspects developed by some scholars. In the process we build a foundation for the use of these terms by the contributors to this book.

Box 1.1 Varying perspectives on polycentric governance

To give some sense of the various definitions given over the last fifty-five years, below are a sample of the ways in which the term polycentric governance (or its variants) has been used.

The traditional pattern of government in a metropolitan area with its multiplicity of political jurisdictions may more appropriately be conceived as a 'polycentric political system'. 'Polycentric' connotes many centres of decision-making which are formally independent of each other. Whether they actually function independently, or instead constitute an interdependent system of relations, is an empirical question in particular cases. (OTW 1961, 831)

[T]he critical variables of concern to scholars in the polycentric tradition include (1) individuals; (2) decision rules; (3) sets of events; (4) outcomes; and (5) measures of performance. (V. Ostrom 1972)

Polycentricity refers to conditions where a pluralistic organizational structure reflects a pattern of power and influence characterized by many interdependent but relatively autonomous organizational units. (Toonen 1983, 251)

Rearticulating the original OTW definition, V. Ostrom says that a polycentric system is a self-organizing system composed of '(1) many autonomous units formally independent of one another, (2) choosing to act in ways that take into account of others, and (3) through processes of cooperation, competition, conflict, and conflict resolution.' (V. Ostrom 1991, 225)

Polycentric 'systems are the organization of small-, medium-, and large-scale democratic units that each may exercise considerable independence to make and enforce rules within a circumscribed scope of authority for a specific geographical area'. (E. Ostrom 2001, 2)

Polycentric 'institutional arrangements [are] nested quasi-autonomous decision-making units operating at multiple scales. They involve local, as well as higher, organizational levels and aim at a finding a balance between decentralized and centralized control'. (Folke et al. 2005, 449)

By 'polycentric' I mean a system where citizens are able to organize not just one but multiple governing authorities, as well as private arrangements, at different scales. (E. Ostrom 2003, in an interview conducted by Paul Dragos Aligica 2003, reprinted in Cole and McGinnis 2015, 61)

A polycentric order is one where the elements of a complex system are allowed to make mutual adjustments to each other 'within a general system of rules where each element acts with independence of other elements'. (Aligica and Boettke 2009, quote V. Ostrom 1972)

[A] truly polycentric system is one in which governmental units both compete and cooperate, interact and learn from one another, and responsibilities at different governmental levels are tailored to match the scale of the public services they provide. (Cole 2011)

Polycentricity thus describes a system of qualified independence among interdependent centres of authority. (Oakerson and Parks 2011, 154)

Polycentricity is a system of governance in which authorities from overlapping jurisdictions (or centres of authority) interact to determine the conditions under which these authorities, as well as the citizens subject to these jurisdictional units, are authorized to act as well as the constraints put upon their activities for public purposes. (McGinnis 2011)

[Polycentricity] is an institutional arrangement involving a multiplicity of decision centres acting independently but under the constraints of an overarching set of norms and rules that restrict externalities and create the conditions for an emergent outcome to occur at the level of the entire system via a bottom-up competitive process. (Aligica and Tarko 2013)

Polycentric systems are complex adaptive systems without a central authority controlling the processes and structures of the system. Polycentric systems are characterized by multiple governance units at multiple scales, with each unit having some capacity to govern at its scale. (Garmestani and Benson 2013)

Polycentric governance systems must fulfil at least two criteria to function as systems: presence of multiple centres of decision-making and coordination by an overarching system of rules. (Pahl-Wostl and Knieper 2014, 140)

1.2.1 Central Aspects

At the core of almost every definition of polycentric governance (or polycentricity, polycentric systems, or polycentric arrangements) is the idea of multiple centres of decision-making, or multiple authorities, no one of which has ultimate authority for making all collective decisions. The specific features of these multiple centres are rarely delineated. The necessary number of these centres in any given governance space is unclear. The basic idea implies that decision-making or service-provision units are likely to vary in size, since not all public goods are most efficiently produced or delivered at the same level of aggregation (cf. Chapter 3). How many centres or how many different sizes exist is less important than the basic idea that multiple centres exist and operate concurrently, within a system in which no single centre has final ultimate authority.

Critical to the original definition from OTW (1961) was the notion that the decision-making centres were formally independent of each other and no single centre had ultimate authority over others. All centres retained significant autonomy from any other centre. At a minimum, formal independence could mean that decision centres could not simply do away with each other, i.e. that they possess enough autonomy to maintain their existence and cannot be abolished without reference to some overarching rules or processes. Beyond that minimum, formal independence could include some ability to contest adverse actions by other decision centres. At the same time, OTW observed that the extent to which these centres acted independently was an empirical question to be investigated in each case.

Similarly, the extent of decision-making autonomy that is required has not been consistently delineated. For the sake of our work here, we treat independence and autonomy as synonymous terms.

Despite the centrality of formal (de jure) independence to the original definition of polycentric governance, we accept that there may be decision centres in such governance that have de facto independence. For example, subordinate units in a hierarchical organization might lack formal independence while also enjoying, in practice, significant levels of decision-making autonomy. For this reason, we include decision centres with de facto autonomy as part of a larger set of polycentric governance arrangements, in which other centres may have clearly defined de jure autonomy and de facto autonomy combined.

Alternatively, it is worth mentioning that there could be cases where decision centres are formally independent of one another, but lack de facto autonomy (e.g. where one centre has come to dominate others despite the formal independence). Such cases may be few, but we would consider them monocentric and not polycentric.

In addition, cases of polycentric governance are rife with jurisdictions whose connections are either formally absent or ambiguous and confusing, often by design. To consider one prominent example, the three branches of the US national government defined in the Constitution are formally independent, though functionally they are interdependent in numerous ways. The US Constitution serves as an overarching set of rules, but there is no higher-level institution that oversees all three branches. In addition, this Constitution leaves space for citizens to work together to establish new forms of collective action that were not specified in that document (including such critically important entities as political parties!). Many of the decision centres subsequently formed focus on matters of economics, professional expertise, religion, or community solidarity, resulting in a dazzling array of institutional diversity that must be considered an important consequence of the way polycentric governance was set up at the constitutional level.

1.2.2 Common Aspects

Somewhat in tension with the notion of decision-making autonomy, OTW also emphasized the importance of the idea that the decision-making centres in a polycentric political system overlap in their areas of responsibility. The combination of autonomy and overlap is a critical aspect of polycentric governance.

The presence of overlapping jurisdictions is critical to the dynamism of polycentric governance, because without it, fewer decision centres would find it necessary to take each other into account when making decisions and taking actions. The sources of their overlap can be many, including interdependence between issues governed, the interconnectedness of the physical jurisdictions (e.g. water), or because functions of governance such as monitoring can be interdependent. Policy issues overlap in numerous ways, as can be seen with human health and environmental conditions. The notion of externalities assumes overlap. Similarly, the interconnectedness of physical jurisdictions is seen readily around water as an environmental concern. Rivers are regularly used as both boundaries and points of connection. Functions of governance such as monitoring and evaluation can require many eyes from multiple locations to better understand the effectiveness of laws. For example, research on river basin management (Lankford and Hepworth 2010) has found that polycentric attempts at river basin management can help in situations where data monitoring is desired but is limited by resource constraints.

Polycentric governance spillover effects can occur between jurisdictions, regardless of overlap. Both overlapping jurisdictions and spillover effects help to increase the likelihood that decision centres will take each other's concerns and actions into account when making their own decisions.

By acknowledging the centrality of jurisdictional overlaps, OTW (1961) sought to counter the pervasive belief (then and now) that governmental overlaps invariably result in wasteful duplication of efforts, and that this duplication justifies movement towards consolidation. OTW argued that these overlaps recognized the reality of interdependencies among formally separate units and encouraged public officials in overlapping units to consider ways in which they might address their common concerns. In effect, overlaps guarantee both the need and the opportunity for authorities to engage in competition and cooperation among themselves. Though neither competition nor coordination will always be productive, there is the (high) potential for either to enhance the quality of the services provided across the jurisdictions. In this way, overlapping jurisdictions are the engine for actions, reactions, and interactions among all authorities involved.

From the earliest days of conceptualizing polycentric governance systems there has been an understanding that multiple decision centres take each other into account to some extent. They do so by engaging in regularized forms of interaction, which might take the form of competition, coordination, contractual relationships, consolidation, and other instruments for collective action. Since different forms of interaction may inspire them to develop different mechanisms for collective action, over time, a pervasive degree of institutional diversity will result. A high level of institutional diversity is a natural consequence of the long-term operation of polycentric processes.

Competition, contracts, partnerships, alliances, collaboratives, joint decision-making councils, the formation of higher-level authorities and other forms of coordination reflect different levels of conscious understandings of the implications of interdependence. Different decision centres can compete, and thus be interdependent, with little awareness of each other.[7] They can react to consumers of their services who, in turn, are the ones interacting across decision centres. Contracts are conscious actions where decision centres come to agreements concerning how each can help the other better achieve its own goals. Contractual relationships may be defined for limited periods of time, whereas partnerships or other forms of coordination require participants to adopt a more long-term and flexible attitude. In some circumstances, formerly independent decision centres may choose to join together into some larger governance units. Over time, new decision units will be formed and old ones dissolve, while others continue as before, or change in response to new challenges and opportunities.

Analysts of polycentric forms of governance stress the importance of low entry and exit costs, since that is the only way that individual consumers or voters, or the groups which represent them, will be able to choose from among alternative service providers or producers. This is an important source of dynamism in polycentric governance arrangements. Some level of competition among producers of similar goods seems inherent in most analyses of polycentric governance. In particular, low entry costs greatly facilitate the continued formation of new decision centres, as well as the innovation of new types of organizations or processes. Several analysts, such as Aligica and Tarko (2012) have insisted that an openness to the formation of new decision units is important to the underlying notion of polycentric governance.

---

[7] In this case, two decision centres may be taking each other into account less and mutually adjusting to one another more in the context of their interdependencies. Though we understand 'taking each other into account' as slightly more conscious and direct than 'mutual adjustment', for the sake of this chapter we treat these phrases as equivalents.

1.2.3 Dimensions of Polycentric Order

Some analysts of polycentric arrangements dig more deeply into the motivating principles that lie behind these patterns of taking each other into account. Do actors adjust to each other only because they have to, once they come to realize the extent of their interdependence? Or do they mutually recognize each other's goals as legitimate concerns, and acknowledge a minimal sense of legitimacy to the actions of others? More generally, are these actors and their strategic options considered only on a one-off basis or are they connected together within a broader sense of community or legitimacy? Whether described as an 'overarching set of rules', an 'overarching set of norms and rules', or even as a 'general system of law', the concern here is whether there is a rule-based structure that manifests a shared sense of connection among these actors. In more informal terms, are they all playing the same game, according to a mutually agreed-upon set of rules for that game, or are they merely engaging with each other because they have to, but otherwise exist in a social vacuum?

When Polanyi discussed polycentric orders in biological or chemical systems, the search for a better understanding of the natural operation of physical laws provided the overarching context. For applications to governance, the nature of the overarching legal and normative context within which social interactions occur is rarely so obvious. For OTW this question was easily answered, because they were investigating forms of governance manifested in metropolitan areas in the United States of America, all of which were, in the final analysis, operating under the same laws, procedures, and shared legal understandings embedded in the US Constitution. When OTW (1961) consider the need for 'recourse to central mechanisms to resolve conflict', they find a ready example in the role of courts in settling both disputes among individual claimants and broader questions related to the Constitution itself. The courts are central authorities, but they derive that authority from the US Constitution, the overarching rules.

When extended beyond this well-defined legal context, the relevant actors may or may not share a common sense of belonging to the same political or cultural system. Ostrom (1972) draws an analogy to Polanyi when he stresses the importance of a general system of rules for the successful operation of any form of polycentric governance. More recently, Aligica (2014) argued that polycentric governance is especially well-suited to multicultural societies, provided those groups have arrived at some minimal understanding of the nature of their constitutional foundation. The origin of this foundational constitutional ordering has been left unspecified in most accounts of polycentric governance, and yet, as the authors of Chapters 9 and 10 articulate, this is something that deserves careful attention in application to any empirical setting.

Polanyi was more directly concerned about establishing the logical basis for a different kind of order, namely, a regularized and persistent pattern of order which emerges automatically from interactions among the component units. The idea that polycentricity might create conditions for an emergent order or spontaneous order is critical in thinking about polycentric governance. Emergence or spontaneity both express the sense that the orderly configuration of arrangements was not designed, directed, or ultimately controlled by any single centre of authority. An order wholly designed and controlled by a single centre is not consistent with polycentric governance as understood here. For example, an empirical example of polycentric order arising through emergence can be seen in Northern Thailand (Tam-Kim, Uravian and Chalad 2003) where water governance has developed through a diverse set of institutional arrangements and networks.

The question of emergence is of long-standing provenance in the study of complex adaptive systems, but this is not a topic that we can address in any detail here (cf. Chapter 4) But we do need to clarify the interrelated meanings of scale, levels, aggregation, and emergence, as they relate to the operation of polycentric governance.

Scholars writing about polycentric governance have at times treated scale and level as equivalents (e.g. Andersson and E. Ostrom 2008; E. Ostrom 2012), but we follow distinctions laid out by Gibson, E. Ostrom, and Ahn (2000). That is, 'scale' means 'The spatial, temporal, quantitative, or analytical dimensions used to measure and study any phenomenon.' 'Level' then means 'The units of analysis that are located at the same position on a scale.' This distinction allows us, in turn, to introduce the phrase 'levels of aggregation', which can be used to refer to the patterns of order that are most clearly perceived when an analyst focuses on interactions among actors operating primarily at the same level on a geographic scale. One complication is that the terms 'scale efficiencies' or 'economies of scale' actually relate to the production levels for goods, and not to the scale on which those efficiencies are to be measured. But these terms are so well-enshrined in the literature that we feel compelled to continue to use them.

With this distinction in mind, federalism requires a spatially based jurisdictional scale in which political authorities have jurisdictions defined at the distinct national, state and local levels. Typically, jurisdictional units at levels located lower on that scale are neatly nested with larger units organized at higher levels. When generalized to a polycentric system of governance, actors operating across those supposedly well-defined levels must also be considered, as would be collaborations involving jurisdictional units operating at distinct levels, or constituents of different jurisdictional levels who have decided to work together for common purposes, rather than trying to work through the leaders of their home jurisdictions.

In situations of emergent order, interactions among units organized at one level tend to generate regularized patterns that can best be observed at a higher level of aggregation. In the most interesting cases, the pattern of order observable at the higher level was not among the goals being pursued by the component parts acting at lower level. For policy analysts, the classic example of emergent order was given to us by Adam Smith, in his concept of market efficiency emerging at the systemic level even though no individual producers or consumers consciously sought that outcome. He famously argued that the desirable outcome at the higher level occurred because lower-level actors were guided, as if by an invisible hand, to take actions that led to overall efficiency. Later economists defined the mathematical conditions under which that kind of emergent order can be assured, as well as identifying several complications that can arise along the way. To take the most notable example, purely voluntary exchange among individuals can rarely ensure the optimal production of goods that would benefit all members of that interacting system. Market failures of this kind need to be addressed in ways that step outside the strict boundaries of voluntary exchange, and this step moves us in the direction of considering broader contexts of polycentric order. We are not arguing that polycentric governance can ensure optimality any more than voluntary exchange. We are suggesting that polycentric governance may enhance other parts of a social system.

1.2.4 Polycentric Governance Systems

As we continue to consider the dimensions of order in a political system, we recognize that some forms of order may have been consciously planned and reflect high-level goals pursued by some, though not all, of the constituent units. Many forms of coordination between actors in small-sized polycentric systems can be treated as a natural part of the options available to those actors. For example, OTW discuss both 'cooperative undertakings' and 'competition relationships' between decision centres, and they left as a question of empirical analysis the extent to which the interactions among multiple centres of limited and overlapping authority constituted an effective level of regular order. For systems of higher complexity, substantial direct efforts at systemic-level coordination may not seem consistent with the notion that order emerges in polycentric systems. But, direct efforts at system-level coordination will in a polycentric governance setting lead to cascading adjustments by other decision centres, who in turn adjust to each other's adjustments, so that the outcome of the coordination effort is ultimately emergent despite any efforts to coordinate in a controlling manner (cf. Chapter 4).

The origin of systemic order is a point of some contention among scholars using the concept of polycentric governance. We think it is important to acknowledge that effective coordination within complex systems may emerge from the bottom up as a side-effect of other efforts (including competition), or it may result from explicit efforts by higher levels within that system (including explicit coordination). Elinor Ostrom and other analysts have demonstrated the ability of small-level community action to generate desirable outcomes on environmental and equity grounds. But there is no reason to presume that a polycentric system can include only small-sized decision centres. Clearly, someone with the wide scope of authority as the US President could engage in explicit efforts to make plans for the nation as a whole. His or her ability to actually implement such plans, however, is sharply limited by the concurrent activities of many other public officials, each with their own sphere of authority. Even so, presidents are often held accountable for facilitating the realization of a certain level of coordination among the various parts of the governmental system. Polycentric governance only precludes the total concentration of power or authority in any single actor. For example, in the area of climate change policy in the United States of America, a group of individual states in the northeast came together and created a regional initiative to cap and trade CO_2 emissions in their states. This action happened in the absence of national policy. Even if national policy were to occur, the work would remain polycentric because of the necessary involvement of multiple levels of government.

Opinions differ on the question of whether system-wide coordination is a required condition for polycentric governance. Most would follow the lead of OTW and Polanyi in saying that even when there is no evidence of conscious efforts at coordination at the systemic level, a substantial level of regularity may still emerge from real-world examples of polycentric governance in action. For instance, OTW expected that public officials operating at lower than metropolitan-wide levels of authority would find ways to work together to realize at least some of their shared aspirations. It is reasonable to presume that similar efforts might take place among public officials with wider ranges of responsibility. When successful, those conscious efforts might well contribute to instances of successful coordination at the level of the political system as a whole.

Some definitions make a point of including coordination of the decision centres as a key characteristic of polycentric governance. For example, Pahl-Wostl (2009) (see Box 1.1 for an example) requires the regular achievement of effective levels of systems-wide coordination for governance to be classified as polycentric. We understand and appreciate her reasoning, but remain unconvinced that polycentric governance must necessarily include a high level of system-wide coordination. On the other hand, the mere existence of such a level of coordination would not disqualify that system from being treated as polycentric (according to how we have distinguished polycentric and monocentric governance) unless the coordination implied an entity that alone assumed a position of ultimate authority over all other decision centres within the system.

One way to balance these concerns is to require that to be considered well-performing, a polycentric governance system must manage, at a minimum, to successfully address at least some of the critical large-scale coordination problems that naturally arise in any complex array of institutional arrangements. Remember that OTW advocate polycentric governance as a means by which a wide range of collective goods, each of which is most efficiently produced or provided for at different levels of spatial aggregation, can be generated more effectively than if the entire governing apparatus was consolidated into a single centre of authority. Systemic coordination itself can be considered, in many circumstances, to constitute a collective good of value to actors who consciously pursue that goal, which suggests that some actors within a polycentric system might choose to directly address this problem, rather than hoping that the required level of coordination will somehow emerge on its own. In practice, both emergence and intentionality could contribute to the realization of coordination at the systemic level.

Another reason to require fully realized polycentric governance to generate at least a minimal level of coordination can be justified by considering a core meaning of governance itself. The nature of political leadership is to find a balance between the competing goals and interests of that leader's constituents, while still managing to pursue the interests they share in common. Governance requires difficult decisions, and thus some may question whether an order that emerges purely spontaneously is worthy of the name governance. Others are quite comfortable calling uncoordinated actions of separate powers a form of emergent polycentric governance. For our part we continue to understand polycentric governance more as process than as end-state. To say that one situation or another constitutes 'governance' is not our primary task, but we do want to note the differences as seen by others (cf. Chapter 2).

When summarizing our discussion about characteristics of polycentric governance, we feel capable of providing a widely agreed-upon basic definition of polycentric, and therefore a basic definition of polycentric governance, but we do not feel capable of providing a highly detailed definition that would be agreed upon by a large variety of scholars.[8] Thus, we offer pared-down basic definitions as follows:

Polycentric: connotes multiple centres of decision-making authority which are de jure independent or de facto autonomous of each other.

Polycentric Governance: governance that has polycentric attributes, where governance is a process by which the repertoire of rules, norms, and strategies that guide behaviour within a given realm of policy interactions are formed, applied, interpreted, and reformed.

These definitions do not capture all of the key relevant characteristics. And we acknowledge that governance is a contested term in the literature. But as a start to understanding polycentric governance, it is solid. Next, we turn to eight characteristics (or dimensions) that in combination may begin to present a fuller, more detailed understanding of polycentric governance. In presenting these eight characteristics, we give scholars an opportunity to better recognize and make sense of governance under numerous contexts and to potentially further conceptualize the polycentric dimensions of governance.

1.3 Dimensions of Polycentric Governance

The preceding discussion identified eight characteristics or properties that scholars have associated with the concept of polycentric governance (albeit while using diverse terms such as polycentricity, polycentric order, arrangements, etc.).

---

[8] For intriguing efforts to more fully characterize the logical structure of polycentric governance, see Aligica and Tarko (2012) and Carlisle and Gruby (2017). For reasons discussed in the text, we remain unconvinced that the literature on polycentric governance is yet ready to converge on any single representation of this complex and subtle concept.

1. Multiple decision centres (which may be of varying sizes and types);
2. De jure independence or de facto autonomy of decision-making authority for each decision centre;
3. Overlapping jurisdictions in the range of authority for different decision centres (in addition to spillover effects of outcomes);
4. Multiple processes of mutual adjustment among decision centres (taking each other into account);
5. Low entry and exit costs for organizations or informal groupings;
6. An overarching system of rules (or laws, norms, and shared values);
7. Emergent patterns of behaviour, interactions and outcomes across decision centres;
8. A combination of emergent and intentional means of effective coordination at all levels of aggregation, from single decision centres to the system as a whole.

We review these conceptual distinctions and operational suggestions, in order to facilitate empirical analyses of how outcomes of polycentric governance arrangements are shaped by the specific combinations of these components that are in place in particular settings. Each of these factors, considered separately, should prove amenable to empirical measurement. In Table 1.1 we provide examples of empirical measures that might be used to evaluate the extent to which the institutional forms in a particular setting exhibit the characteristics identified above. For reasons of space we cannot investigate these measures further in this chapter, but we note that several contributors to this book consider specific measures in detail (cf. Chapters 5–8 in Part II).

If we were to offer our own, more detailed definitions of polycentric governance and polycentric governance systems, we might start with the following points. First, polycentric governance would be any form of governance that has a mixture of the dimensions described above, but at the least would include the first and second characteristics. Each dimension can be logically arrayed from 'less' to 'more' in a way that is consistent with the basic definition of polycentric governance. Second, polycentric governance systems would be based on the first four characteristics, at the least, but could include some degree of each of the second four characteristics. Third, we do not have the sense that more of a characteristic translates into a better outcome. Further empirical work is needed to better understand the relationship of the dimensions to outcomes. Finally, we have an underlying assumption for polycentric governance systems that they provide options for individuals to potentially reach preferred outcomes,

Table 1.1 *Potential measures for the eight characteristics of polycentric governance*

Multiple decision centres (of varying sizes and types)	Multiplicity of decision centres: number of relevant units, distribution of size of each (number of people, spatial scale, magnitude of resources, scope of functional responsibilities); distribution of decision structures (decision processes, degree of formality, are decisions compulsory or voluntary?)
Formal independence/de facto autonomy	Range of decision latitude of each unit; measures of hierarchical structure or resource dependence across decision units.
Overlapping jurisdictions (and spillover effects)	Proportion of people or resources under jurisdiction of multiple decision units; number of decision units involved in specific types of policy interactions or other measures of degree of functional interdependence.
Multiple processes of mutual adjustment among decision units	Number and diversity of communication channels available to (and used by) decision centres; number and relative use of mechanisms to establish contracts, collaboratives, partnerships, mergers, councils; number and relative use of legal forums, options for arbitration, mediation, and other forms of alternative dispute resolution.
Low costs of entry into or exit from decision centres	Economic, legal, and social transaction costs for joining or leaving new decision centres (or for dismantling existing ones).
Overarching system of rules or law	Degree of convergence of beliefs, values, shared understandings, values, norms, rules, and laws; extent of similarity in internal structures of organizations or institutional processes (institutional isomorphism).
Orderly patterns of behaviour, interactions, and outcomes (may be emergent)	Regularity and predictability of behaviour of decision centres and collective outcomes, such as stability of communication networks and patterns of social interaction.

Table 1.1 (*continued*)

Emergent or intentional means of effective coordination and decision-making at systems level	Measures of successful achievement of goals shared by a high proportion of individual citizens and/or decision centres; number of decision units with authority that spans multiple decision units, proportion of regulations enacted or implemented by higher authorities; proportion of resources collected/spent by central authorities.

including the option of collectively developing new kinds of options when other options fail. Failure remains an outcome, but futility does not.

Other relevant considerations remain for subsequent investigators. In order to evaluate the normative implications of different kinds of polycentric governance in different settings, for example, analysts would need to specify exactly which evaluative criterion should be considered.[9] Trade-offs between desired criteria would, of course, be inevitable. Consider the question of the 'optimal' level of complexity in a given empirical setting. A more complex system of decision units would be more costly to keep running, for instance, but increased transaction costs could be offset by potential gains if the greater complexity provides improved resilience to changing circumstances.

Yet, there may be settings in which a specific kind of polycentric governance would be deemed preferable. For example, since coordination costs necessarily increase with the number of units participating in a given activity, in times of existential threat to an entire community it may be useful to concentrate decision-making authority more centrally than might be prudent in more ordinary times. Even so, there may be reasons for ensuring that other authorities maintain some oversight over the actions of central authorities, even in desperate times.

Although it would be premature to state conclusions at this early stage, we expect that each of the eight characteristics will need to be present, to at least a minimal degree, to ensure effective governance in any significant sector of policy concern. But before we can even ask questions concerning

---

[9] See Carlisle and Gruby (2017) for an interesting effort to trace out the normative implications of each contextual attribute that helps enable polycentric governance on three evaluative criteria: enhanced adaptive capacity, good institutional fit, or mitigation of risk on account of redundancy. Their analysis makes it clear that there is no configuration of polycentric governance that can simultaneously optimize all three criteria.

the 'optimal' degree of polycentric governance, we need solid measures of its magnitude in different cases, and along all relevant dimensions.

Although the values of different cases on any one characteristic might be relatively easy to compare, in terms of which case more fully exhibits that characteristic, we leave as a question for subsequent researchers to determine how the overall multidimensional configuration of characteristics found in specific cases might be compared. We are confident that contributors to this book have provided useful clues towards subsequent investigations along those lines.

Ultimately, polycentric governance can be understood as an intrinsically dynamic process embedded within a contingent type of structure that is difficult to capture in simple measures. Yet this task may be critically important for anyone seeking to understand the foundation and the future evolution of political systems, democratic or not. Our belief is that this book goes a long way towards a theoretically rich, and an empirically grounded, understanding of polycentric governance. The next chapter concentrates on how an analyst might use the aspects and dimensions we have presented, in order to try understand a governance situation involving multiple centres, and to determine whether and how it exhibits characteristics of polycentric governance.

2

Seeing Polycentrically

Examining Governance Situations Using a Polycentricity Lens

William A. Blomquist and Nadine Jenny Shirin Schröder

2.1 Introduction

Stephan, Marshall, and McGinnis observed: 'Polanyi focused on polycentricity as a form of emergent order, in the sense that a complex system of component parts may exhibit regularized patterns which are only apparent if one looks at the system as a whole.' This chapter deals with identifying regularized patterns in complex governance situations and, more specifically, with what it means to examine those situations by thinking about them as potentially polycentric. We call this approach 'seeing polycentrically'.

A multitude of governance types qualify as polycentric. In this chapter we consider polycentricity as a particular lens through which to view governance arrangements. Given the ubiquity of governance arrangements involving multiple semi-autonomous but functionally interdependent actors, we believe it to be important to consider how thinking polycentrically might help in understanding and evaluating how they interact and perform.

The chapter proceeds as an inquiry. There is no classic or ideal type of polycentric governance, and polycentric order generally emerges rather than being planned using an a priori design. The analysis of how and in what ways a particular governance situation is polycentric, therefore should not be conducted deductively by starting with a model of a polycentric governance system and then determining how closely the situation under scrutiny fits the model. To some extent, developing an understanding of emergent situations needs to be emergent also.

An inquiry-based approach can be conducted as a kind of diagnostic assessment, guided by questions that draw out information that can be used to develop an overall depiction of the situation.[1] The results from such an inquiry may also be useful in analysing the governance arrangements and contemplating modifications to them, as discussed in Chapter 11. The definitions and dimensions of polycentric governance presented in Chapter 1 can aid in identifying and organizing the inquiry one would undertake.[2]

In what follows, we imagine that one has come across a complex situation involving multiple centres of decision making, and then works through an inquiry process by which one might determine the extent to which that situation resembles polycentric governance. More directly, we would say that upon encountering any multi-organizational governance structure, an analyst needs to consider whether it is a polycentric governance arrangement or a fragmented and uncoordinated, polycentric mess.[3] We present and discuss a sequence of questions that an observer can ask before reaching conclusions about the nature, operation, and effects of complex governing arrangements. The order of the topics and the sequence of questions have been considered carefully and adjusted from time to time during the drafting of this chapter, and we recognize that the questions are so interrelated that the answer to one question will entail or pre-empt others. This will not always or necessarily be the case, however, so the questions still need to be identified separately so they can be addressed as needed or relevant. In each of the six following sections of the chapter, the reader will find a set of questions grouped by topic; the questions are listed together at the beginning of each section and then discussed.

2.2 Questions about the Centres Themselves

- What centres influence the governed good/service/resource?
- What are their functions?
  - Do larger centres perform functions or provide services that are beneficial for smaller centres, or vice versa?
  - Are some centres primarily provision units and others primarily production units?

---

[1] For recent examples of inquiry-based approaches to analysing complex governance situations, see Buytaert et al. (2016), Kerber (2017), and Kiparsky et al. (2017).

[2] We are setting aside the topic of research methods, i.e., the means by which an analyst might collect and analyse data on these inquiries.

[3] Of course, these are not the only options and may instead be seen as poles of a spectrum along which actual governance arrangements lie.

- o Are functions concentrated in a few centres or widely spread among centres?
- o What rationales underlie functional separation and functional integration among centres?
- Do the centres operate at different scales or levels?
- Is there actual duplication among the centres, and to what extent?
  - o Are they identical, i.e. doing the same things in the same way?
  - o Do centres that do the same things serve differing areas or clienteles?
- Is there overlap?
  - o Do centres do some of the same things but not all of the same things?
  - o Do centres overlap in affecting the good/service/resource but do very different things?
  - o To the extent there is overlap, does there appear to be any rationale for it?
- Is there redundancy in the sense of a default actor in case another centre fails or ceases to act?
  - o Where there is actual duplication, does it appear to be entirely needless or does it serve as potentially useful redundancy?
  - o Do centres have overlapping authority or responsibilities formally but not necessarily in practice?

One's first impression of polycentricity may be of multiple identical centres. A polycentric structure composed of matching organizations is imaginable, but seems inconsistent with (a) processes of design, spontaneity, and emergence involving (b) intendedly albeit boundedly rational individuals, capable of engaging in (c) multiple levels of action. It is unclear why or how people would create and maintain copies of the same centres, despite being able to adapt them over time or eliminate them, or how and why any spontaneous or emergent processes of organizational creation and adaptation would produce and keep producing identical organizations.

Organizational diversity is a foundational concept for understanding polycentric governance. Instead of presuming or anticipating a set of replicas performing the same functions and operating identically, polycentric governance presumes and anticipates that the centres are differentiated. Empirical studies of polycentric structures, as well as theoretical explorations of why and how such structures would come into existence and persist over time, converge to a common view, namely, that most (and perhaps all) actual polycentric arrangements are comprised of distinct units operating at different levels and/or performing different functions. Visualizing the polycentric governance of a region, for instance, Elinor Ostrom (2009, 753) wrote:

> In a polycentric system, some units are general-purpose governments, whereas others may be highly specialized. Self-organized resource governance systems, in such a system, may be special districts, private associations, or parts of a local government. These can be nested in several levels of general-purpose governments that also provide civil equity, as well as criminal courts.

Governance functions may be distributed among centres, and if so, it can be important to inquire whether there have been reasons for arranging governance responsibilities in this fashion. For instance, one or more centres may be charged with regulating the activities of others, so that centres which provide goods and services are not policing themselves. The literature on local public economies (which are examples of polycentric arrangements) has emphasized the distinction between provision and production functions – provision decisions involving what goods or services to acquire, in what amounts and with what quality, how to pay for them, etc., and production functions being the actual transformation of inputs into the outputs that are those goods or services (Oakerson 1999; United States Advisory Commission on Intergovernmental Relations 1987). This distinction may help an analyst to begin to sort through the centres that are present in a complex situation to see whether some of them are provision units and others are production units.

Centres performing production functions may have different requirements and constraints. Roe and Schulman (2008) introduced the concept of 'high reliability organizations', meaning those that produce goods or services for which even slight deviations or errors may have disastrous consequences. This idea may help an analyst to make sense of the differentiation of functions across centres even when, at first glance, they are production units involved in 'the same' good or service or resource. On a given stream or lake, for instance, production of drinking water for public consumption may be an example of a 'high reliability' task, where treatment and distribution processes have to be executed the same way every time with minimal to no error, because any slippage could result in a public health epidemic, and any process changes have to be introduced carefully after extensive testing. Alternatively, the operation of facilities that manage stream flows or lake levels may be conducted within acceptable ranges, and might even be experimented with under limited conditions as part of an adaptive management approach. A complex governance situation within which high-reliability tasks are distributed to one centre and more flexible and adaptive tasks to other centres may make sense if personnel needs, operating procedures, and performance standards differ in important ways from task to task.

It may be, and often is, the case that centres exist and operate at different levels (often referred to as 'scales' in the literature, although we follow the distinction of levels and scales used in Chapter 1). This observation does not assume and should not be confused with a claim that polycentric arrangements naturally or inevitably take advantage of scale efficiencies or result in appropriate matching of levels. Mismatches and inefficiencies are possible as well.

There are several ways in which levels and scales may come into play. One way is through the idea of scale of production. Conceptually at least, any good or service can be produced at levels ranging from individual to global. We can readily anticipate and observe that diverse levels of production will come into existence, whether through deliberate choice, trial-and-error adaptation, or sheer happenstance. To the extent that diversity of levels of production translates into the creation of multiple producer organizations, it is one source of polycentricity as organizations take others into account.

Scale of effects is conceptually distinct from scale of production, although as a practical matter they are often connected. Scale of effects involves the question of who benefits from or is otherwise affected by some good or service (compare with the concept of externalities, e.g. Bromley 1989). Scale of production and scale of effects do not have to match. The set of human or other beings who are affected – positively, negatively, or some combination of both – by any good or service may also range from very small to global levels. Impacts may be substantial or attenuated, and indeed, what it means to be 'affected' at all by any phenomenon is constructed and contestable. The inclusion of positive or negative externalities adds further complexity to an arrangement in ways that often give rise to felt needs for regulation and/or conflict resolution. As people organize processes and structures for demand articulation, demand aggregation, cost allocation, regulation, and conflict resolution, we can readily anticipate and often observe that those entities will exist at various levels corresponding not only with characteristics of the goods and services in question, but also characteristics of the communities that are perceived to be affected.

Organizationally diverse arrangements may exhibit duplication, overlap and redundancy. This is important to the understanding and analysis of polycentric arrangements, in ways that go beyond normative judgements. Analysts sometimes use these terms interchangeably, or use one term when one of the others would be more accurate. There are important differences among the three, but our purpose is not to parse the terms. Instead, we are interested in how all three are connected with understanding polycentric governance.

All three terms have had negative connotations and have been used in critiques of multi-organizational settings. Viewed from the perspective of a Weberian ideal type of organization, all three characteristics are problematic and should be targeted for elimination. Rhetorically, just to apply the words duplication, overlap, or redundancy to a situation is to indict it as deficient and inefficient without any need for further inquiry.

Other scholars, however, have discovered some virtues in duplication, overlap and redundancy. Martin Landau's defence of redundancy (1969, 1973) is especially notable in this literature. He emphasized the value of back-up systems in complex structures to reduce their fragility and vulnerability, and his arguments became a building block of later work on robustness and resilience. Also during the 1960s and 1970s, in their studies of water resource management and of public service delivery in metropolitan areas and federal systems, both Vincent and Elinor Ostrom presented theoretical arguments and empirical support for arrangements that others had assailed for duplication and overlap. (Both often cited Landau, also.) They repeatedly connected duplication and overlap with the importance of contestation through the existence of overlapping forums for conflict resolution and the enforcement of rules guarding dissent and diversity (e.g. E. Ostrom 2009, 753). Another important thread of supporting argumentation is seen in the work of public administration scholars such as Peters (2015, 129) who have emphasized the importance of multiple channels of information and communication in complex and multi-organizational structures (see also Buytaert et al. 2016, 3).

One need not take sides among these contesting views in order to incorporate and apply the concepts of duplication, overlap, and redundancy in the effort to understand polycentric governance. Rather, one can recognize that (a) these characteristics are typically present in polycentric arrangements, (b) their presence is a matter of degree, such that there may be greater or lesser amounts of duplication, overlap, and/or redundancy in a particular setting, and (c) whether the duplication, overlap, and redundancy that are present have net positive or negative effects is an empirical question, the answer to which will depend on both the situation and the evaluative criteria the analyst applies.

2.3 Questions about the Social Problem Characteristics

- What biophysical characteristics of the problem/good/service/ resource affect how the governance arrangement functions?
- Are there multiple possibilities to fulfil the function of the problem/ good/service/resource that people are trying to address, and, if so, how does the multiplicity of decision-making centres align with those possibilities?
- How are characteristics of the problem/good/service/resource that people are trying to address multi-functional?
  - ○ Is the problem/ good/ service/ resource used or valued in more than one way?
  - ○ Do the multiple decision centres correspond with these multiple functions/uses/values?
- Are multiple scales of the problem/good/service/resource conceivable, such that it can be governed at smaller or larger scales and by lower or higher levels?
  - ○ Do scale differences of centres appear to correspond in some manner with relevant differences in social problem characteristics?
  - ○ Do scale differences of centres capture scales of production or scales of effects and, if so, in what ways?

The structure and functioning of governance arrangements strongly relates to the characteristics of social problems/goods/services/resources addressed, people's knowledge about those characteristics, and differing perceptions of them. This is an important focus of Chapter 3. The problem characteristics may change over time, and the knowledge and perceptions about them may change even more or faster. It is likely that governance arrangements reflect these processes and exhibit a multiplicity of settings with centres corresponding with different scales, levels, functional alternatives, as well as with the multifunctionality of a problem/good/service/ resource. The plurality of possibilities to fulfil a function is a source for the variety of polycentric governance arrangements. For example, the function of producing drinking water may be fulfilled by using local groundwater resources, treating surface waters, transporting bottled water from a distance, etc. Governance arrangements might involve one or several of these possibilities in varying combinations, and one or more centres may come into being to pursue these possibilities separately or in a coordinated manner.

When dealing with complex and differently defined social problems, we should not expect a set of diverse and formally independent yet functionally interdependent centres to be harmonious. As Cash et al. (2006) observed, 'Knowledge is often held, stored, and perceived differently at different levels, resulting from differences across levels about what is perceived as salient, credible, and legitimate knowledge, or what is perceived as the important scale or level of the problem.' They referred to this as 'the plurality challenge'.

Differences in information and interpretations of information can and should generate some exchange, and this exchange is what we call contestation. The term is broader than the simpler 'conflict', and therefore preferable for our purposes here. (Chapter 6 focuses more directly on conflict between centres.) Contestation over differences in information or interpretations can be illuminating and can generate ideas and insights. It can also deteriorate into mere rebuttal, refutation, and rejection. What transpires in actual settings with respect to information and contestation is an empirical question. The variety of information at work in polycentric arrangements, and contestation among centres over its meaning and significance, may lead to positive or negative outcomes or a combination of both. The presence and patterns of information and contestation about the social problem, but also about governing processes are essential characteristics to be examined and assessed in any polycentric arrangement. Recent emphasis on adaptive management and collaborative governance should sharpen scholars' focus on the vital roles of information generation, exchange, and interpretation for understanding polycentric governance.

The goods and services that people produce and enjoy, the natural resources they value and with which they interact, and many other aspects of their environments are multi-functional. Very few if any phenomena of significant interest to us (including human beings) are just one thing or have just one aspect. As Norberg and Cumming (2008, 9) observed:

Each individual component of a complex system may have many properties and many functions; for example, an antelope is simultaneously a grazer, a food source, a disperser of nutrients, and a producer of methane. Any component of a complex system may have properties that are redundant (i.e. that are duplicated by other system components) and others that add diversity to the system.

A watercourse may be regarded and valued as an aesthetic treasure, a conduit for navigation, a source of drinking water, of hydropower, of waste disposal, of spiritual renewal, of recreation, of irrigation, and so on, as well as a habitat for a variety of plants and animals. Furthermore, each of these uses and their effects may be experienced and governed by different but overlapping groups over different areas.

From a prescriptive perspective, multifunctionality may be the basis of arguments for a single integrated centre to govern and manage the watercourse in its entirety and for all uses and all users. Empirical observation has tended to reveal the opposite, however. More commonly, people have established multiple overlapping centres, organized around particular groups or areas and focused on certain functions or values of the resource (Boelens, Zwarteveen, and Roth 2005; Kerr 2007; Lankford and Hepworth 2010). Such arrangements are a principal source of the overlap that occurs in polycentric governance arrangements. Whether they function well or poorly is an open question to be addressed.

The concept of scale, already discussed, has further relevance here to the existence of polycentric arrangements for the governance and management of natural resources. Natural resources tend to be interconnected, nested, and overlapping. At a broad and relatively abstract dimension, ecosystems and habitats illustrate this point. Ecosystems may contain habitats, but a habitat is not necessarily confined within a single ecosystem. Within a habitat we might identify critical zones (e.g. nesting grounds, spawning areas). The contours of those zones may change over time, as do the extent of habitats and ecosystems. We could go on, but the theoretical and analytical significance of this point for understanding polycentric arrangements can be stated directly. Natural resources exist at multiple scales and are impacted by dynamics occurring at and across multiple scales. Whether human beings are trying to exploit, preserve, or recover natural resources – and especially when human beings are trying to perform some combination of these, as is often the case – it is likely that they will organize decision making and action in multiple, overlapping centres along different scales. Inquiring about the connections between the centres in a complex governance situation and the scales and functions of a good or service is an important step in attempting to understand it from the viewpoint of polycentricity.

2.4 Questions about Independence and Interdependence among Centres

- How independent are the centres in their decision making?
  - To what extent and in what ways do they control their own resources (funding, personnel, etc.)?

- o What kind of questions may centres autonomously decide on, i.e. what range of discretion do they have?
- o To what extent and in what ways are they able to reach their goals on their own?
- What forms do relationships among the centres take?
  - o Are there formalized relationships such as contracts between centres, membership of one or more centres in another centre, etc.?
  - o Are there informal forms such as interpersonal relationships, over-lapping members or constituents, etc.?
  - o Are some centres nested within others and, if so, in what ways, and for what apparent reasons?
  - o Are some centres in competitive relationships to each other and, if so, in what ways? Does competition generate any useful informa-tion or choices and, if so, for whom and in what ways?

A diverse set of units would not necessarily constitute a polycentric structure. If a single authority can create and eliminate each unit, establish every unit's structure and define the scope and processes of its operation, which the units themselves possessed no discretion to change, such an arrangement would be more nearly monocentric than polycentric. In polycentric arrangements, the centres exhibit at least some independence or autonomy. The centres can to a greater or lesser degree adopt and alter their functions and processes. The use of qualifying expressions such as 'at least some' and 'to a greater or lesser degree' is deliberate – independence does not have to be total and usually will not be.

The other side of the coin is the interdependence of decision-making centres – various relationships among centres that constrain their inde-pendence. Biophysical characteristics of a problem/good/service/ resource may relate centres to each other, but centres are also socially embedded and sometimes institutionally interconnected, generating additional interdependencies. This idea is picked up, for instance, by the literature on cross-scale and cross-level linkages (see Adger, Brown, and Tompkins 2005; Berkes 2006). The conceptions of those linkages range from broad characterizations of 'institutional interplay' among centres to more intentional 'co-management' and concrete 'bridging organizations' that are created to forge and maintain relationships among centres.

As stated in Chapter 1 and elaborated further in Chapter 3, as well as in Chapters 9 and 10, the idea of an 'overarching set of rules' appears in several important definitions of polycentricity. In actual settings, such rules may be expected to place some limits on what centres can do and in what ways. This may encompass formal and informal rules giving some sort of order between centres (E. Ostrom 1983). However, contesting rules might also create conflicts e.g. through institutional interplay (Young 2002). Some rules may apply to the whole arrangement, others only to parts of it, e.g. rules within a hierarchy. A hierarchical structure may have elements that can be considered as separate decision-making centres if they exhibit at least some independence in decision making from the higher level.

Relationships between centres may also be shaped informally through activities and memberships of individuals. Those information relationships might change faster than an overarching rule system and can be hard to control endogenously and exogenously. They offer the chance to find governance solutions based on personal trust and to exchange information, but may also be sources of additional conflicts (E. Ostrom1986).

Competition may be inherent to all kinds of relationships mentioned. It is a common feature of polycentric arrangements, and is the focus of Chapter 7. Relationships between centres in polycentric governance arrangements will feature various combinations of competition and coordination at a given time, over time, and from one polycentric governance arrangement to another. The question for scholars then becomes how to incorporate the concept of competition into their analyses of polycentric governance. Part of the answer lies in considering what the centres may be competing for or about, and there is a broad range of possibilities.

Centres may compete with one another for power and influence, for more material matters such as revenue or territory or personnel, or even for constituents. In polycentric governance, some centres may function as producers of public goods or services and thus may compete in ways similar to rival producers in market-like settings (e.g. Bendor 1985; Tiebout 1956). They may be imagined also as nations or states competing on the international stage, or as agencies competing for control over policy making. Any number of analogies is possible and, for a given governance situation, some will be more apt and useful than others.

The effects that competition produces in any governance situation are both contingent and a matter for empirical inquiry. It may yield benefits – competition is often said to generate information and innovation, for example (Low, E. Ostrom, and Wilson 2003, 101; Vanberg and Kerber 1994, 216). It may be detrimental, as in the often-remarked 'race to the bottom' phenomenon (e.g. Konisky 2007). In complex actual settings, both benefits and drawbacks are likely to be observed, and discerning the overall effect becomes a challenging evaluation task.

We need not, however, consider competition and its effects solely from the perspective of the outside analyst observing and evaluating a polycentric governance arrangement. Competition among centres will be experienced and evaluated by the participants themselves. Accordingly, competition can also be incorporated into our analyses and understanding of polycentric arrangements as an endogenous driver of change. People may respond to competition by creating or modifying or eliminating centres, changing their operations, or shifting levels of action and altering the rules governing centres and their interaction. Competition and the setting of other relationships are therefore also essential for understanding polycentric arrangements and how they change over time.

2.5 Questions about Coordination

- Are there identifiable ways in which centres coordinate?
  - Do they share information and, if so, about what and in what ways?
  - Do they collaborate on projects/programs/activities and, if so, in what ways?
  - Do they share or exchange resources such as funding, personnel, facilities, etc., and, if so, in what ways?
  - Do they appear to coordinate their respective functions, i.e. to identify and to some extent agree upon which centres may/must/must not do what and under which circumstances?
  - Do centres at different levels coordinate with each other?
- Are there decision centres working at more than one level of the problem/ good/ service/ resource and, what is the rationale for that and how does it affect coordination and conflicts?
- How have conflicts among centres arisen and been addressed?
  - Have conflicts had only negative impacts, or have they reflected potentially useful contestation about alternative perspectives or values?
  - Are there centres that perform conflict-resolution functions and, if so, in what ways or under what conditions?
  - Can individuals or centres challenge a decision or action that was taken at another level?

How centres take each other into account may derive to some degree from their use and pursuit of information in relation to problems, goals, strategies, and outcomes (see Chapters 5–8 in Part II). Interactions among centres may become cooperative, competitive and, to greater or lesser extents coordinated, depending on complementarities or incompatibilities in the information they generate, exchange, withhold, and use and in how they interpret and understand it. In addition to competition, as discussed, coordination is a way that centres 'take each other into account'. Each centre does not have to coordinate with all the others in order to constitute a polycentric arrangement, but a collection of centres that was devoid of coordination would not be a polycentric governance arrangement.

Searching for, characterizing, and assessing the coordination occurring in a polycentric governance situation is important but not simple. Coordination can appear in many forms. There are formal types of coordination, such as approval processes, and informal ones, such as consultation among peers. Coordination may be mandated (even legislatively; see Schafer 2016) or voluntary. It may be institutionalized in associations, task forces, working groups, and the like. The variety is immense, and the specific manifestations so diverse that Peters (2015, 128) has observed, 'although we certainly know coordination when we see it, measuring that coordination in other than a qualitative sense is at present difficult if not impossible'. An added complication for the analyst is that in some situations one or more mechanisms of coordination may have been established formally, but no one is participating in them and no actual coordination is occurring in practice, so one must look beyond surface appearances.

Although coordination, cooperation, and collaboration are all used frequently and sometimes treated as synonyms, they are not the same. All cooperation/collaboration may be coordinative, but not all coordination is cooperative/collaborative, especially to the degree that cooperation connotes voluntariness – one may imagine, for instance, individuals or organizations coordinating their activities so that they can avoid each other. Coordination is therefore a characteristic property to be found at least to some extent in any polycentric governance situation, while cooperation and collaboration, although important, will be frequently but not necessarily present. Cooperation among centres is the focus of Chapter 5.

Coordination has a favourable connotation in many usages, but for our purposes we are not suggesting that it is inherently or necessarily good or efficient, fair, inclusive, etc. A cartel, for example, or a criminal syndicate involves very high levels of coordination among the centres involved. The effects of coordination are contingent and a matter for empirical investigation. The key is for analysts to look for and identify the forms and extent of coordination that are present in a polycentric governance situation as part of the attempt to understand and explain it and assess its functioning and effects (Berardo and Scholz 2010). Berardo and Lubell (2016), and others, emphasize the bridging and bonding capital inherent to coordination processes in polycentric governance systems and the role of risk perception for organizing these processes. As noted briefly, these processes may also manifest in the establishment of specific 'boundary or bridging organizations' (i.e. additional centres). Cash et al. (2006) identified and characterized such organizations as one answer to the pervasive scale and plurality challenges playing intermediary roles in the exchange of information among centres. It should be considered that these organizations may have substantial independence and need to be counted as additional centres in a governance situation with their own goals, means, and power.

Furthermore, we make a distinction between coordination processes and whether the polycentric arrangement, as such, can be called coordinated overall. Conflicts may in some circumstances indicate a lack of overall coordination. As we have stated, conflicts are inherent to any governance situation and a dynamic component, with a strong temporal dimension, so it is relevant how conflicts arise and how they are resolved. Regularly occurring conflicts may render institutionalized conflict-resolution processes necessary. Conflicts resulting from dynamic processes, such as changing needs, changing perceptions and changing contexts, may be addressed through changes of the governance arrangements. Like competition, conflict and coordination may be endogenous drivers of change within polycentric arrangements. Individuals experiencing the presence, absence, extent, or effects of coordination and conflict may become motivated to create new centres or modify or eliminate existing ones, or shift levels of action and engage in rule adaptation for purposes of trying to alter the existence, nature, or operation of coordination in that polycentric situation. Section 2.6 elaborates these dynamisms further, and Chapters 5–8 in Part II use empirical cases to discuss, illustrate, and compare cooperation, conflict, and competition among centres.

2.6 Questions about Emergence, Transition, and Decline

- How do centres come into existence or dissolve?
- Are they able to change their organizational structures and/or their decision-making processes and, if so, how?
- Are they able to change their functions (activities performed, services provided, areas or constituencies served, etc.) and, if so, how?

- How have relationships and interactions between centres changed over time, and for what reasons?
- Do changes of centres or relationships reflect changed understandings of scales of problems, scales of production, or scales of effects?
- Have conflicts among centres resulted in changes to the number, composition, functions, and/or interactions of centres? If so, how did those changes occur and with what apparent consequences?

Fundamental to understanding polycentric arrangements is the recognition that both the units (centres) and their relationships can and do change. This is a focus of Chapter 4. These changes are not always or necessarily exogenously driven. Individuals within polycentric governance structures may and do generate changes. Processes of emergence, change and decline can be captured by the concepts of design and spontaneity. Because the centres in a polycentric structure are human creations, it is essential to view them as deliberately created, and therefore designed, at least, to some extent.

This does not, however, necessarily imply that a polycentric arrangement composed of those centres was designed. The structure is not merely the additive sum of the centres, but also the composite of their interactions with one another. It is possible, and even likely, that centres have been designed but the interactive system they comprise has not. Furthermore, the internal dynamics of any polycentric arrangement can be expected to change over time through the appearance or disappearance of centres and alterations in their individual operations and in their interactions with one another, and it is possible and even likely that these changes are also not designed.

Scholars have used terms such as 'spontaneity', 'spontaneous order', 'emergence', 'emergent structure', etc., to try to capture and convey the idea that even though there may be identifiable patterns in a dynamic structure, they do not necessarily reflect or result from an act or a process of design. It may also be the case that some aspects of polycentric arrangements have been designed and others have emerged so the structure has designed and undesigned elements. The multitude of polycentric arrangements that exist in the world is better approached with a conceptual toolkit that includes design as well as spontaneity or emergence, and where many polycentric arrangements belong somewhere on a spectrum between being fully designed and completely spontaneous.

Some contributors to the literature on polycentricity have argued that it is a practical impossibility for any one person to design a structure as complex and dynamic as a polycentric governance system (e.g. Boettke and Coyne 2005, 154; McGinnis 2005, 168). Polycentric arrangements are complex, having been composed by multiple 'designers' who have established centres and developed and altered their relationships over time. The levels of action concept[4] aids in understanding and explaining scope, extent and mechanisms of endogenous change in polycentric arrangements. It was presented in 1982 by Kiser and E. Ostrom (1982) and since then has been used in many theoretical and empirical examinations of institutions and their functioning. It is also one of the core elements of the Institutional Analysis and Development (IAD) framework, although it can be used and applied outside of an IAD approach as well.

What centres exist, how they came into being, and how they are altered, are functions of actions taken at a *collective-choice level*. Similarly, what centres must, or may or may not, interact with other centres, and in what ways, depend upon rules adopted at a collective-choice level. Changes that are made at a collective-choice level feed into and shape the *operational level of action* of a polycentric structure by affecting the number, types, and functions of the centres and the manner in which they take each other into account. The *constitutional-choice level of action* is also important to understanding polycentric arrangements because decisions made at that level determine whether and how easily people may make changes at the collective-choice level. In communities (of whatever size) where the constitutional-choice level of action allows wide latitude for individuals and organizations[5] to establish and alter centres and their relationships, the dynamics of stability and change of polycentric structures can and should be expected to differ from those that are observed and experienced in communities with stronger constraints on institutional modification.

One seeks to understand a polycentric structure through an examination of the centres, their functions and operations, their interactions, effects, and adjustments over time as individual actors and organizations pursue their aims, try to solve problems, and adapt. Any unit may fail, or may succeed at others' expense, or may find ways to succeed through cooperative ventures that advance others' well-being too. More likely, a polycentric structure at any given time will include all of those experiences plus others,

---

[4] Remember that the concept of levels of action is not the same as levels of government.
[5] Remember that each level of action does not entail a different set of actors. Individuals working at the operational level may decide to shift to collective-choice actions to modify centres and relationships, and to constitutional-choice actions if they wish to address the processes by which such changes may take place.

which is another reason why polycentric arrangements change over time even though no single designer is adjusting the structure as a whole.

2.7 Questions about Effects

- How has the governance arrangement helped or hindered efforts to improve conditions and solve problems?
- In what ways and to what extent has this governance arrangement facilitated information generation, learning, error correction, and adaptation?

To this point, the inquiry has been directed toward understanding elements, context, and dynamics of the governance situation – allowing the analyst to see it in terms of polycentricity. At this stage, the analyst may pose questions about the governance arrangement as a whole and how to think about the effects it generates.

Evaluating a governance arrangement differs from evaluating a particular good or service, a programme or a policy. Citing McGinnis (2011), Koontz et al. in Chapter 8 observe, 'Scholars of polycentricity, and governance more generally, have identified a wide range of performance criteria.' Those authors apply multiple criteria – some emphasizing processes and others focused on outcomes – to the cases they present in Part II. These performance criteria are accountability, social learning, adaptability, representation, consideration of appropriate knowledge in decision making, network building, and coherence (both among decision centres and across levels), in addition to the familiar evaluation criteria of efficiency and efficacy. This combination of criteria is compatible with prior work by Blomquist (1992), Pahl-Wostl and Knieper (2014), Pahl-Wostl (2014, 2015) and with the recommendation of Low, E. Ostrom, and Wilson (2003, 86) that performance of management arrangements for complex resource systems can, and should, be assessed in terms of their ability to cope with risk, uncertainty, and exogenous shocks, reduce errors through learning, address local as well as subsystem and system level problems, and avoid system collapse or failure. Accordingly, the questions listed address a myriad of effects that a governance arrangement may have.

In regard to complex systems, adaptive capacity is a vital criterion. It connotes purposeful adjustment in light of updated information. In the governance context, we may link it to the concept of levels of action mentioned in Section 2.6. In a governance structure that exhibits adaptive capacity, people would be able not only to make behavioural adjustments at the operational level in response to changed understandings, but also to shift to the collective-choice level to alter rules governing behaviour and to the constitutional-choice level when necessary to alter decision-making processes. Pahl-Wostl has linked the concept to the importance of single-loop, double-loop, and triple-loop learning as characteristics of adaptable complex governance structures.

Adaptation by governance arrangements in response to updated information and revised understandings depends necessarily upon both information generation and the interpretation of information from multiple viewpoints. Assuming that fuller information is beneficial for effective governance, arrangements that more effectively promote the generation of information from different levels, about various dimensions of problems, performance and about alternative practices would be preferable. Similarly, since information admits of multiple meanings, governance arrangements featuring diverse channels through which people can express, exchange, and even contest about the interpretation and significance of that information would be preferable to governance arrangements that limit such flows.

These criteria are readily linked to another, i.e. error reduction. Human-created structures are unavoidably error-prone to greater or lesser degree, both in bringing about undesirable results and in failing to achieve desirable ones (Bendor 1985). Error elimination may be impossible, but error reduction is nonetheless desirable and a legitimate criterion on which to evaluate the demonstrated performance of governance systems. Whether a governance arrangement enables or inhibits learning and contestation is therefore an important area for inquiry.

The examination of effects of polycentric governance arrangements in specific settings will often – perhaps always – generate mixed findings. Naturally, some trade-offs may be identified between the openness of a governance system to change and its robustness to maintain functions and withstand disruption. It is worthwhile to take both into account when evaluating governance arrangements, to consider how they are situated between rigidity and flux. Furthermore, Milman and Scott's (2010) cogent assessment of trade-offs in the water-management context is valuable. They noted that the overlap and redundancies of polycentric arrangements may enhance resilience, but also raise transaction costs and the prospects of conflict and confusion over authority and responsibility. Overlap among centres may be incomplete: 'gaps in jurisdiction' may occur where 'some aspects of water management do not fall under the purview of any water management agency' (2010, 532). The dynamic nature of polycentric arrangements is surely an advantage in some respects, but it can also be the case that '[r]apid evolution leads to ambiguity (ill-defined roles) [that] in turn leads to legitimacy claims that can result in overlapping mandates and program implementation working at cross purposes' (2010, 532). Noting both the pitfalls and the promises of polycentricity, Milman and Scott reach a conclusion similar to that of Elinor Ostrom when she wrote 'there is no guarantee that such systems will find the combination of rules at diverse levels that are optimal for any particular environment' (E. Ostrom 1999, 39).

2.8 Conclusion

Since polycentric governance is widespread, it is essential to have some way of identifying and characterizing it. This is challenging, however, because of the countless forms and variations that actual polycentric arrangements may take and their continuous change over time. The diagnostic inquiry-based approach laid out above therefore has many parts and steps.

However, making this effort to 'see polycentrically' should generate insight into the ways in which the various aspects and dimensions of polycentric governance manifest themselves in a complex governance situation. What should emerge in the composite result of these inquiries is an understanding of governance in a particular setting that helps to indicate whether, to what extent, and in what ways it resembles a polycentric governance system, an uncoordinated and fragmented jumble, or something in-between. We encourage the use and refinement of this inquiry-based approach in future research on polycentric governance across a variety of settings, which will enhance the accumulation of knowledge.

Developing that kind of overall portrait of a complex governance situation, by assembling this information, is also vital to any prospect for an accurate and empirically grounded evaluation of how the governance arrangements perform and of the prospects for positive change. If we make such pronouncements without undertaking the inquiry, we run the risks not merely of failing to understand the governance arrangements, but also of substituting ideological judgements for actual analyses – i.e. (a) dismissing as undesirable all polycentric governance situations, regardless of how well or poorly they may actually operate, or (b) embracing as desirable all polycentric governance situations, regardless of how well or poorly they actually operate. Neither is the appropriate stance for committed researchers or practitioners.

Other chapters in this book use empirical cases of water and other governance situations to discuss, further illustrate and compare the elements laid out in this inquiry. How polycentric governance functions in any actual setting depends on more than the characteristics of the governance arrangements themselves. It also depends on the overarching rules of the polity, the nature of the problems being addressed, and the communities in which governance arrangements are embedded. These are the focus of Chapter 3.

Foundational Aspects of Polycentric Governance

Overarching Rules, Social-Problem Characteristics, and Heterogeneity

Andreas Thiel and Christine Moser

3.1 Introduction

Our question in this chapter is very simple: why is governance of water and other natural resources structured differently in different biophysical and socio-political contexts? Such differences, we argue, tend to be most pronounced where public, private and civil society actors have the opportunity to decide flexibly how their interests and tasks are to be represented. In such cases, actors at least have the option to modify how they want to organize provision and production of (collective) goods and services. Overall, we argue that three foundational components of polycentric governance can provide a useful structure for understanding differences in the ways natural-resource management is addressed.

First, autonomous decision-making and independent self-organization by public and/ or private agents needs to be considered legitimate (i.e. both allowed and recognized) for polycentric governance to emerge. However, the existing institutional scaffolding that structures self-organization, which we summarize as overarching rules, presumably differs across jurisdictions. As a result, the human, physical, and social resources and capacities of agents and communities may also differ. These differences in the features of underlying institutions and degrees of agency are presumably responsible to some extent for the variability of polycentric governance. For example, differences in how constitutional rules are legitimized and their implications on polycentric governance can be illustrated via examining differences in the ways water management is set up across Europe. In Northern Europe, we predominantly observe territorial water management (i.e. administrative boundaries independent from the boundaries of water bodies, usually consistent with boundaries of interrelated sectoral responsibilities for land management, agriculture, public health), which tends to lead to difficulties in coordinating relevant actors responsible for the water quality of a particular water body (e.g. a basin), though it does ease coordination across sectors that shape the overall performance of water management. In contrast, in Southern Europe, basin management can be observed in many countries. Here, surface-water-related management issues are more easily coordinated, while cross-sectoral coordination is much harder to achieve (Thiel 2015).

A second key component shaping differences in polycentric governance structures and outcomes is what we call social-problem characteristics. Societies identify problems deriving from deviations between the status quo and a socially desired state of affairs, including environmental issues such as water quality and the like, and the characteristics of these problems then shape decisions and performance expectations regarding governance arrangements. Thus, for example, water governance in relatively humid and highly industry-driven Germany differs from water governance in arid, agriculture-dependent Southern Spain. Also, associated water management challenges differ. Farming in Southern Spain depends on intense extraction of water for irrigation, making water-quantity management a question of economic survival in this area. In contrast, in relation to surface-water management in Germany, flooding and water pollution from industry are perceived as the principal threats to the economy, but also, and even more so, to public safety and ecosystems. The perceived characteristics of these social problems greatly differ, which, when given the chance, tend to lead to different approaches for addressing them through polycentric governance (Thiel 2015).

The third set of factors that we want to address is heterogeneity in terms of the characteristics of actors and groups. The socio-economic characteristics of communities, as well as the distribution of values and preferences within them, can differ widely in ways that affect governance structures and evaluation of governance performance. For example, studies of the politics of (transboundary) rivers that cross state or country borders illustrate that communities sharing water and natural resources have heterogeneous features and, therefore, also claims on these resources.

Thus, for any given time and place, governance of water and other natural resources does not emerge in a void but is, rather, configured by combinations of (a) overarching rules (b) social-problem characteristics, and (c) community heterogeneity – all of which influence the emergence and functioning of polycentric governance and can account for variations across locations and change over time.

Against this background, this chapter proceeds as follows: we begin by briefly situating our argument in relation to previous work on polycentricity. Subsequently, we elaborate on the three aspects we consider foundational to polycentric governance: first exploring overarching rules as a necessary condition for the emergence of polycentric governance, then examining perceptions regarding social-problem characteristics and, finally, illustrating the role of community heterogeneity when organizing in relation to provision and production of collective goods. Throughout the text, specifically in two vignettes, we refer to examples illustrating our argument.

We consider it important to reiterate these foundational issues, not only for didactic reasons and as a contribution towards the comprehensiveness of this book, but also to trigger future research on some thus-far underrepresented aspects of polycentricity. Therefore, to end the chapter, we discuss how the three components that we consider foundational to polycentricity interact in governance and point towards future research needs from this perspective.

3.2 Polycentric Governance as Dependent and Independent Variables and Its Internal Dynamics

A number of scholars wonder whether polycentric governance is present or not in particular constellations. We consider this to be a mostly descriptive understanding of polycentric governance (McGinnis 2016; Thiel 2017), as outlined in Chapter 1 in relation to polycentric governance arrangements. Meanwhile, Chapter 2 proposes a different perspective, which seeks to understand particular dimensions of polycentric governance and identify explanatory factors that shape their form. In this chapter, we want to deepen our engagement with this perspective and argue for a differentiated research programme, seeking to conceptualize the foundational co-determinants of polycentric governance.

We consider (polycentric) governance to be both a dependent and independent variable. In particular, following the early writings of the Ostroms, we focus on categories of variables co-determining different forms of polycentric governance along with their functioning and performance (cf. Ostrom and Ostrom 1999b). Overarching rules have also been referred to by Ostrom et al. (1961), characterized as the normative preconditions for the emergence and dynamic functioning of polycentric governance, possibly entailing combinations of what have also been called constitutional and collective choice rules (Ostrom, 1999b).

Polycentric governance theorizes the way actors develop activities in relation to particular social problems. Corresponding polycentricity theory (Jordan et al. 2015) subscribes to a relatively precise but ontologically open conception of the actor. This conception has been laid down in what have been called metaconstitutional assumptions[1] (Ostrom 2005a). Specifically, actors are conceptualized as being boundedly but intendedly rational and fallible learners who, in consequence, are able to undertake measures to effectively improve their well-being over time. Further, as members of particular communities, agents need to be aware of the assumed need to share common values in the interest of realization of collective well-being.

To exemplify how overarching rules, social-problem characteristics and social heterogeneity jointly shape governance, we can mention here water-related private goods, the characteristics of which are rivalry and excludability, making them prone to transactions through markets. However, markets emerge only in contexts where property rights and their transfer are constitutionally granted, highlighting the role of overarching rules. In particular cultural contexts, private goods, such as water once it has left the tap, may, for ethical reasons, be considered a good to which everyone should have access. Thus, in the end, social-problem characteristics, overarching rules and (cultural) heterogeneity of communities may lead to very diverse forms of (polycentric) governance of goods and services.

Governance and differences in the ways it operates have different behavioural implications for public and private agents involved in providing and producing public goods and services. To greater or lesser degrees, providing and producing agents may be contested by citizen–consumers regarding the ways they provide goods and services, potentially leading to a kind of evolutionary change of polycentric governance arrangements (see also Chapter 4). Further, involved agents can apply different criteria for evaluating polycentric governance performance; as illustrated by the brief example of tap water, different evaluative norms may be culturally bound. Ostrom et al. (1968) argue that particular types of polycentric governance emerge from continuous confrontation among partially conflicting evaluative criteria – such as efficiency, effectiveness, equity, political representation, or resilience – held by different constituent groups. Figure 3.1

---

[1] In this book we distinguish between metaconstitutional assumptions and metaconstitutional conditions. The former refer to assumptions about actors that inform the analysis of the Ostroms. Instead, the latter, metaconstitutional conditions are referred to as observed empirically on the metaconstitutional level of analysis. They refer to culture, beliefs, etc. Chapter 9 by Marshall and Malik particularly refer to this concept.

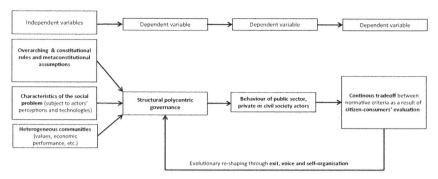

Figure 3.1 Conceptual map of variables emphasized in polycentric governance research
Source: Authors

schematically maps out our understanding of polycentric governance as both an independent and dependent variable. In what follows, we want to detail our treatment of foundational factors and describe how they determine particular forms of polycentricity.

3.3 The Overarching Rules of Polycentric Governance

The original 1961 publication about polycentric governance by Vincent Ostrom and colleagues does not say much about the underlying conditions of day-to-day practices of polycentric governance (Ostrom 1999a). Nonetheless, it argued that polycentric governance is related to functionally interdependent but formally independent decision-making centres. Particularly in the realm of water or other forms of natural-resource management, functional interdependence means that governance and its performance are affected by a multitude of activities. For example, consider cases where agricultural development policy in an area affects water use, policy and their performance. Formal independence may, in turn, be related to de facto decision-making powers and responsibilities in relation to, for example, creating certain kinds of infrastructure, allocating specific amounts of water to particular uses, or implementing specific legislation. However, in many cases it could be argued that independently administered sources of revenue are equally as important as legal rights. Further, under polycentric governance, decision-making centres may have the option to enter into contractual and cooperative undertakings, as well as resort to central mechanisms to resolve conflicts between centres. Thus, the day-to-day functioning of polycentric governance requires overarching rules that set up the corresponding options.

To clarify his stance in regard to these overarching rules, Vincent Ostrom largely relied on the work of Michael Polanyi (1953) and Alexander Hamilton and James Madison (Ostrom 1999b). In later publications, the Ostroms referred to the kinds of rules we want to examine here as constitutional rules. However, in this chapter, we would like to avoid the use of language associated with levels of institutional analysis and rules, as referred to by the Ostroms (Ostrom 2005), because the conditions and overarching rules we discuss could presumably take effect at any level. Further, we want to make clear that we refer to what the Ostroms and others have called 'rules in use', such as the rules actually underpinning the ways co-users of a water reservoir organize its maintenance, which may differ substantially from what is prescribed by the relevant formal rules (Ostrom et al. 1994).

We consider Vincent Ostrom's position on overarching rules to entail tensions between three approaches: (a) theories and descriptions regarding what polycentric governance is, (b) propositions for empirically testing how polycentric governance is brought into being, as well as (c) normative ideas regarding the superiority of polycentric over monocentric governance. The description of polycentric governance has already been elaborated upon in Chapter 1. Here we propose to understand the rules that underpin polycentricity as empirically generated normative propositions, with regards to what brings polycentric governance about. In our view, they have not yet been subjected to enough systematic examination. Thus, from our perspective, it has not been satisfactorily empirically proven that corresponding rules or conditions are necessary and/or sufficient for polycentric governance. Nonetheless, Vincent Ostrom seems to see these prescriptive rules as necessary conditions for proper functioning of types of governance that rely heavily on decentralized self-organization of actors. In contrast, where these conditions are not in place, he would probably expect such forms of governance to not work well. Thus, in relation to many social problems, the desirability of forms of governance that emphasize self-organization and favour autonomous decision-making centres can be considered to be related to value judgements, meaning that they cannot simply be taken as given. Consequently, we argue that rigorous research should be undertaken before claims are made concerning what particular governance arrangements may be most desirable, in particular contexts.

Finally, we presume that the already reported overarching rules and metaconstitutional assumptions that co-determine polycentric governance may lead to greater probabilities of emergence and proper functioning of polycentric governance (Ostrom 2007), but they do not guarantee it. Thus, in many cases where polycentric governance operates, we may not readily observe all of the expected rules or conditions. Similarly, we may encounter situations where sufficient rules appear to be in place, yet polycentricity does not emerge. Taken together, these problems indicate to us a need for deeper scrutiny of the roles of social-problem characteristics and the heterogeneity of communities and actors, leaving us with a research puzzle concerning the relationships between the socio-economic contexts, configurations of formal rules and day-to-day rules in use connected to polycentric governance.

3.3.1 General and Domain-Specific Rules

In this section we present an account of overarching rules that structure polycentric governance. In this regard, we distinguish between general and domain-specific rules. General rules are unspecific to a particular domain. Oriented by 'the principles of federalism and separation of powers within a system of limited constitutions' (Ostrom 1999a, 57), general rules are meant to ensure that tendencies towards monocentricity in one domain are counterbalanced by polycentricity across domains for polycentric governance to operate well. The underlying idea is that, if any among the judicial, political, economic, and public-service spheres were to move towards monocentricity, system-wide polycentricity could not be maintained, because the mechanisms for system-wide self-correction and self-regulation would be disturbed (Ostrom et al. 1961; van Zeben 2013).

For example, it is claimed that, if polycentric governance were to be embedded in a system with monocentrically organized political or judicial spheres, this would undermine competition associated with the ways in which provision of public goods are organized in the water sector, because either would instil a dynamic tending towards one large provisioning entity or type of governance. This dynamic has been observed in the drinking-water and water-treatment sectors in Portugal, where, over the past two decades under a centralist state, the national state-driven foundation of public-service companies quasi-automatically led to one large country wide provider, held in check by a weak, national state-affiliated regulator (Thiel 2010b). We hold that, in this manner, the potential for polycentric governance was to some extent weakened. However, we have not been able to assess the actual performance implications of this development. In fact, it could well be that, for the particular case of Portugal and for that particular period of time, the corresponding set-up was performing as the best solution on several counts.

The constitutional domain structures the affairs of government and public and private entities, as well as its relation to citizens, consumers and interrelated public and private actors. It sets up independent decision structures and enables the vetoing or contesting of others' decisions. Ideally, a division of authority implies segmentation of the components of the provisioning function such that governance functions (e.g. monitoring, information-gathering, financing, conflict resolution, producing, financing, coordination) are spread across agents (McGinnis 2016; McGinnis and Ostrom 2012; Paavola 2007; Thiel 2014). The resulting independent and potentially overlapping decision-making structures then allow actors to access legal, political, administrative, and constitutional remedies afforded by different units of government. Further, in cases of violation of constitutional provisions, individuals need to be capable of and willing to exercise disobedience.

In fact, we can observe countries that have experimented with different arrangements for water-governance functions across jurisdictions. In the 1990s for example, Portugal integrated the responsibilities for water, previously vested in administrations and jurisdictions over land and environmental management, into one entity, but then, in the middle of the last decade, it separated water management among administrations guided by basin principles, from land and environmental management. Spread of governance functions across different entities also makes threats to exit from a particular jurisdiction, or coordination and collaborative arrangement, and switch to another one more credible (Ostrom 1999a, 63). Combined with multiple decision-making mechanisms and cultures, this can lead to shifting coalitions and externally imposed requirements being put upon public-service agents to constantly scrutinize their operations.

In addition, larger units of governance need to be put in place to provide institutional arrangements for the resolution of conflict between entities. For example, if farmers were to be discontent with their water allocations during droughts, they need to be able to turn to higher jurisdictions and courts in order to have their claims verified against the corresponding water-allocation body. Such nestedness is particularly necessary to maintain the polycentric order (Ostrom 1999a, 72) and is also one of Elinor Ostrom's design principles, meant to secure successful collective self-organization.

Further, agents at higher, more-encompassing levels need to have access to procedures to reform rules constituting governance and to knowledge constituted, for example, by sciences seeking to uncover causal relations between the way governance is organized and its outcomes. Further, individual agents need to have the right to contest governmental decisions in courts and seek remedies.

In addition to these summarized general rules, Vincent Ostrom elaborated a number of domain-specific rules referring to the political, judicial, public-service provision, and market domains (Ostrom 1999b). Following the general critique that in Ostrom, Tiebout and Warren 1961 he and his colleagues had left open what brought polycentric governance into being and what sustained it, he elaborated upon domain-specific rules in a number of publications, with the most concise overview being provided in Ostrom (1999b). These initial ideas were later complemented by a variety of authors (for an overview, see Thiel 2017). In summary, across domains these rules seemed to be modelled on an idealized conception of the United States' democratic federal state. Beyond rules structuring the polity, particular emphasis was attached to the formation of particular characteristics of agents as preconditions for democratic societies that can sustain critical engagement and self-organization in relation to collective affairs (Ostrom 2014). Although, due to lack of space, we will not expand further on domain-specific rules, to make the concept clearer, we shall provide some examples of how they play out in particular realms of society.

For the public-service provision and production domains, for example, individuals in polycentric governance, relying on autonomous self-organization, need to be both entitled and enabled to self-organize. Jurisdictions also need to be entitled to coordinate and contract with other jurisdictions, in order to realize economies of scale. Further, in relation to the economic domain, secure property rights and freedom of contract are key, including mechanisms to sanction their infringement, as both are preconditions for economic exchange and effective threat of exit – basic conditions underlying capitalist competition. Within the particular field of water provision, such constitutional rules form the backbone of schemes to trade water rights, in order to increase efficiency (Garrick 2015).

Box 3.1 Vignette: Polycentric governance in Germany and China – the role of constitutional rules

Da Silveira and Richards (2013) studied polycentricity in the European Union and China, looking at water governance in the Rhine and Pearl river basins and coming to the conclusion that in both cases polycentric governance existed, although this was more pronounced and successful in the case of the Rhine. They judge success in terms of the presence of institutions that encourage actors to share the monitoring of data and information, noting that the actors have greater motivation to collaborate in the Rhine basin, where the European Union Water Framework Directive (WFD) and the European Court of Justice provide institutional incentives for law enforcement. This is quite different in China, where actors compete with each other and, thus, do not share information readily, and few levers exist that the central government may use to establish order within the governance system, which suffers from multiple actors with overlapping duties. Da Silveira and Richards (2013) note the paramount importance of policy networks in both cases. The processes of Europeanization and decentralization have played an important role in what may be seen as an emergent form of polycentric governance that is being promoted by inter-basin networks (INTERREG), the WFD, and other pan-European legislation. Meanwhile, a networked nature of governance is also being increasingly observed in China, where 'personal relationships' play a key role (da Silveira and Richards 2013).

Da Silveira and Richards' study is useful in highlighting the role of constitutional rules in water governance. In Europe, formally codified constitutional conditions and the Ostroms' propositions on overarching rules facilitating polycentric governance that is characterized by autonomous, decentralized self-organization approximate each other to some extent empirically. In contrast, this is far from the case for the Pearl River in China. What are the differences in the nature of polycentricity in both cases? First, we find it striking that in both of these highly diverse formal constitutional configurations, da Silveira and Richards (2013) found significant traits of self-organization in forms of polycentric governance. Therefore, for us questions emerge regarding what further traits distinguish kinds of polycentric arrangements and how these traits are connected to overarching rules. Also, the role of contextual factors needs to be assessed. In our view, da Silveira and Richards' study (2013) reveals that, when we examine the role of overarching rules for polycentric governance, we also need to pay attention to agency, context and contingent events (Thiel and Mukhtarov 2018).

3.3.2 Overarching Rules and the Selection of Preferred Polycentric Governance Arrangements

Ideally, the general and domain-specific rules tend to facilitate multifaceted, differentiated and nested polycentricity, as a means to flexibly organize governance responses in consonance with actors' purposes (Ostrom and Ostrom 1999b, 41). Within such polycentric constellations, exit, voice, and self-organization are mechanisms through which actors can contest the actions of other functionally interdependent actors, who are all connected via governance structures and processes. Aligica and Tarko (2012) have, in our opinion, adequately summarized these mechanisms underpinning polycentric governance. On the demand side, voicing concern about public-goods provision through political channels or exiting from a jurisdiction reminds us of discussions initiated by Hirschman (1970). The Ostroms added the possibility of self-organization as a strategy for consumers to establish supply side alternatives for public-goods provision and production. It highlights the radical dimension of polycentricity, distinguishing polycentric governance as an alternative within debates at the time – and largely continuing today – that posited market forces (where exit options are supposed to be readily available) and state governance (where voice is supposed to be available) as the two principal alternatives. Specifically, self-organization under polycentric governance hinges on the question of whether and to what degree the overarching rules encourage, allow, discourage, or prohibit it, along with exit and voice. These mechanisms allow agents, in their roles as citizens or consumers for example, to select the governance features and performance levels they prefer, albeit drawing on very different ways of legitimizing their forms of contestation, either abstaining from consumption (as consumers) or withdrawing support (as citizens). Such mechanisms can also be invoked by actors co-providing and provisioning on the supply side.

For example, in relation to self-organization, one question is whether decision centres such as citizens or consumers are encouraged to voice discontent with providers, leave them physically or withdraw their membership, and if they are granted the rights and capacities to do so. Ideally, they would have the rights and necessary capacities to self-organize service provision. In relation to water governance, this might for instance mean that citizens or consumers themselves take over sewage-water treatment or drinking-water supply. Self-organization matters because, as in much of water management, polycentric governance addresses the provision and production of collective goods, requiring rules that can sustain self-organization such that collective action dilemmas can be overcome in the long-term (Ostrom 2007). Correspondingly, the overarching rules ideally enabling and guiding polycentric governance need to allow a role for self-organization, so that consumers and citizens can flexibly associate in what they consider to be the most suitable and efficient ways.

Further, rules should foster the exercise of a credible threat to providers and producers through which individuals, in their positions as citizens or consumers, will be potentially able to politically delegitimize providers and producers and, when deemed necessary, withdraw their financial support.

Through such available avenues, citizens and/or consumers are presumed to be potentially effective in influencing the day-to-day operation of polycentric governance by making providers and producers respect their preferences. In contrast, under monocentric governance, where 'the governmental prerogatives ... are vested in some single office or decision structure that has an ultimate monopoly over the legitimate exercise of coercive capabilities' (Ostrom 1999a, 55), alternatives to central public-service provision and production cannot be credibly put forward. In addition to these citizen- and consumer-oriented features of polycentric governance, the Ostroms have also discussed the relevance of mechanisms of exit, voice and self-organization on the *supply side* of public goods and services. In the water sector, this would include actors involved in securing water-related nature conservation, provision and production of drinking water or suppliers of hydropower as well as agents monitoring water use or gathering information about the status of resources. We consider such supply side mechanisms as standing for checks and balances within a polycentric governance system. Ideally, because of the stratification of governance functions under polycentric governance, actors can mutually scrutinize each other and, consequently, options for switching provisioning partners may emerge. As a corollary of this state of flexibility, in their struggle to meet the preferences of citizens and consumers, public enterprises have the option to autonomously select their collaborators, which is especially relevant if they become discontented with their performance. Providers themselves can also check on each other's performance in their efforts to secure continued support from citizens and consumers. A relevant example here would be tendering processes to determine operators of water-related public infrastructure, where providers of water services regularly check the performance of producers in terms of the ways they deliver water services to citizen–consumers.

Simultaneous operation of these mechanisms on the demand and supply sides requires the support of the formal and informal, general and domain-specific overarching rules. For example, overarching rules under polycentric governance can enable the involvement of numerous actors in the roles of provisioning or producing collective goods, giving citizens and consumers greater options for contracting specific services and, thereby, making possible contestation of existing relations through their opting for easily accessible alternatives. Such rules can lower transaction costs for questioning providers and producers and, in that way, make threats of citizens and consumers more credible; but it may also increase other transaction or production costs, due to economies of scale foregone. At the same time, among provisioning actors, a greater number of potential collaborative partners may come into play across governance functions, which can strengthen the checks and balances exercised by providers and producers in seeking different contracting options.

3.4 Social-Problem Characteristics

Similar to rules, social problems, that we want to treat in this section, are socially constructed (Ostrom 2005a). Social problems represent cases where actors' observations do not correspond to what they desire as states of affairs. Social problems are culturally and historically co-determined, as much as ways to address them depend on social constructions such as values, perceptions, rules and technologies available that allow people to redress social problems. Disputes over ways to resolve challenges to governance emerge as groups of actors from various layers of society may want governance to perform well in relation to different performance criteria, such as cost-effectiveness, fairness, resilience, positing different tasks for it. In relation to polycentric governance, we also want to highlight a second sense of the concept of social-problem characteristics, based on the fact that the effects of and possible solutions to problems such as water quality, ecosystem health, habitat values or recreational values reach beyond the individual, making them collective goods (public good or common-pool resource problems; see Ostrom and Ostrom 1999a).

Naturally, large-scale issues like this can be considered problematic for very different reasons. An intuitive and common categorization is to distinguish between the social, economic and ecological aspects of such problems. Thus, for example, lack of water often affects actors unequally, hinders economic production, and undermines intact, water-related habitats. A great deal of interdisciplinary work has been undertaken based on the assumption that the dimensions of large-scale problems are often interconnected (e.g. resilience studies, political ecology, sustainability sciences).

Polycentric governance keeps open the kinds of underlying motivations actors may pursue in addressing problems through self-organization. It expands possibilities in all directions, positive or negative, for addressing questions concerning whose values will be counted in determining the ways problems are to be approached, who should carry the financial costs of alternative solutions, how will all be related to existing forms and scales of governance, and how governance should perform in addressing given problems. This multidimensional quality of polycentric governance has clear implications for the economics and politics of the ways social problems may be addressed.

A number of authors have examined how particular social-problem characteristics affect the challenges to and performance of (polycentric) governance. Here we illustratively discuss four core categories under which the effects of social-problem dimensions on different performance criteria can be subsumed. Research on these issues in relation to social-ecological systems remains new, and the categories borrow heavily from literatures outside of the natural-resource governance domains (e.g. industrial organization; Williamson 1991). First, we discuss the spatial scale of social (-ecological) problems and its relation to the scale of different governance functions and the effects it can have on the efficiency, control and representativeness of governance; second, we outline factors affecting agents' opportunistic behaviour and the cost-effectiveness of governance; third, we examine factors affecting the cost-effectiveness of modes of coordination; and then, fourth, we highlight factors that can influence the costs of credibly contesting polycentric governance. How these and other dimensions affect other performance criteria, such as sustainability or resilience, is a task for further conceptual and empirical research (see Carlisle and Gruby 2017).

3.4.1 Mismatches between Scales of Exclusion and Efficiency and Control and Political Representativeness in Governance

In relation to *scales of governance*, social-problem characteristics refer to a scale where exclusion from positive and negative, indirect and direct effects from provision and production of goods and services is technologically and affordably possible, meaning where spatial externalities (spillovers) are internalized. Following Gibson (2000), we use *scale* here to represent a type of dimension of a problem (e.g. excludability), whereas *level* represents the particular values that characterize a problem at a given scale (e.g. high or low excludability). For example, drinking bottled water has no externalities beyond the individual, whereas a farmer polluting a lake has negative externalities on further users interested in obtaining clean water from it. To cease drinking bottled water is easily possible at the level of the individual, while monitoring pollution is easiest in relation to actors distant from the lake, for example through control of access roads as a means of exclusion. Thus, the level of exclusion is higher for the lake.

Lack of excludability at the level of the individual, as exemplified by the case of the water quality of a lake as opposed to bottled water, can lead to impracticalities when trading goods in the market that may turn into collective action problems concerning, for example, good quality water production and provision. To internalize the costs and benefits of such common-pool resources, the levels of financing, provisioning and evaluation should match the levels at which a resource has effects on users. However, over time, exclusion from goods and services can become more or less feasible and affordable and more or less valued by particular groups within a society, due to changes in technology and values. Monitoring of water consumption through remote sensing can be considered an example of progress in terms of exclusion technologies that illustrates such change.

What matters in terms of identifying the appropriate scale of exclusion for a particular good is its relation to the scale of financing it, the scale of deciding about its provision (in terms of quality and quantity), and the scale chosen for evaluating its performance. Depending on the relation of levels of these different governance functions/scales and the technologically determined scale of exclusion, we encounter situations of either match or mismatch of scales, with matching implying that the levels of different scales coincide. According to Ostrom, Tiebout, and Warren (1961), where the level of exclusion and the levels of financing, provisioning and evaluation decisions in relation to a good coincide, we can then consider this to be a governance performance situation that exhibits efficient allocation combined with optimal political representation and control, standing here for internalization of external effects.

The above discussion is intended to show that, in order to overcome problems of mismatch for a particular good (Ekstrom and Young 2009; Young 2002), governance needs to be organized at diverse scales that coincide with the level at which exclusion is possible, which may itself vary over time. As a result, we expect an ever-changing scalar configuration of polycentric governance (see also Chapters 2 and 4). Nonetheless, empirically, the scale of governance functions is generally built upon existing administrative levels. Thus, theoretical considerations of scale may need to be oriented in relation to existing local, regional, state, or federal levels of governance. Diverging from these scales may require the establishment of additional, potentially duplicate, administrative structures, as noted by Ostrom's theory of polycentric governance (Ostrom et al. 1961). A case in point is the discussion of river basins as a scale at which countries often do not have capacities and responsibilities allocated, other than those related to water management, so questions emerge regarding how this scale of governance is related to, for example, existing territorial and water-provision levels of jurisdiction (Moss 2012).

3.4.2 Opportunistic Behaviour and the Cost-Effectiveness of Types of Governance

Polycentric governance not only refers to situations of complex governance architecture across scales and levels, but also to a diverse spectrum of forms of governance arrangements. According to Williamson (1985), the characteristics of social problems generally affect the cost-effectiveness of *controlling actors' attempts at opportunistic behaviour* through governance, such as in relation to moral hazard problems (Fritsch 2014). Thus, in seeking to provide cost-effective governance, a diverse set of possible governance arrangements will need to be selected from to match particular social-problem characteristics.

In this regard, Williamson particularly refers to asset-specific investments, which lead to unilateral dependence of one actor upon another, therefore creating risks of exploitation due to opportunistic behaviour. This can occur, for example, where water users decide to adapt their facilities to meet the technical specifications of water providers. Such measures tend to limit their flexibility in switching providers and increase exposure to risks of opportunistic behaviour (rising sunk costs). Further, Williamson refers to uncertainty and the difficulties of measuring transaction results, which can also increase the risk of opportunistic behaviour. We can observe this where consumers have difficulties pinning down responsibility for widespread health problems that may potentially be related to water-pollution problems. In such situations of great uncertainty, Williamson advocates, for example, hierarchical kinds of governance, which are expected to be better at holding actors accountable. Finally, he also refers to frequency, describing how greater expenses entailed by governance structures seeking to more effectively monitor agent behaviour can be better compensated through gains from diminishing opportunistic behaviour if a transaction takes place more frequently. This can be observed in the monitoring of private water consumption in households, as opposed to occasional consumption of water for private purposes (e.g. car-washing) on the premises of a publicly owned company. Williamson suggests that for social problems (which he calls transactions) that are ridden by high asset specificity, great uncertainty and frequency, a hierarchical type of governance tends to be justified in terms of cost-effectiveness, whereas markets are most cost-effective where asset specificity, uncertainty and frequency are low.

Thiel et al. (2016) have added relational distance as a factor for evaluating the likelihood of opportunistic behaviour, proposing the idea that monitoring compliance becomes more costly when interdependent actors (social relational distance) or activities (physical relational distance) become more distant from each other. For example, monitoring water use within a limited irrigation perimeter is much easier than monitoring water use from a large river. Therefore, we hypothesize that, all other things being equal, increasing physical and social relational distance tends to decrease the cost-effectiveness of all governance arrangements.

3.4.3 Requirements for Coordination and Cost-Effectiveness of Governance

The social-problem characteristic jointness of production (or its opposite, separability) has been shown to have significant implications for cost-effectiveness and efficiency of different governance arrangements for coordination in polycentric governance (Thiel 2016). Chapter 2 captured it as multifunctionality (Vatn 2002). It describes that while deliberately undertaking activities that involve natural resources in complex ecosystems, actors often jointly produce interconnected goods and services combining public and private goods (Thiel 2010a; Vatn 2002). Vincent Ostrom referred to this as interrelatedness of uses (Oakerson and Parks 2011; Ostrom 1962). Many jointly produced or interrelated effects may be unintended or even unknown. For example, applying nitrogen fertilizers on a field might result in higher crop yields and, thus, increase farm income. As an unintended side effect, some of the applied fertilizers might end up in the groundwater or – directly or indirectly – in a nearby river imposing additional (cleaning-) costs on actors using the river as a source for drinking water. Jointness of production, no doubt, could be described as a specific kind of externality. However, we prefer its description as jointness in production because this does not suggest conventional market solutions discussed in environmental economics, such as for example standard price approaches. In contrast, similar to Hagedorn (2008), description of this phenomenon as jointness opens the thinking up to consideration of other kinds of coordinating/internalizing governance structures. Its systematic analysis has often been overlooked in recent literature (for exceptions, see Falconer 2002; Hagedorn 2002; Vatn 2002). In cases where those joint effects are presumed, precautionary elements of coordination in governance may be put in place in addition to attempts to account for positive and negative spatial externalities (spillovers). For different kinds of jointness of production Hagedorn (2008, 2015) suggests different kinds of governance arrangements to allow for the realization of benefits of coordination across interdependent effects at the expense of increases in transaction costs. For example, along with others, he argues that the family farm, following multiple objectives, integrates jointness of production better into decision-making than private companies, primarily optimizing revenue (Hagedorn 2008).

3.4.4 Structure of Governance Alternatives and the Costs of Contesting Governance

Social-problem characteristics also affect the way citizens or consumers are able to contest governance. They affect the shape and performance of polycentric governance indirectly. Specifically, we presuppose the contestation mechanisms of exit, voice and self-organization are legitimately available to citizen–consumers in polycentric governance but argue that particular characteristics of social problems affect their accessibility. Thus, what we call the characteristics of place-boundedness and discreteness of the production function of goods and services lead to constellations of governance, where citizens have no alternatives of production and provision readily available. Options to exit and switch provision relations or to self-organize are limited, and the principal option available to citizens is voice, i.e. influencing provision and production politically. Scholars of the Bloomington school, in particular Oakerson, named such constellations as alternating because at any one time and in one place, only one provider or producer is available (Advisory Commission on Intergovernmental Relations 1987).

An example from the water sector would be flood protection. It can only be provided and produced once for each location and, in most cases, it is associated with indivisible investments (i.e. a discrete production function). In contrast, where benefits from goods and services are not bound by a specific place and their production function is continuous, which implies that incremental increases in production also benefit actors, they can rely on exit and easily switch to other providers or even self-organize. Such a constellation relates to enhancing water security worldwide through water-saving technologies paid for by a price premium on purchases of bottled water (cf. www.vivaconagua.org/ accessed 16 June 2016). It allows consumers to opt for retailers that promise the greatest water-security contributions. Writings on local public economies call this a duplicate constellation of governance (ACIR 1987). It facilitates contesting the way goods and services are provided and produced because sunk costs associated with opting for alternative provisioning actors are relatively low. Yet, our vignette on a biofuels case shows that duplication alone is not sufficient to enable contestation (Thiel and Moser 2018).

We learn that in polycentric governance, we expect that differences in characteristics of social problems require diverse governance arrangements at multiple scales, respectively affecting their performance in diverse ways. We consider the categories of scale of exclusion, opportunistic behaviour, joint production, and structural accessibility of governance alternatives to be important for the way the multitude of social-problem characteristics affect governance. Arguably, most characteristics of resource units and resource systems that Ostrom later depicted in her social-ecological systems framework can be grouped according to these categories (Ostrom 2009). Figure 3.2 summarizes the characteristics presented here (cf. Thiel 2016).

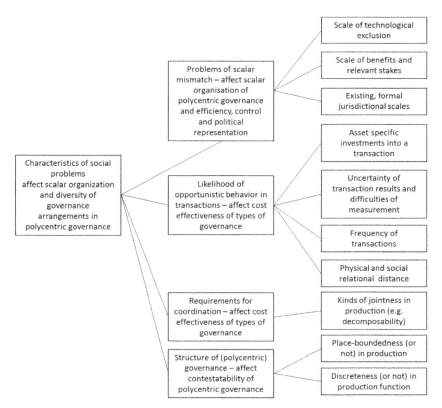

Figure 3.2 Social-problem characteristics that shape the performance of polycentric governance
Source: Authors

Altogether, we see an important research agenda in this field of research on polycentric governance, where the guiding question should be how particular social-problem characteristics affect performance of polycentric governance in relation to different normative criteria and what this implies for the shape of polycentric governance.

Box 3.2 Vignette: Contrasting social-problem characteristics and constitutional rules – the EU's governance for sustainable biofuels

The case of the EU's governance for sustainable biofuels production highlights the underpinning role that both social-problem characteristics and constitutional rules play for the emergence, structure and performance of polycentric governance arrangements. Climate change mitigation, i.e. the reduction of Greenhouse Gas (GHG) emissions relative to conventional fuels, is one of the main goals stipulated by the EU's biofuel deployment policy. Reacting to evidence of adverse effects of biofuel production, it introduced what has been identified, at least structurally, as a polycentric governance approach. That is, the 2009 Renewable Energy Directive provided that biofuels are to be produced in accordance with sustainability criteria that refer to GHG emission caps mainly. To this end, the entire biofuel production chain is to prove compliance, for which the main trajectory is certification in accordance with private, voluntary standard systems, of which the European Commission recognized a total of nineteen as eligible.

Thiel and Moser (2018) show that social-problem characteristics affect the structure of the governance arrangement. First, climate-friendly biofuels are a result of joint production, i.e. the production of the private good is to result in GHG savings and hence the (global) public good of climate protection. Hence, there are multiple producers of the public good. Also, it requires coordination along the biofuel production chain.

As biofuels do not necessarily result in positive, climate-friendly externalities, there is need for regulatory action. This, in turn, refers to a second problem characteristic: while biofuels are sold and combusted in the EU, their potentially detrimental effects on GHG emissions stem from agricultural feedstock production, which in turn makes it necessary that EU regulations become effective extraterritorially to yield compliance in countries of feedstock production.

Employing private certification schemes allows EU regulators to monitor and enforce compliance transnationally. While, in this function certification schemes help to overcome information asymmetries, their multiplicity results in search and information costs for both companies and citizen–consumers, with the high amount of coordination and blurring further contributing to opacity. Thiel and Moser highlight that transparency and therefore also accountability of biofuels governance in the EU is insufficient. Hence, duplication is not a sufficient condition for satisfactory functioning contestation mechanisms.

This refers us to how EU's biofuel governance exemplifies the effects of constitutional rules on the structure of polycentric governance, as the market stimulus for certification leads to the proliferation of certification schemes catering to the new demand. More importantly, however, this case shows how constitutional rules are crucial for performance of polycentric governance. In recognizing private certification schemes, the EU regulators did not institute transparency and accountability rules that would allow for contesting performance of certification schemes. As a result, biofuel certification systems compete for customers and engage in a 'race to the bottom' that puts to question their effectiveness in verifying climate-friendly biofuel production.

The example further illustrates the description of social-problem characteristics and their implications for governance arrangements (i.e. multiple providers of goods that are considered equivalent). In contrast, many water-related collective goods, e.g. ecosystem health, and sufficiently maintained groundwaters provide for place-specific collective goods. It therefore displays characteristics of an alternating Public Service Industry.

3.5 Community Characteristics: Heterogeneity

Besides diversity in social-problem characteristics and overarching rules, polycentricity provides scope for responding to heterogeneous actors and actor groups (Ostrom 2002). Heterogeneity among actors can refer to their capabilities, interests, beliefs and information (Poteete et al. 2010), wealth or income, costs and benefits from activities, or locational differences (Bardhan and Dayton-Johnson 2002), values, norms and mental models (cf. Van Riper et al. 2018). Because of described heterogeneities, preferences of actors and perceptions of social problems and their characteristics may differ. Correspondingly, actors and actor groups diverge over ways to solve social problems and outcomes of governance (Aligica and Tarko 2013). Aligica writes 'heterogeneity and institutional diversity are two sides of the same problem' (Aligica 2014, 22), meaning where self-organization is possible, heterogeneity leads to diverse institutional arrangements, as we can see in the urban melting pots of this world.

In relation to water, for example, in Germany, people are expected to pay for a glass of water in a restaurant, thus, people perceive it as a commodity. In contrast, in Spain, the United States of America or Great Britain, water is provided free of charge; people see it as a human right. Another example may be provision and production of water quality, for example in the EU, in which farmers play an important role. Conventional farmers organize production in a way that uses fertilizers and pesticides within the limits imposed by the government. In turn, governmental agencies control compliance with these rules. Alternatively, organic farmers, to which alternative value sets are usually ascribed (Moschitz 2009), from the start do not risk using detrimental input factors to the extent conventional farmers do. Thus, partly because of diversity in values, water quality monitoring is less of an issue in this case. In contrast, products and the production processes themselves are monitored concerning compliance with organic farming regulations.

Evidence on the implications of heterogeneity for collective action and polycentric governance is inconclusive. Hereby it is important to distinguish between heterogeneity within the group and across groups. Aligica's review (Aligica 2014) found that the majority of the evidence points in the direction that heterogeneity at the group level inhibits collective action. Specifically, in relation to the role of heterogeneity, context seems to greatly matter to the way it plays out in collective action.

According to Aligica, the fundamental concern of polycentricity with heterogeneity across groups implies a significant departure from conventional political science approaches that consider processes that create homogenous perspectives of actors (such as voting procedures) as core of the subject (the 'homogenization' or 'normalization' thesis) (Aligica 2014). In contrast, Aligica interprets the Ostrom's perspective and polycentricity as an approach in which diversity is 'instrumentally important'. It embraces pluralism and diversity and entertains 'a predilection toward negotiation and commonly agreed solutions' (Aligica 2014, 22). Polycentricity for him implies 'a process able to capture it [(heterogeneity)] as a resource, while minimizing its unavoidable drawbacks' (Aligica 2014, 22).

We do not subscribe to this normative perspective that polycentricity is necessarily the best way to deal with heterogeneity. We consider this to be an unfounded panacea (Ostrom et al. 2007). Instead, from the perspective of polycentricity as a lens, we suggest heterogeneity as a foundational component of emergence, change and performance of governance. Further, in line with other authors we consider it grossly undertheorized and under-researched. Engagement with it is important if we follow the observation that we live in a world in which diverse values, identities, principles, and cultures are entangled with unprecedented intensity (Aligica 2014, 26).

Box 3.3 Vignette: The role of social-problem characteristics, identity politics and constitutional provisions in the transformation of water governance in Spain and Germany

A comparison between water governance in arid Southern Spain and humid Germany, both of which are federal states, illustrates the role of social-problem characteristics, constitutional rules and heterogeneity of communities in the dynamics of governance. The largest Southern Spanish basin, the Guadalquivir is at the same time a transboundary river within Spain. The ministry governs the basin within basin boundaries. Extraction of water for irrigation in agriculture and exploitation of its hydrologic potential are greatly developed. Changing use patterns, promoted by the regional government, required the redistribution of water to irrigation in olive farming. Further, it requested greater attention to groundwater, which was increasingly overexploited. The idea was to shift towards territorial management of water by localities, in order to better match governance to the groundwater scale at which exclusion was necessary and in order to better coordinate with consuming agricultural and tourism uses that similarly followed a territorial logic. Thus, when political majorities at the national level allowed for it, the region vehemently claimed responsibilities for water distribution, and introduced an Andalusian legislation. Publicly, these moves were legitimized by appeals to identity politics (reinforcing heterogeneity), which emphasized that Andalusians had rights to self-determine water policy in the interests of their economic well-being. Constitutional law, however, in the end inhibited self-governance of Andalusian waters, as much as it inhibited self-governance among sharing states. Instead, the national level maintained control over water in the Guadalquivir. In contrast, in Germany, for decades, asymmetric spread of pollution from upstream to downstream made basin-wide collaboration difficult. Since the nineties, however, pollution has dramatically decreased and efforts focused on the improvement of the ecological status of the River Elbe, shared by ten German states. Upstream states became dependent on downstream states, as opposed to the previous constellation where downstream states depended on upstream states in the way they provided for water quality. Incentivized by the participatory process of implementation of the WFD, and legitimized by rights to cooperate among states, territorial water governance at the state level was complemented by bottom-up driven self-organization of collaboration and coordination at the basin level at which corresponding ecosystem services were produced, with only a marginal role of the national ministry.

This comparison shows how public-goods provision like ecological status at the basin scale, as opposed to extraction status of groundwater (social-problem characteristics) shape dynamics of conflict and cooperation in a basin. Further, it shows how a combination of identity politics (heterogeneity in values between Andalusia and the rest of Spain) and constitutional rules (inhibiting decentralization and decentral collaboration between states) determined the unsuccessful drives towards decentralization in Spain and how it determined successful basin-wide collaboration between sharing states in Germany.

3.6 Conclusions: Politics of Problem-Solving as Interaction of Foundational Components of Polycentricity

In this chapter, we have built on the conception of thinking polycentrically. We detailed what we named foundational components leading towards the emergence of particular forms of polycentric governance and shaping its performance. Particularly, we described (a) necessary overarching rules that allow for multifaceted governance because of (b) variable social-problem characteristics and (c) heterogeneity of communities. The way actors engage with polycentric governance as a result of these foundation components is conceptualized by metaconstitutional assumptions (underlying agents' behaviour).

While overarching rules of polycentric governance have to be socially upheld, diversity of social-problem characteristics, and heterogeneity of communities can be assumed as given, naturally leading to polycentric governance. If self-organization at various levels of social aggregation was permitted, a form of governance would emerge that is not only shared among multiple autonomous but functionally interdependent actors, but that is also characterized by involvement of multiple levels of governance, by multiple forms of governance, by differential involvement of public, private, voluntary and community types of organizations, and in which different actors may specialize in different functions of governance (monitoring, enforcement, financing, production, etc.) (McGinnis 2011b). Variations in problem characteristics and community attributes may also lead to alternative, more hierarchical forms of governance for certain types of problems. For example, issues of redistribution to maintain social peace or national defence, a classic public good, may fall into this category. However, also in relation to such goods intermediate governance functions (e.g. monitoring and information-gathering) may be spread across levels in a way that they are implemented in a polycentric fashion.

We derive that the study of polycentric governance entails an interest in the interplay of overarching rules, social-problem characteristics and perceptions thereof, and community attributes in the way people organize provision and production of predominantly collective goods. In an insightful contribution, McGinnis (2015) characterizes the novelty of this approach in political science at the time of its inception. In our view, it still holds great promise today as a future research agenda.

First, already long before many others acknowledged this (cf. Marsh 1992; Peters and Pierre 2004) this approach recognized that governance is much more than the activities of governments. Instead, it conceived governance as the 'politics of problem-solving', primarily also of non-governmental actors and communities (McGinnis 2015, 295). In that sense, the Ostroms' perspective suggests a functionalist dimension. Nonetheless, the struggles over rules, governance and their diverse implications for participants take centre stage. Therefore, it is far from being a context-neutral, structural-functionalist explanation of governance (Obinger 2015). Instead, in our view the analysis of collective problem-solving addresses well, particularly the (local, community level) dimension of problem-solving and its underlying politics. Thus, the prominent analysis of collective action, for example through the Institutional Analysis and Development (IAD) framework, asks how problems are solved in particular contexts, as much is it wonders why they are solved in a particular way, which (dominant) coalition of actors imposed it and whom it serves.

Nonetheless, in order to enable such flexible politics of problem-solving through polycentric governance, it rapidly becomes normative with 'subtle implications for democracy' (McGinnis 2015, 298). As detailed in this chapter, as well as in some of the following chapters, the Ostroms held that flexible self-organization at various levels of social aggregation requires particular overarching rules and capabilities of actors involved. As Aligica (2014) notes, maintaining such conditions equates polycentricity to a kind of context-specific democracy. It does not impose particular grand ideas of democratic governance on communities, but it enables actors to choose their own appropriate ways of governance. In such polycentric governance arrangements overarching rules may facilitate creative problem-solving, public entrepreneurship, and protect the rights of groups to self-organize. In that way, also the problem of overriding transaction costs of coordination across autonomous but functionally interdependent actors may be balanced by actors' desire to organize the provision and production of goods and services (McGinnis 2015, 299; Oakerson 1999).

On the whole, in our view, from the foundational perspective on polycentricity that we elaborated in this chapter, a rich research agenda emerges, not least because it received little attention thus far in governance research. The foundational aspect that has probably been addressed most intensely is that of heterogeneity of groups. However, questions in this regard concern the relationship between performance of self-organization and heterogeneity of actors within a collective (Bardhan and Dayton-Johnson 2002). In contrast, how different constellations of heterogeneity among groups relate to types of polycentric arrangements and their functioning remains hardly researched. The other two foundational elements, perceptions of social-problem characteristics and overarching rules (in form or in use) have also been little researched. In addition, the interaction of these three elements has received little attention (for exceptions see Becker et al. 2015; Boelens et al. 2015). We would argue that, particularly in relation to social-ecological system research, this promises a rich research agenda for what some have termed Comparative Institutional Analysis (Aoki 2001; Williamson 1991).

While this chapter has focused on the determinants of a particular configuration of polycentric governance arrangements, in Chapter 4 we outline a preliminary conceptualization of how institutional change develops in polycentric governance.

4

Evolutionary Institutional Change and Performance in Polycentric Governance

Andreas Thiel, Raúl Pacheco-Vega, and Elizabeth Baldwin

4.1 Introduction

In water governance, the spatially diverse and temporally integrative nature of the hydrological cycle can lead to the formation of polycentric structures of governance. In these polycentric institutional arrangements, multiple actors with potentially overlapping roles have limited individual authority over the provision and production of collective goods, and therefore may perceive that collaboration is in their best interest. For example, water quality that individuals enjoy is affected by a large number of current and past users, by institutions that regulate their functional or biophysical interdependence (e.g. due to the hydrological cycle), as well as by public, private, and civil society groups who may choose to collaborate on institutional development and regularization. Thus, in this chapter, we start with the observation of polycentric governance as a phenomenon, and intend to provide the building blocks for theorizing its change. Such an understanding is useful we argue for crafting and modifying polycentric governance arrangements. While we consider polycentric governance potentially more desirable than other governance arrangements, in line with the overall argument of this book we also recognize the desirability of polycentric governance as an open question subject to future research.

In this chapter, we ask: how and why do institutions that mediate actors' interdependence change in polycentric settings? We start by considering situations where humanly recognized interdependencies have been long recognized and institutionalized. We also explore the conceptually similar phenomenon of institutional emergence, where humanly perceived interdependencies among actors' activities are newly recognized and initially institutionalized (North 1990). The latter cases occur where humans only recently became aware of specific interdependencies and/or their relevance for human well-being. Examples include climate change, whose regulation has only emerged during the last twenty years; or contamination of drinking water with antibiotics, whose institutionalization is even more recent.

Polycentric governance structures have sometimes been described as Complex Adaptive Systems (CAS) whose change is evolutionary (Aligica 2014; V. Ostrom 2015) and whose institutional arrangements, networks and interactive, cross-scalar dynamics are emergent properties of evolutionary selection. Therefore, our second aim is to substantiate this claim and to spell out its implications for assessing the dynamics of polycentric governance. Particularly, we spell out what it means for the assessment of polycentric governance that its change is evolutionary, variable in relation to level of aggregation at which selection takes place, and path-dependent. Indeed, the question emerges if particular sequences of events lead to polycentric governance while others do not.

With these aims in mind, we structure the chapter as follows: first, we describe institutional change in polycentric governance as centred on the analysis of individual negotiations over institutions; we connect this understanding to the analysis of different roles and relations that polycentric governance addresses and to a set of endogenous and exogenous factors shaping institutional change in polycentric governance. Second, we elaborate on polycentric governance as CAS and connect it to theories of evolutionary institutional change. In the last section of the chapter, before we conclude, we elaborate on how institutional change in polycentric governance affects performance assessment of the corresponding dynamics. Further, we illustrate our argument through two vignettes (see Boxes 4.1 and 4.2) that briefly summarize our insights by looking at the issue of water governance in Kenya (institutional change) and Mexico (the role of timing and sequencing for institutional performance).

4.2 Mechanisms of Institutional Change in Polycentric Governance

In Chapter 3 Thiel and Moser highlighted an understanding of polycentric governance that, on the foundational level, emphasizes the role of constitutional rules, social-problem characteristics, and heterogeneity of communities. The polycentric governance arrangement (multiple, potentially overlapping, formally independent, but functionally interdependent decision-making centres that take each other into account) that emerges from these categories of factors is considered to be stratified across multiple governance functions. To delineate polycentric governance arrangements, Public Service Industries (PSIs) are defined as 'areas of productive activity involving interrelationships among many different agencies and units of government concerned with the provision of similar public services' that function at an 'intermediate level of organization' (V. Ostrom and E. Ostrom 1999b). We use this heuristic concept in order to delineate the (social) boundaries of the governance situation in which we want to understand institutional change. Given that PSI actors may be involved in both provisioning and production of collective goods, the heuristic includes consumers and stakeholders that hold an interest in the provision and consumption of said collective goods (Advisory Commission on Intergovernmental Relations 1987).

Following Ostrom (E. Ostrom 2014b; cf. E. Ostrom 2011) we consider implicit or explicit negotiation processes over institutional arrangements to be at the core of institutional change. We suggest conceptualizing these negotiations as action situations following the Institutional Analysis and Development (IAD) framework.[1] Thus, our analysis of institutional change returns to the micro-analytical approach of the Bloomington School of Political Economy and places methodological individualism at the centre of our analysis. In our view, this micro-analytical approach entails a detailed reconstruction of actors' choices as a result of their preferences, and the options available to them as a result of particular institutional configurations. Nevertheless, the framework and its subsequent extensions (Basurto and E. Ostrom 2009; E. Ostrom 2009) also recognize that structural and context-related aspects of the action situation shape individual actors' perceived net benefits of institutional change.

Thus, we consider the action situation as one useful way to operationalize Knight's distributional theory of institutional change (Knight 1992). Knight's theory conceptualizes institutional change as 'bargaining problems' (Knight 1992, 210) between boundedly rational actors and invokes 'the asymmetries of power in a society as primary source of explanation' (1992, 210). Institutions, and their development, are thus 'best explained as a by-product of conflicts over distributional gains' (Knight 1992, 20). Institutional change happens when actors' positions in distributional conflicts change, or when expected substantive social outcomes of institutional arrangements change, in either case changing the net benefit of institutional changes. We illustrate this with an example from the water sector.

---

[1] To note, we do illustrate IAD in this chapter. We only use its elements to provide theoretical and analytical guidance to help us explain how institutional change would work. We refer readers to fundamental articles on IAD (e.g. McGinnis 2011, 796).

A consumer group may, for example have an incentive to change the rules according to which water companies calculate water tariffs for two reasons. First, they may obtain a veto position on a consultative board that agrees on changes in water tariffs. Second, community characteristics such as wealth distribution may change, allowing large numbers of consumers to easily organize themselves in protest and lowering the transaction costs of collective action for the consumer association.

The distributional theory of institutional change seemingly aligns with New Institutional Economics (NIE) (Lin 1989), given its rational choice understanding of how and why actors employ institutions as instruments for maximising benefit in light of stable preferences. However, by elaborating specific meta-constitutional assumptions for human agents, the Ostroms defended a more complex model of individual behaviour. While this model adds theoretical fuzziness to the conventional NIE view, it has the benefit of empirical validity and also supports the analysis of polycentric governance as a CAS. In the Ostroms' model, actors are not only boundedly rational, but are also fallible learners that correspondingly experiment with rules. Further, the Ostroms point to the role of shared basic cultural values as a necessary component underlying actors' operations in polycentric governance. Correspondingly, for example, Elinor Ostrom (2005a) devised a detailed model of how actions, belief systems, mental models, culture and institutions interrelate that goes far beyond the usual rational choice perspective on agency.

In another publication, Ostrom enlarges the mechanisms of institutional change to include those suggested by classical institutionalists and anthropologists (Cleaver 2002; Hodgson 2004; E. Ostrom and Basurto 2011; Schmid 2004). Thus, institutional change becomes an outcome of a combination of social learning, evolution and emergence (E. Ostrom 2014b). Specifically, conscious forms of institutional change are distinguished from unconscious forms of institutional change (E. Ostrom and Basurto 2011). Conscious forms express humans' ability to learn. For example, they entail experimenting with institutions, imitating rules, deliberately negotiating favourable institutional arrangements or competitive selection of consciously devised rules. This includes the above rational choice perspective of institutional change. Ostrom and Basurto (2011) further qualify this perspective when they highlight that the sheer number of institutional options available in a complex system such as in polycentric governance necessarily overburdens actors' capacities to adopt an optimal choice. Therefore, through institutional change actors never optimize but, at most, improve their situation in relative terms.

In contrast, unconscious rule changes go beyond rational choice. They result from variations in interpretations of rules, from unconscious, slowly developing adaptations or even neglect of rules. Ostrom and Basurto highlight that the pace of change of endogenous or exogenous drivers of institutional change could potentially make the difference between conscious and subconscious institutional change (E. Ostrom and Basurto 2011). In agreement with many other authors, Ostrom admits that no conclusive theory of institutional change exists that would help us understand how the different mechanisms interlink and lead to a renegotiation of institutions (North 2005; E. Ostrom 2014; Schmid 2004). Nevertheless, in this brief summary we highlight what we can learn from these: that institutions evolve, individuals learn, and rules adapt under a broad range of stressors to a variety of conditions.

Of all the processes described earlier in this book, in this chapter we focus on conscious institutional change driven by boundedly rational agents. This process presumably plays an important role in polycentric governance also because of the important role of public agents that, at least in part, operate based on formal rules. In addition, we expect that a whole range of subconscious processes may drive institutional change. However, we do not claim to be sure about the underlying mechanisms of institutional change in all of these cases. In the subsequent description of drivers of institutional change we distinguish between the exogenous and endogenous drivers.

4.2.1 Endogenous Drivers of Institutional Change in Polycentric Governance

Institutional change can be triggered by changes endogenous or exogenous to the action situation, pertaining to a particular PSI. In most cases it is difficult to detach these from each other. Also, what is endogenous and what is exogenous depends on the way an analyst draws the boundaries around a PSI.

Overall, as a rule of thumb, we would consider those changes that affect the provision and production of collective goods resulting from more than one PSI as exogenous to a particular PSI, while those that predominantly affect one PSI to be endogenous.

In relation to endogenous factors, the IAD describes negotiations among actors through a set of seven rule types that structure an action situation and specify what actions specific actors can, or cannot, or must take, along with consequences for failing to follow the rule.[2] Together with social-problem characteristics, these rules determine to what extent actors can exercise the contestation options of exit, voice and self-organization. Besides the IAD, many other frameworks and typologies have been developed to categorize the variables that endogenously affect institutional change. Several authors have devised typologies of 'power resources' that cut across rule types and whose change may lead to institutional change through renegotiation of institutions (Knight 1992; Schlüter 2001; Theesfeld 2005). Thiel (2014), for example, identifies four categories of factors whose change might affect power relationships by changing the costs or benefits of renegotiating institutions: (a) transaction costs, for example of organizing actors supporting institutional change, (b) credibility of actors partaking in negotiations to actually opt out of an existing institutional arrangement (e.g. because of available alternatives), (c) network membership that affects the availability of information about institutional alternatives, and (d) time preferences, which stand for actors' ability to survive without being part of a particular transaction and institutional arrangement. In whatever way they are categorized, endogenous drivers of institutional change shape the positions of actors in various roles in polycentric governance arrangements. In the next section we want to describe how we can conceptualize this idea.

4.2.2 Embedding Endogenous Drivers of Institutional Change into a Polycentric Perspective

To analyse polycentric governance, we need to analyse the interdependence of action situations (E. Ostrom, Gardner, and Walker 1994). More recently, several authors have developed frameworks that tie action situations together, including Networks of Adjacent Action Situations (McGinnis 2011b), Lubell and colleagues' Ecology of Games framework, and Feiock and colleagues' Institutional Collective Action (ICA) framework (Feiock 2013).

The frameworks focus on a particular moment in time; their extension for understanding institutional change is no doubt conceptually ambitious. A framework that has tried to do so, predominantly from a learning perspective, is Pahl-Wostl's Management and Transition Framework, which similarly borrows ideas from the IAD (Pahl-Wostl 2009; 2015).

---

[2] These rule types are boundary rules, position rules, choice rules, information rules, aggregation rules, scope rules, and payoff rules (Ostrom, 2005a).

However, its application focuses on assessing the outcomes of change (Huntjens et al. 2011).

We consider these frameworks to be path-breaking advances in conceptualizing polycentric governance and particularly to stimulate research on types of relations between actors involved. Further, we consider them as promising starting points for (a) advancing our language on institutional change in polycentric governance, and (b) mapping precise hypotheses on pathways of institutional change. We have not yet found, however, a research programme that spells out a strategy for theory building on institutional change. First steps in this regard were made by Elinor Ostrom herself, when she suggested mapping and typifying rule changes in action situations before researchers systematically engage in understanding the underlying determinants (E. Ostrom 2014b). Such an approach presumes that findings from the micro-analysis of institutional change can be upscaled. Others have questioned this because of differences in the powers associated with actors and in the characteristics of communities at different levels (Cash 2000).

The roles that different actors have in institutional change are especially important in polycentric governance. Authors have distinguished between top-down or imposed institutional change, in which public agents trigger institutional change, and bottom-up, induced or even spontaneous institutional change, where private or civil society actors trigger institutional change (Lin 1989; Schmid 2004; Vatn 2005). These categorizations may underestimate the complexity of processes of institutional change, and they fail to differentiate the jurisdictional level from which institutional change originates from particular types of actors and mechanisms of change. Further, empirically, bottom-up and top-down institutional change are often interrelated. Therefore, we argue that particularly in polycentric governance, analysts need to consider the way that different actors' divergent perspectives and roles relate to each other in institutional change.

From the perspective of polycentric governance, the roles of and relations between citizens, consumers, providers and producers particularly stand out. We suggest that these actor groups' negotiations over institutional change can be conceptualized and analysed as action situations. We presume these actors to be intendedly and boundedly rational, capable of learning as they pursue institutional change. Nevertheless, interest formation differs among the different roles of actors. We also presume that actors do not all have identical – or necessarily compatible – interests.

For example, in market economies, producers are assumed to be profit-oriented. We presume individual consumers and citizens pursue institutions that align with their substantive preferences; for collective public or private actors, we suggest collective action theory to understand the way interests are represented in negotiations over institutional change (Olson 1994; E. Ostrom 2007). Further, for public agents involved in provisioning, we suggest taking account of the way public choice has theorized public agency, as oriented by maximizing votes or prestige (Mueller 2003; Niskanen 1994; Tullock, Seldon, and Brady 2002). The approach we therefore suggest to model institutional change in polycentric governance clearly highlights an understanding of polycentric governance as a framework that brings together various perspectives on actors' role-associated behaviour and which share some core assumptions.

Each actor group has potentially three pathways for contesting the way a PSI provides for collective goods, expressing their discontent, and thereby triggering institutional change. First, voice entails attempts to delegitimize PSIs through 'political' or administrative channels. A more radical option is 'exit'. It involves physically or socially exiting from a relationship with providers and/or producers, thereby weakening their positions through the withdrawal of funding and support. It includes physically moving away or withdrawing from cooperation. Third, consumers, providers or producers, may couple exit with self-organization, i.e. the establishment of alternative entities for provisioning and producing collective goods in order to replace existing relations with which they were discontent. We detailed these options for contestation and their functioning in Chapter 3.

A necessary precondition for polycentric governance and institutional change is that the de facto constitutional rules fulfil (at least to some extent) preconditions for polycentric governance to emerge (cf. V. Ostrom 1999a). Further, the transaction costs that actors in different roles encounter when they want to use these different pathways to influence institutions depend on the particular way in which social-problem characteristics and community features constitute a PSI (cf. Chapter 3). Social-problem characteristics shape the credibility of the threat to delegitimize provisioning or production arrangements through exit. They determine to what extent readily accessible alternatives are available to replace existing providers and producers of collective goods. For example, consumers and citizens usually have few alternatives for procuring water supply and sanitation services. The reasons are economies of scale and network economies that characterize water supply and sanitation services as social problems. This limits their contestation options to voice. In contrast, consumers have relatively easy access to multiple providers for foodstuffs produced in an environmentally conscious manner. In such competitive situations, where a multitude of alternatives for collective goods provision and production are available, consumers' and citizens' threat of exit is much larger. As a result of this heightened credibility of the threat to contest provisioning relations, institutional change that matches consumers' or citizens' preferences is a much more likely outcome (see also Chapter 3). Following efficiency theories of institutional change (Lin 1989), we presume that institutional change will be more likely to produce efficiency improvements where numerous alternative options are available to citizens and consumers.

Institutional change may also originate from the heterogeneity of communities, which was described in Chapter 3. Heterogeneity potentially leads to diversity in problem perceptions, preferences and governance arrangements concerning the way collective goods are provided, if social-problem characteristics allow, i.e. if such differentiation was physically possible. Thus, on the one hand, institutional change may be more likely in highly heterogeneous societies because actors have a broader set of governance arrangements with which to compare (Bednar 2009). Further, where levels of heterogeneity change, for example as a result of widening income gaps, institutional change may be the outcome. On the other hand, as our discussion of polycentric governance as a CAS shows, high levels of heterogeneity may also increase inertia in institutional change.

4.2.3 Exogenous Drivers of Institutional Change in Polycentric Governance

In the IAD framework, the structures that exogenously shape actors' perceptions of net benefits of governance arrangements include resource characteristics, characteristics of the community affected by institutions and interdependencies, and rules structuring the action situation. While we recognize that rules can be both exogenous and endogenous to an action situation, depending upon the perspective of the analyst, we consider pre-established rules that structure an action situation to be exogenous factors. As noted, however, these exogenous rules are sometimes shaped by processes endogenous to a PSI, for example when actors renegotiate institutions as described in Section 4.2.2.

The similarity of named categories to those we also highlighted in Chapter 3 as underlying polycentric governance (constitutional conditions, heterogeneity of actors and social-problem characteristics) is obvious.

Economic theories of institutional change designate another set of exogenous factors. They highlight the role of (a) interrelated institutional options available, (b) changes in technologies of governance, (c) changes in factor or product prices of assets transacted through particular governance structures, or (d) changes in overarching mental models and values that shape perceptions of net benefits of particular governance arrangements (Lin 1989; North 1994, 2005; Thiel 2014) .

On the one hand, the availability of interrelated institutional options may depend on knowledge about alternative ways of regulating interdependencies that may trigger institutional change. For example, in the Federal State of Germany, participatory processes in river basin management are structured very differently across the sixteen Länder. Accordingly, each Land has potentially fifteen role models on which it can draw when devising participatory processes, which may trigger institutional innovation. On the other hand, institutional options available may also relate to changes in interdependent institutions outside of the PSI. For example, if responsibilities for land-use management were changed, we would expect that this also affects the way water is governed, restructuring the corresponding PSI. Changes in technologies of governance can also affect transactions or governance costs. For example, GIS technology and remote sensing have reduced the costs of monitoring illegal irrigation in arid zones in ways that probably could not have been anticipated when the technologies were initially developed. Similarly, twenty-five years ago no one imagined the Internet's potential to disseminate information inexpensively to stakeholders. Both technological changes have changed the costs of governance by changing what actors considered to be cost-effective institutional arrangements for governance to fit their purposes.

Changes in value perceptions of products and input factors similarly affect the net benefit that actors associate with governance. In the case of water or natural resource management, these may entail changed perceptions about scarcity of water, for example, because of increasingly intense drought periods. Where actors' valuation of water or natural resources increases, it is presumed that they are willing to shoulder greater costs of governance for controlling the resource (Williamson 1991). Finally, the category of changes in mental models or values encapsulates societal changes in perceptions. For example, in relation to water governance, the mental model may shift from a focus on supply management, including the provision and production of clean drinking water, to a paradigm of demand management, where needs for drinking, but also irrigation, water are to be reduced. These broad changes in social perceptions would

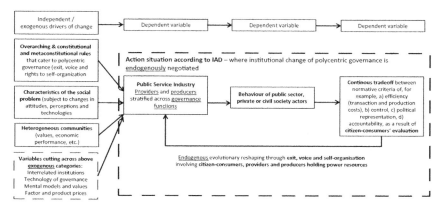

Figure 4.1 Institutional change in polycentric governance
Source: authors

subsequently shape actors' preferred institutional arrangements among the multitude of institutional options available. In Figure 4.1, we depict the way we see drivers and agents of institutional change embedded into polycentric governance.

4.3 Institutional Change in Polycentric Complex Adaptive Systems

On a variety of occasions, polycentric governance development settings have been equated with Complex Adaptive Systems (CAS) (Aligica 2014; McGinnis 2016). According to Arthur and colleagues (1994) cited in Levin (1998, 432), CAS are characterized by 'dispersed interaction, the absence of a global controller, cross-cutting hierarchical organization, continual adaptation, perpetual novelty, and far-from-equilibrium dynamics'. Based on these features, polycentric governance constellations certainly qualify as CAS. Thus, as we learnt from Chapter 1, defining features of polycentric governance include dispersed interactions among many centres of decision-making of limited authority and absence of a single centre of control.

Since polycentric governance arrangements are not deliberately coordinated, dispersed interactions between centres of decision-making facilitate the emergence of diverse patterns of cross-scalar and horizontal organization. Actors experiment with governance arrangements to adapt to new challenges or to improve their well-being, and to continually adapt and develop novel institutional arrangements. Indeed, given the multitude of ongoing interactions and the huge number of possible combinations of governance arrangements, we can presume that institutions do not ever reach an equilibrium, but rather that institutional change becomes continuous. McGinnis (2005b) aptly described the resultant equilibrium properties as follows: 'As long as a polycentric system is in operation we should expect to observe unending processes of change and renegotiation, as new collective entities are formed, old ones dissolve, and new bargains are arrived at to deal with an unending series of new issues of public policy. If this can be said to be an equilibrium, it is a radically dynamic one with nothing fixed except the underlying complexity of the system as a whole.' In such CAS, aggregation of actors in communities and governance arrangements is the result of self-organization; hierarchies in organization emerge from below, instead of being imposed from above (Levin 1998, 433). In result, path dependence and incrementalism characterize institutional change in polycentric governance (McGinnis 2016).

Path dependence suggests that modification of structures in CAS is constrained by previous structures (Kauffman and Levin 1987). For deliberate institutional change, path dependence highlights the importance of the status quo, as net benefits of institutional change depend on the point of departure of institutional change. Challen (2000) therefore argues that in explaining institutional change, the analyst must not only compare the net gains from alternative institutional arrangements, but also the costs of transitioning from one arrangement to another (North 1994; Pierson 2000). As we argue in Section 4.4, when we look at timing and sequencing, path dependence may help us understand why institutional architectures evolve into polycentric governance systems or not. Second, because of multiple entanglements of centres of decision-making in complex relational architectures, we expect incremental, slow-moving change of institutions in polycentric governance as a result of constant and ever-present needs of adjustment. McGinnis explains this with the large number of veto-points in polycentric governance (McGinnis 2016; Tsebelis 2002). Nonetheless, occasionally CAS are also subject to dramatic shifts. This possibility of sudden and dramatic shifts in CAS gave rise to the now extensive literature on resilience and robustness (Anderies and Janssen 2013; Folke 2006).

Key in understanding change in CAS are evolutionary selection processes at different levels of aggregation of populations. In evolutionary systems, members of a type (e.g. institutions) are similar in key respects and represent a population. For a system to follow an evolutionary path, Knight points out that three aspects need to be present (Hodgson 2010; Knight 1992, 87):

(a)   Variation in relevant traits of a population either as result of chance, or as a result of deliberate innovation by human agents.

(b)   A method of inheritance of successful traits whereby selection of the fittest members of the population becomes an integral part of inheritance.

(c)   A method of selection such as (i) random variation, (ii) decision-making (guided trial and error involving innovation, or individual decisions about existing variants based on some fitness criterion), or (iii) natural selection.

There can be little doubt that institutional change in polycentric CAS fulfils these criteria. Thus, variation in the population of institutions (a) is created by dispersed interactions. Inheritance (b) is secured by the information contained in institutions and governance arrangements, for example through written documents or through word of mouth, passed on to following generations of actors. Either as part of the process of inheritance or through (c) (ii) selection by decision-making (guided trial and error by fallible learners or conscious evaluation by boundedly but intendedly rational actors), those institutions are expected to survive in polycentric systems that actors (consumer–citizens, providers or producers) consider most beneficial and fit for their particular purposes. Alternatively, a particular variation may be (c) (iii) 'naturally' selected, independent from people's choices (unconsciously). Such selection takes place because of broader social or biophysical processes such as competition over scarce resources. An example may be the disappearance of water-user associations because of vanishing agricultural practices in times of drought.

Box 4.1 Vignette: Institutional change in Kenyan water governance

In Kenya, water is critical for small-scale agriculture, but its availability varies across space and over time. While upstream water users have consistent and reliable access to water, downstream users may lack access entirely unless upstream users curtail their use significantly, particularly during annual dry seasons and periodic droughts. Centralized water governance institutions in place from the 1960s to the 1990s were ineffective at allocating water equitably, leading to prolonged periods of conflict (Baldwin et al. 2016).

Beginning in the late 1990s, the country replaced its centralized and bureaucratic approach to water governance with a multi-level, polycentric approach, one in which decisions about water allocation are shared between local, regional, and national actors. This change was the result of both endogenous and exogenous factors. Reform emerged at least partially in response to the failures of the prior system. In the late

1990s, farmers, government officials, and NGOs in Kenya's Ewaso Ng'iro Basin began to experiment with Water Resource Users' Associations (WRUAs), organizations that bring upstream and downstream users together to negotiate locally appropriate water allocation during times of water scarcity. Encouraged by the success of these regional experiments, national officials adopted regulations that formalize WRUAs' role in water allocation and encourage their use throughout Kenya (McCord et al. 2016).

These reforms were enabled by a broader shift in the country's mental model for governance and its constitutional-level rules. In 2002, a new ruling party came to power in Kenya, devolving significant authority from national to local officials and emphasizing local participation over technical expertise. In this political climate, local water users in the Ewaso Ng'iro Basin augmented a failing set of institutions with a more effective and participatory approach to water allocation.

While Kenya's experiment with water reform is too new to be declared a definitive success, there are initial indications that polycentric governance emerged and continues to develop as an evolutionary process. It is clear that the polycentric approach embodied in the WRUA system emerged in response to the prior institutional systems' failure to distribute water equitably. Preliminary evidence from fieldwork suggests that the current approach – while imperfect – has reduced water conflicts, increased equity of water distribution, and allows local actors to develop diverse institutions in response to local conditions, and experimentation with innovation. Research also suggests that the process is dynamic and iterative; both local actors and national policy makers can change institutions over time in response to changing conditions and through a process of policy learning.

Despite this dynamism, however, it may be premature to conclude that institutional variation among Kenya's WRUAs will automatically lead to institutions that are well-adapted to local and changing conditions. The evolutionary process suggests that ineffective or inflexible institutions will be replaced with others that are a better fit for local and changing conditions. Our research does not yet show whether this is happening in Kenya. In fact, there are some examples of institutional inertia – for example, while local WRUAs are allowed to engage in institutional experimentation, they often do so slowly; many have adopted organizational forms recommended by national officials, modifying their approach only when necessary or when problems occur. Thus, the support from national officials that enables and encourages the formation of WRUAs may also provide incentives for WRUAs to adopt similar institutional structures, at least initially. Continued observation over time may be necessary to determine whether Kenya's WRUAs evolve and adapt in response to changed conditions.

4.4 Evaluating Performance of Evolutionary, Complex and Adaptive Polycentric Governance

Understanding institutional change in polycentric governance is an important epistemic basis for crafting institutions that serve democratic values in society (Bromley 2012; E. Ostrom 2014; Thiel, Mukhtarov and Zikos 2015). Thereby, institutional configurations will always trade off performance criteria such as efficiency, equity, representativeness, resilience, flexibility or others that actors involved or analysts consider important (Ostrom, Tiebout, and Warren 1961). Further, to identify the targets of deliberate institutional crafting, knowledge on the performance of particular constellations and dynamics they unleash is necessary.

In this book, we mention the challenges of evaluating institutional performance at various occasions. In the last section of the chapter we want to spell out the implications of our understanding of institutional change in polycentric governance for assessing its performance. Specifically, we argue that two issues come to the fore, both of which are tightly connected with the evolutionary nature of polycentric governance. First, we want to look at the assessment of performance of polycentric governance in light of questions concerning the scale of aggregation and the temporal scale for assessing performance of polycentric governance. Second, we want to discuss how path dependence and evolution shape opportunities for gathering knowledge on performance of polycentric governance.

Before we address these issues, we state underlying assumptions of the discussion. First, among the many possible vantage points one could adopt on governance, we assume that of an external observer that evaluates performance in relation to particular criteria. Thus, we neglect the perspective of individuals involved in governance and assess performance at the level of the PSI as a whole. Further, we assume that despite all difficulties, we can delineate a governance arrangement through the heuristic concept of the PSI. Finally, we recognize that different analysts may wish to employ different assessment criteria to evaluate performance of polycentric arrangements, including effectiveness, efficiency, and equity. Nonetheless, the following discussion is not affected by the choice of performance criteria, although we offer additional possible criteria that assess not only current performance, but also the ability of governance arrangements to adapt and respond to changes over time. The reason is that the issues raised affect any system that can be conceptualized as CAS. We consider our points specific to conceptualizing governance arrangements as polycentric because we are not aware of another approach that wholeheartedly embraces the ideas of a CAS for conceptualizing governance. We argue that this raises awareness of a set of difficulties in assessing polycentric governance that go beyond the problem of operationalizing performance criteria and gathering appropriate data that are addressed in Chapters 2, 5–8.

In relation to the scale of aggregation, the question is, at what level do we expect governance to perform well in order for the overall PSI to perform well; this also relates to the question at what level governance arrangements are selected (Knight 1992). In other words, we cannot be sure if PSIs on the whole perform better in the long term if individual institutions compete against each other, as a sign of selection at the level of individual institutions, or if the PSI performs better if institutional arrangements are coordinated among each other and selection therefore takes place at a higher level of aggregation. The former would be the case, for example, if bulk water consumers each negotiated contracts with water providers in a watershed; the latter would be illustrated by a case where representatives of bulk water consumers in a flexibly arranged region negotiate institutions with water companies. The level of competition would be higher in the former case, which in the end may lead to better results, while at the same time, economies of scale of the second set-up, for example may be advantageous. To different degrees, either would be considered polycentric. This problem cannot be overcome, because we can never be sure at what level selection is most beneficial in the long run.

In relation to timing, the evolutionary perspective highlights problems of choosing any one particular moment or period for assessment. In fact, it questions the worthiness of static assessments of governance altogether. It relates to the described idea that, on a deeper level, structural and agency related features are never in equilibrium. Therefore, whatever timescale we select for assessment, ongoing sequences of operational governance are always part of more extensive dynamics of selection, making it difficult to conclusively assess a sequence. For example, any sequence in which performance of a PSI rapidly deteriorates may be part of a longer-term dynamic necessary to establish a better performing PSI. In other words, from any perspective only history will tell about the value of any polycentric governance constellations for overall performance on a larger temporal scale. Clearly, stated in these ways the problem is exaggerated, but nonetheless, determining the correct period for assessing dynamic performance is unresolved.

There are several ways to address but never to solve this dynamic problem of assessing polycentric governance. First, one could address development trends of outcome-related criteria, such as efficiency and equity. Second, one could move away from absolute evaluation criteria such as efficiency and equity of water provision and outcomes and move into the assessment of operational, process-related criteria that are of particular relevance for polycentric governance. We could imagine that intensity of bottom-up innovation or self-organizing capacities of actors fall into this category.

The latter already hints at another approach to the problem. Rather than assessing the actual operational performance of polycentric governance, evaluation could focus on the de facto observation of the principles that are foundational to well-functioning polycentric governance. Thus, the analyst could assess the structure and agency related abilities of actors to exit, voice and self-organize, thus assessing the system's potential for inducing self-correcting dynamics. For example, in relation to water governance, performance assessment might focus on questions about whether providers and producers of collective goods were accountable to citizens and consumers, or whether citizen–consumers were able to evaluate information and motivated to act upon it if necessary. Further, the barriers to politically influencing the way collective goods are provided (voice), or barriers to self-organization and exit would need to be assessed. Nonetheless, such an assessment would only address the potential of governance to fulfil the presumed connections between polycentric governance and its desirable performance; a relation which still needs to be tested for many issues in our view (Anderies and Janssen 2013; Carlisle and Gruby 2017; Huitema et al. 2009).

Timing and sequencing of institutional change raises additional issues that may call into question the described reasoning about the impossibility of conclusively assessing a period of polycentric governance (Grzymala-Busse 2011). Timing and sequencing implies that there are certain formative junctures where events occur that have a long-lasting impact on the developmental trajectory of a political system (Pierson 2000). These junctures may have an impact on whether a system becomes polycentric or not. Path dependence, which we associated with the nature of polycentric governance as evolutionary CAS, holds that among the large number of potentially possible governance arrangements, over time a decreasing subset is realistically in reach. This creates lock-in situations (Beyer 2011; Pierson 2000; Sydow et al. 2009). The question remains whether certain development paths lead to more desirable lock-in situations than others, what these development paths look like, and how we can observe them. Altogether, this raises questions about whether path dependence, associated transaction costs, and tendencies towards incremental change in polycentric governance might entail a serious obstacle to desirable performance of governance. In such situations, more centrally organized governance arrangements may better deal with undesirable lock-in situations. In fact, we consider this issue concerning polycentric governance as an important research gap that also poses important methodological challenges, given the problem of counterfactuals and limited availability of real-world comparative cases.

Box 4.2 Vignette: Timing and sequencing in Mexican water governance

Understanding, assessing and evaluating policy change implies being able to comprehend a broad range of mechanisms of institutional change (Capano 2009). How policies are built is partly a product of how institutions are created and constructed. As we have indicated, institutional arrangements (including, and for the purposes of this book, fundamentally polycentric governance) may emerge through top-down or bottom-up mechanisms. This is quite clearly the case in Mexico, where policies on water governance based on international water-resource-management paradigms were implemented through a top-down approach (Benson et al. 2015; Giordano and Shah 2014; Pacheco-Vega 2012). The first river basin council in Mexico, the Lerma-Chapala Basin Council (Consejo de Cuenca Lerma-Chapala) emerged in 1993 as a multi-stakeholder roundtable tasked with managing water across five states. Created through a top-down mandate driven by the National Water Commission of Mexico (CONAGUA), the Lerma-Chapala river basin included a broad range of stakeholders, from academics to agricultural, industrial and service water users, to government officials across all three levels of government.

An experiment in what would end up becoming networked (polycentric) governance, the Lerma-Chapala river basin continued as the sole Integrated Water Resources Management (IWRM) project in Mexico until 1999, when the OECD published a document encouraging countries (especially Mexico) to adopt IWRM and 'governing by river basin council' paradigms (Pacheco-Vega 2013). This is a clear example of where timing and sequencing is important. Had Mexico not experimented with the IWRM model of river basin council governance a few years beforehand, implementing the OECD's directives would probably have been more complicated. As it turns out, twenty-three out of the current twenty-six Mexican river basin councils were established by CONAGUA after the OECD report. Sequencing was also quite important given that the Lerma-Chapala river basin council helped model those emerging after 1999.

Tracing back the history of how river basin councils in Mexico emerged enables us to hypothesise where timing and sequencing could have had a role in the way in which polycentric governance emerged (Trampusch and Palier 2016). As Jensen and Wu indicate, in the water sector, it is quite important that we pay attention to the timing and sequencing of multiple governance interventions (Jensen and Wu 2016). The same logic of process tracing could be applied to understand the role of timing and sequencing in other cases of emerging polycentric institutional arrangements through the study of causal mechanisms (Grzymala-Busse 2011)

On a broader level, the discussion in this chapter relates to the question of institutional design (Aligica 2014; Goodin 1996; Thiel et al. 2015), and emphasizes the quagmire of whether, in addition to promoting institutions that condition favourable outcomes, we need to be attentive to the timing and sequencing in which institutions are introduced or selected. Thus, we argue that we ought to take a historically grounded, time-sensitive approach to the study of institutional change that follows not only how institutions change, but at which points (junctures) they face particular challenges, how they respond to these challenges and what the implications are in the medium- to long term. This approach is championed by scholars of comparative historical analysis (Rast 2012; Thelen 2000, 2003), mechanisms and temporality (Beach 2016; Beach and Pedersen 2016; Buthe 2012; Falleti and Lynch 2008; Grzymala-Busse 2011; Levi 2009; Walt et al. 2008) and path dependence (Bennett and Elman 2006; Rixen and Viola 2015). Such understanding can help facilitate the emergence of 'stronger, better performing polycentric governance' that is not only robust in terms of compliance with rules, but also flexible enough to be nimble and adaptive, both characteristics of complex adaptive systems.

To use an example from the water field, a resource governance scheme where control of the resource is centralized and licensing is governed by a national agency can begin to show polycentric characteristics when, politically, citizen participation is encouraged through changes in policies. Such changes may become formalized. However, if the political economy, financing model, and centralized accumulation of knowledge and data counteract decentralization and citizen participation in water management – perhaps because interests of resourceful industry are best represented at the national level – then management may be locked into a centralized system and polycentric governance involving citizens cannot be realized. Therefore, we need to pay attention to timing and sequencing in designing polycentric governance systems.

4.5 Conclusions

In this chapter, we have described our conception of institutional change in and of polycentric governance. We have pointed out that while numerous conceptual starting points exist for understanding such institutional change, we are far from having a consolidated theory in place that could explain how institutional change occurs in certain situations and why. Particularly, we have little understanding of the way situational context affects institutional change respectively when different mechanisms of institutional change apply and how they relate to each other. Further, we elaborated our understanding of polycentric governance as evolutionary, complex adaptive systems. Insights from the vignettes of case studies we analysed and include in this chapter lead us to believe that the arguments presented here are beneficial for understanding institutional change in polycentric governance.

Our discussion also suggests that when considering constellations of polycentric governance, we ought to pay attention not only to the way in which institutions evolve, but also to the exogenous and endogenous factors that shape institutional evolution. We call on scholars to pay particular attention to how these rules, norms and strategies impact actors, how the resource to be governed is shared among appropriators, and how political and other forms of power are shared among actors. These factors shape the negotiations among actors that lead to institutional change.

While we reiterate the importance of assessing performance of polycentric governance systems, we also note that the features of polycentric governance pose significant methodological and research design-related obstacles in relation to assessing its performance. In particular, evaluative criteria such as effectiveness or equity that are typically used to assess performance are typically the product of a particular moment in time. In addition to this typical approach to performance assessment, we need approaches that assess the governance system's ability to adapt and respond to exogenous and endogenous changes, and that recognize how the timing and sequencing of institutional change may be shaped by path dependence. To do this, we require more conceptual and empirical research work on institutional change and performance in polycentric governance. We thus call for the research community to develop conceptual and methodological stepping stones for analysing and assessing institutional change in polycentric governance systems, embedded into a research programme that is logically designed to advance our understanding of institutional change in polycentric systems.

All chapters in Part I of this book have attempted to advance our understanding of polycentric governance, its analysis and mapping, its determinants and change. Building on this perspective, Part II addresses the operation of polycentric governance focusing on the interactions of cooperation, conflict and conflict resolution and competition.

PART II

Interactions and Performance in Polycentric
Governance

Tomas M. Koontz and Dustin E. Garrick

OVERVIEW AND INTRODUCTION

Tomas M. Koontz, Dustin E. Garrick, Tanya Heikkila, and
Sergio Villamayor-Tomás

Part I of this book laid out foundational concepts in polycentric governance. A core definition of polycentric governance systems is that multiple
centres of decision-making are formally independent of each other but
interact within a system of overarching rules. These interactions, also
known as 'taking each other into account', can be thought of as three main
types: (1) cooperation, (2) conflict and conflict resolution, and (3) competition (Ostrom, Tiebout, and Warren 1961). Although intertwined, these
types of interactions can be analysed distinctly.

Cooperation involves multiple centres working together to advance
shared goals. Centres seek common ground to mutually advance their
goals by coordinating, communicating, and possibly sharing resources with
each other. This form of interaction has been growing in practice and
scholarship under a variety of terms, especially 'collaboration' and 'collaborative governance'. An important element of collaborative governance is
the interaction of not only government, but also non-governmental actors
including the private and non-profit sectors. This diverse array of participants moves beyond the narrower definition of polycentric governance as
only those actions taken by formal political units of government. Instead,
both government officials and non-governmental actors can play critical
roles, as described in Chapter 1.

Conflict can be defined as a dispute or disagreement among actors over
how to provide a good or service, or over the rules, policies or institutions

for addressing a governance issue (Weible and Heikkila 2017). Conflict occurs in polycentric governance systems, as decision centres within polycentric systems have competing interests or goals with respect to governance choices (Ostrom et al. 1961). Generation of externalities, disagreement about the need for public goods, free-riding on the investments of other centres, and questions about who has appropriate authority over which decisions can spark conflict. Conflict resolution, on the other hand, involves an agreement or decision where actors or decision units no longer have incentives to engage in conflictual behaviours, or where they are willing to compromise on an issue.

Competition provides a market logic for different decision-making centres to respond to demands. Competition is one means by which centres in a polycentric governance system are pressured to provide public goods and services efficiently. As centres seek to provide and/or produce public goods and services, competitive interactions can arise, and these interactions are sensitive to information availability.

To analyse how centres in a polycentric governance system take each other into account, we identify and describe three key elements affecting incentives and interactions among multiple centres: authority, information, and resources.

Authority is key in structuring how multiple centres of decision-making are permitted or forbidden from interacting with one another. For example, a state regulatory agency with authority to limit pollution might forbid a municipality from contracting its waste water treatment with a neighbouring city, or it may grant local governments authority to enter into joint agreements for public service production (Oakerson and Parks 1988). Large scale, metropolitan-wide sole authority precludes lower-level units from cooperating to provide services (Ostrom, Tiebout, and Warren 1961).

Information is critical for motivating public organizations to be efficient and responsive. Information provides citizens with leverage to hold public officials accountable, especially in comparing costs and benefits in their jurisdiction with costs and benefits in other jurisdictions (Ostrom, Tiebout, and Warren 1961). Such leverage can motivate independent centres of authority to seek cooperation with each other to improve performance.

Resources are needed to generate public benefits in polycentric governance systems. Overlapping and parallel government jurisdictions may cooperate in sharing resources for joint production or pay other organizations through contracting to produce services ranging from police and fire to waste- water treatment and trash removal (Ostrom, Tiebout, and Warren 1961).

Overall, authority, information and resources are key elements shaping incentives and interactions in polycentric governance systems. These elements are examined across the chapters in Part II of this book. We begin with a description of cooperative interactions, drawing on a case of cooperative ecosystem restoration efforts in the Puget Sound, Washington (USA). Next is a chapter focusing on conflict and conflict resolution in the case of oil and gas development in two US states: New York and Colorado. This is followed by a chapter focusing on competition across two water supply cases, the Ebro River in Spain and the Columbia River in the Pacific Northwest (USA and Canada). We conclude Part II with a chapter on measuring performance of interactions, drawing on case material from the prior three chapters. In all, our aim is to explore how authority, information, and resources affect incentives and interactions, as multiple decision centres of a polycentric governance system take each other into account. We also suggest performance criteria appropriate for each type of interaction.

For analytical consistency and comparability across the cases, we employ the Institutional Analysis and Development (IAD) framework. This framework, often employed in polycentricity studies, helps organize concepts related to interactions and performance. As shown in Figure 4.2, we conceptualize the action situation as including actors who possess and create authority, information, and resources. These action situations are affected by exogenous factors (e.g. community attributes and features of

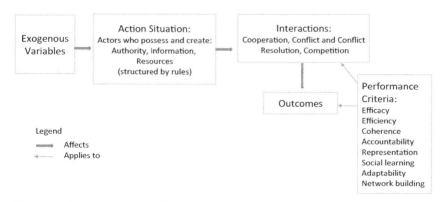

Figure 4.2 Interactions in a polycentric governance system
(adapted from the IAD framework)

the biophysical context). An action situation leads to interactions among actors; these can include cooperation, conflict and conflict resolution, and competition. These interactions lead to outcomes, which can be evaluated via performance criteria. Outcome criteria centre on the question: what results did the system produce? Are these results efficient and coherent with other levels of the system? Additionally, processes can be evaluated: was the decision-making process accountable and representative to those affected? Did the process generate opportunities for learning, adapting, and growing networks for future interactions? These criteria are explained in detail in Chapter 8, which synthesises Chapters 5–7, and we use preliminary empirical data from the cases to suggest how performance might vary across the cases. These exploratory analyses provide a basis for future work on the emerging research challenge of performance.

Another feature of the IAD framework is multiple levels of action: operational, collective choice, and constitutional (Ostrom 1990; Ostrom Gardner and Walker 1994). The operational level is where actors carry out actions on the ground that directly affect people and the natural world, such as planting trees along an estuary shoreline or conducting a stream clean-up day. The collective choice level is where actors craft the set of rules that will steer operational level actions, such as deciding how to allocate their organization's budget or making a rule that landowners shall receive a subsidy of 50 per cent of the cost of the tree seedlings they plant along the shoreline if the trees are of a specified variety. It is also where they develop plans that identify, prioritize, and strategize implementation of actions to improve environmental and social conditions. The constitutional level is where actors constitute the decision-making body that will collectively make rules, such as deciding that the decision-making body shall include two representatives of the farming community and one member of the local soil and water conservation district board of directors.

To examine the different ways decision centres take each other into account, how these ways are affected by authority, information, and resources, and what performance criteria to consider, we next turn to three focal action situations. The first focuses on cooperation in the Puget Sound Basin.

5

Cooperation in Polycentric Governance Systems

Tomas M. Koontz

5.1 Introduction

In polycentric governance systems, multiple centres of decision-making are formally independent of each other but interact within a system of over-arching rules. These interactions can be grouped into three main types: (1) cooperation, (2) conflict and conflict resolution, and (3) competition (V. Ostrom 1994, 225; Ostrom, Tiebout, and Warren 1961). The focus of this chapter is cooperation. A case study of one government agency working within a polycentric governance system reveals how a cooperative approach can encourage local organizations to develop plans and carry out actions in keeping with agency priorities. The performance of these arrangements across levels of action is measured to build theory about interactions in polycentric governance systems.

5.1.1 Cooperation and Collaboration

Cooperation is not unique to polycentric governance. A rich body of theory and practice describes cooperation across a variety of settings. In thinking about cooperation in environmental governance, a key thread of scholarship centres on what has been termed 'collaborative governance', or, more simply, 'collaboration', which is an increasingly prominent form of cooperation. Collaboration scholarship, though vast, seldom explicitly situates collaboration within the framework of polycentricity. By so doing, we can better understand how features of polycentric governance affect collaborative performance and how cooperation plays out in a polycentric governance system.

Collaboration involves multiple parties working together to pursue a goal that none could achieve alone. Participants representing government, non-profit, and industry organizations, as well as individual stakeholders, work across boundaries to plan and carry out actions. Collaboration is particularly prevalent in efforts to address problems in complex social-ecological systems such as watersheds. Scholars have examined key elements of collaboration including authority, information, and resources. These three elements are instructive for understanding how collaboration plays out and for analysing its performance.

5.1.2 Authority, Information, and Resources

Authority structures are important both within collaborative efforts and in the larger political context. Within collaborative efforts, authority structures are marked by lack of vertical hierarchies, at least in theory. Multiple stakeholders should participate together and share power in a collaborative setting. Power imbalances within a collaboration can stifle dialogue (Innes and Booher 2010) and bias decisions towards participants with greater resources (Purdy 2012). Thus authority within a collaborative effort greatly affects its performance.

Authority structures in the larger political context can hinder or incentivize collaboration. For example, Wegerich (2007) argues that attempts to collaboratively manage water use in Uzbekistan were limited by the lack of horizontal-authority structures in the country. This is because authoritarian, vertical-power structures put different jurisdictions at the same level (e.g. cities) in competition with one another for scarce resources from the top, rather than encouraging their cooperation. Authority structures outside the collaboration can also hinder collaboration in contexts such as the USA, where stakeholders may choose to pursue victory in alternative venues including courts and legislation (Koontz et al. 2004). In other words, the authority structures in these alternative venues encourage stakeholders to engage in more conflictual rather than collaborative behaviour. In contrast, sometimes the threat of outside regulatory authority can incentivize parties to come together and seek collaborative solutions instead (Prokopy et al. 2014; Thomas 2002). This threat is likely in governance systems with overlapping authority, as multiple sources of potential regulation may motivate participants to seek collaboration as an alternative. Thus authority structures that provide multiple alternative venues, such as polycentric governance systems, can both encourage and discourage collaboration.

Information is the lifeblood of collaboration, as many such efforts focus on planning and information-gathering. Through deliberation, participants share values, beliefs, and goals to forge common understanding and interests (Brunner 2002; Innes and Booher 2010). Not only is information-sharing a key component of collaborative processes, but it also generates an important type of benefit, social learning (Innes and Booher 2010; Koontz 2014). Information and learning have been described in polycentric scholarship as critical for the success of polycentric governance, allowing citizens to hold public officials accountable and press for more effective and efficient policies. But collaboration scholars have also identified a disadvantage of information-sharing: it can lengthen the time required to come to a decision, criticized as 'all talk and no action' (Lubell 2004). This is especially prevalent as more and diverse stakeholders are engaged.

Studies of information flows in collaboration have identified several obstacles. The first obstacle is related to representation. Collaborative efforts typically fail to include all perspectives, such as racial and ethnic minorities, women, and lower socioeconomic class (Koehler and Koontz 2008; Purdy 2012). This lack of inclusion can limit the amount and breadth of information considered in decision-making. Another obstacle is the science–non-scientist divide. Many collaborative efforts task scientists or other experts with analysing data to share with non-experts, rather than co-producing knowledge. This practice can reduce information exchange and understanding (Innes and Booher 2010; Koontz et al. 2004).

Resources are a key element in collaboration. They provide capacity for collaborating organizations and individuals to do their work together. The lack of resources to accomplish a desired goal on their own can incentivize stakeholders to join collaborative efforts, and the promise of funding can catalyze the formation of collaborative groups (Prokopy et al. 2014). In a review of the empirical literature on factors for success in collaborative watershed partnerships, Leach and Pelkey (2001) found the most frequently cited factor for success was adequate resources, a theme supported by a number of subsequent studies (Koontz and Newig 2014; Lurie and Hibbard 2008; Ryan and Klug 2005; Yaffee and Wondolleck 2003). Similarly, actors in polycentric governance systems cooperate in large part by sharing resources for joint production or to contract for services. In the USA, millions of dollars are spent each year under the Clean Water Act for states to address nonpoint-source water pollution through collaborative efforts (Hardy and Koontz 2008).

The source of resources is a crucial factor affecting collaborative partnerships. If resources come from just one or a few sources, collaborative partnerships are more fragile and susceptible to disbanding (Koontz and

Sen 2013). Also, if a collaborative organization becomes beholden to one or a few sources, then it might face 'mission creep' to align with the funders' approaches rather than generating more creative solutions (Bidwell and Ryan 2006).

Taken together, authority, information, and resources shape cooperative efforts. This chapter examines cooperative interactions in a polycentric governance system, to explain how authority, information, and resources affect cooperation across levels of governance. Moreover, it explores how we might measure the performance of such a system across several criteria.

5.2 Methods and Study Context

This chapter examines a complex case of collaborative watershed management, the Puget Sound Partnership. It focuses on key elements of polycentric governance systems including authority, information, and resources. Cooperative interactions occur across vertical and horizontal levels of government, as well as among special purpose and multiple purpose jurisdictions (Hooghe and Marks 2003). Analysis using the Institutional Analysis and Development (IAD) framework brings these elements into focus.

As described in the Overview and Introduction to Part II, the IAD framework focuses attention on operational, collective choice, and constitutional levels of action (Ostrom 1990; Ostrom Gardner, and Walker 1994). The operational level is where actors carry out actions on the ground that directly affect people and the natural world. The collective choice level is where actors craft the set of rules that will steer operational level actions and develop plans that identify, prioritize, and strategize implementation of actions to improve environmental and social conditions. The constitutional level is where actors constitute the decision-making body that will collectively make rules and develop plans.

Data for the analysis come from reports, guidelines, plans, meeting minutes, and interviews with key informants in the Puget Sound Partnership (Koontz and Thomas 2018), as well as a separate study of collaborative networks in the region (Scott and Thomas 2015).

5.2.1 Background: Puget Sound Partnership

Located in the State of Washington, the Puget Sound is one of the United States of America's largest estuaries, covering more than 2,600 km^2. The broader Puget Sound Basin includes more than 35,000 km² of land draining into the Sound. Over 4.5 million people live in the basin, and the population is projected to grow to nearly 6 million by 2025. The health of the Puget Sound is threatened primarily by nonpoint-source pollution from storm water run-off and urban development that alters natural habitat. In addition, stream flows and structural barriers threaten wildlife such as the iconic Chinook salmon.

The Puget Sound is governed within the context of the US federal system. Water management is governed by the federal Clean Water Act, which gives states primary authority for regulating nonpoint-source water pollution. Two state agencies, the Washington Department of Ecology and the Washington Department of Fish and Wildlife, have regulatory authority related to the Puget Sound ecosystem. In addition, federal authority is important to water resources in the region through regulation of endangered species (including some salmon populations) and their habitat, as well as hydroelectric dam construction and licensing. Local jurisdictions are also involved, including county and municipal health departments, utility and waste water special districts, conservation districts, and local ordinances regulating building construction, housing density, and impervious surfaces. Native American tribes also have jurisdiction and treaty rights relating to certain land areas, as well as to salmon and other fish and shellfish in the Puget Sound.

Given the complexity of jurisdictions and actions affecting the health of the Puget Sound, the Washington State Legislature established the Puget Sound Partnership agency in 2007 to foster cooperation for Puget Sound recovery efforts. These efforts focus on improving ecological conditions for salmon, shellfish and other marine wildlife, as well as human well-being. One goal was to implement the Puget Sound Chinook Recovery Plan under the federal Endangered Species Act. The Puget Sound Partnership (PSP) develops biannual reports on the state of the Puget Sound, creates and monitors progress on indicators of ecosystem and human health, guides local organizations carrying out planning and actions, and updates its Action Agenda every two years to promote recovery of the Puget Sound ecosystem. It has given grants to thirty-four different organizations pursuing collaborative watershed restoration efforts (Scott and Thomas 2015). As a state agency, the PSP is funded by the State of Washington ($7.5 million for 2015–17) as well as the United States Environmental Protection Agency's (USEPA) National Estuary Program ($9.9 million for 2015–17) and the National Oceanic and Atmospheric Administration (NOAA) ($1.4 million for 2015–17).

5.2.2 Overlapping Authority and Multiple Decision Centres

By definition, a polycentric governance system has decision centres with formal independence at the same time as overlapping authority. This does not mean that all centres have equal power, and thus it is important to examine which centres have jurisdiction over which actions.

As a coordinator and facilitator, the PSP does not have formal authority over other jurisdictions. Rather, it fosters cooperation by developing plans and funding strategies to incentivize others to undertake particular actions. PSP operates within an existing institutional landscape of federal, state, local, and tribal jurisdictions. These jurisdictions deal with endangered species protection (especially with regard to salmon), water-pollution control, hydroelectric power production, water-quantity planning, and northwest Puget Sound recovery. Their existence predated the Puget Sound Partnership efforts, and their authority overlaps with PSP authority.

Endangered species protection falls under the US Federal Government. Starting in 1991, seventeen distinct population units of salmon in the Pacific Northwest were listed as endangered or threatened under the federal Endangered Species Act. Under this Act, the National Marine Fisheries Service (within the NOAA) must create conservation plans for species recovery. The State of Washington took action to recommend recovery plans involving local and regional stakeholders. The state Salmon Recovery Planning Act of 1998 created Lead Entities: watershed-based organizations funded to develop and manage salmon habitat protection and restoration projects. Each Lead Entity comprises a coordinator from a county, conservation district, tribe, or regional organization, plus a technical advisory group and a citizens committee. Lead Entities recommend projects for funding to the Washington State Salmon Recovery Funding Board. The twenty five Lead Entities are nested within eight geographical salmon regions across the state.

Water pollution control is regulated under the Clean Water Act of 1972. This federal law established US Environmental Protection Agency regulatory authority over point sources of water pollution throughout the country, such as factories and waste water treatment plants. It granted states authority to regulate nonpoint sources of pollution, such as storm water and run-off from agricultural lands. Section 319 of the Clean Water Act provided a mechanism for states to receive federal funding to clean-up waterways, and this funding is often used by states to promote locally based collaborative watershed management (Hardy and Koontz 2008).

The State of Washington generates 30 per cent of the nation's total hydroelectric power from dams throughout the state. These dams are subject to the Federal Energy Regulatory Commission's (FERC) licensing and relicensing requirements. As a condition of approval, FERC requires dam owners and operators to demonstrate how they will reduce the environmental impacts of dams, including fish passage. Since 1992 FERC has encouraged licence applicants to collaborate with resource agencies, non-governmental organizations, and tribes to determine environmental impacts and mitigation measures (Ulibarri 2015).

Local collaborative water quantity planning was established under the State Watershed Planning Act of 1998. Under the law, public and private stakeholders were encouraged to form collaborative partnerships to assess water quantity, develop watershed management plans, and carry out measures to address local water issues. The 'initiating governments' in a given watershed (all counties, the largest city, and the largest water supply utility) constituted a Planning Unit, which applied for funding to support watershed assessment, planning, and implementation within a Water Resources Inventory Area (WRIA). A WRIA may include all or portions of one or more counties, cities, utility districts, and tribal lands. Planning Units are empowered to make plan recommendations, but county legislatures retain sole authority to enact or adjust local ordinances. By 2012, watershed management plans had been adopted in thirty-three of the state's sixty-five designated WRIAs (Washington State Department of Ecology n.d.).

Another jurisdiction for Puget Sound Partnership recovery efforts comes from an initiative to improve the northwest portion of the Puget Sound. In 1998 Congress established the Northwest Straits Marine Conservation Initiative. Under this programme, the Northwest Straits Commission provides funding and training for Marine Resource Committees (MRCs) in seven counties in the northwestern part of Washington, including some in the Puget Sound region. MRCs comprise citizen volunteers appointed by local elected officials. They collaborate with diverse community partners for restoration, conservation, and education projects.

Finally, Native American tribal jurisdiction comes from a 1974 Federal Court Case reaffirming native tribes' treaty fishing rights. Tribes are recognized as natural resource co-managers with the State of Washington and entitled to half of the fisheries. Besides negotiating with the state to set annual salmon harvest limits, tribes undertake land use and restoration projects to improve fish habitat and reduce storm water pollution.

Taken together, overlapping jurisdictions exemplify the complexity of polycentric governance systems for social-ecological systems. Within the Puget Sound system, they provide authority, information, and resources that shape cooperation and the performance of collaborative efforts. Cooperation takes place at constitutional, collective choice and operational levels, as the PSP attempts to steer the behaviour of local organizations.

5.3 Results

5.3.1 Constitutional Level: Creating Local Integrating Organizations

In 2010, the PSP began constituting nine Local Integrating Organizations (LIOs) throughout the region. LIO geographic boundaries were based on seven ecosystem-based 'action areas' specified in the PSP-enabling legislation, with two action areas requesting to be subdivided into two separate LIOs based on social and community boundaries (Puget Sound Partnership 2014). Ideas for LIO establishment came from task force meetings and a public workshop, and eventually the PSP and US EPA together established the LIOs, by setting aside $75,000 annually for each of nine LIOs. The PSP Leadership Council received proposals from potential LIOs and decided which to approve, based on recommended criteria of 'strong support from the local community and are broadly inclusive' combined with a 'strong capacity to execute roles, responsibilities, and the scope of work' (Puget Sound Partnership n.d.). LIOs could be newly formed or existing organizations.

LIOs were charged with advising the PSP on local priorities in the Puget Sound Partnership Action Agenda, providing assistance to local groups conducting restoration work, implementing strategic actions in the Puget Sound Partnership's Action Agenda, and evaluating progress on such implementation. Following PSP guidance, the LIOs comprise a variety of organizations, some of which have authority to make and enforce laws, regulations, and programmes outside the LIO. Typically, LIOs are led by an executive committee comprising one elected county government official and one Native American tribal representative from each county and tribe operating in the geographic location of the watershed. These leaders have formal authority over multiple government functions of their home jurisdictions, but they do not have jurisdiction over the watershed as a whole. Within the LIO they have authority to oversee implementation of the LIO's work plan and fiscal matters.

Since LIOs are situated within a polycentric governance system, the authority structures include some LIOs that fulfil roles in other decision centres, e.g. one LIO serves as the designated Lead Entity for salmon recovery under the state Salmon Recovery Planning Act, while another LIO is a WRIA under the State Watershed Planning Act. Moreover, some LIO members represent other collaborative groups, which themselves comprise representatives from a variety of jurisdictions (e.g. MRCs).

At the constitutional level, the PSP's authority in constituting the LIOs was based on cooperation rather than coercion. The PSP did not have the authority to require any LIOs to form, but it did have the authority to selectively award grants to proposed LIOs. In choosing which LIOs to create, the PSP also shaped how the LIOs structured themselves with regard to leaders and members. In other words, the PSP relied on resources (grants) to incentivize the voluntary formation of LIOs, who would cooperate with the PSP in ecosystem recovery planning.

5.3.2 Collective Choice Level: Ecosystem Recovery Planning

At the collective choice level, starting in 2015 the PSP encouraged LIOs to create 5-year Ecosystem Recovery Plans. Since polycentric governance systems like the one for Puget Sound recovery have multiple independent centres of decision-making, plan creation was not accomplished by command. Rather it was incentivized by information and funding to steer LIOs to create Ecosystem Recovery Plans in the direction that PSP preferred. While LIOs rather than the PSP held the authority to develop their own plans, PSP influenced plan contents through information and resources.

Within each LIO, participants share information across local jurisdictions horizontally. This includes multiple-purpose jurisdictions such as municipalities and counties, as well as special-purpose districts such as marine resources committees, water resources committees, and salmon recovery Lead Entities. The inclusion of a wide range of stakeholders and representatives in the LIOs who attend regular LIO meetings provides opportunities for such information exchange.

In addition, information flows vertically between the PSP and the LIOs. In creating 5-year Ecosystem Recovery Plans, LIOs are guided by PSP to rely heavily on PSP-recommended documents to inform the plan (Koontz and Thomas 2018). This guidance is supported by workshops, meetings, and feedback on draft plans, with information flowing primarily top down (from PSP to LIOs) during plan creation. Subsequently, the completed local plans are sent up to the PSP, where the PSP intends to incorporate the information into basin-wide implementation plans, the Action Agenda, and regional scale adaptive management (Puget Sound Partnership 2016).

Resources, especially funding, were of critical importance for Ecosystem Recovery Plans. LIOs receive funds from the PSP to support personnel. Each LIO receives $75,000 annually for base coordination (e.g. hiring a coordinator). Also, each LIO received $170,000 for one year (September 2015 to September 2016) to prepare Ecosystem Recovery Plans. These funds provided staffing for moving LIO planning forward as well as incentives for LIOs to follow PSP guidelines in crafting plans.

Overall, at the collective choice level, information and funding are powerful tools in shaping locally created Ecosystem Recovery Plans. Across nine draft plans, each contained the same format, sections, and type of information, and each linked specifically to PSP priorities (Koontz and Thomas 2018). This kind of government-encouraged collaboration is common in collaborative watershed and other environmental management efforts (see Koontz et al. 2004), and it fits the description of collaborative public management as steering, rather than directing, the actions of others (Keast et al. 2004; Milward et al. 1993). Without command authority, the PSP incentivized the creation of plans that reflected PSP priorities through its use of information and resources in cooperation with the LIOs.

5.3.3 Operational Level: Ecosystem Recovery Projects

At the operational level, LIOs are on the front lines of carrying out ecosystem recovery actions. They match resources with local actors to conduct project work ranging from data collection and monitoring to pollution clean-up and habitat improvement. Although LIOs lack authority to compel others to act, they encourage others through information use and resource-sharing. In addition, the LIO itself carries out some activities such as outreach to local governments, holding public science forums, sending representatives to other collaborative efforts, and hosting workshops on restoration topics.

LIOs gather information to carry out restoration activities. This includes information about local contractors who can carry out the work, timelines, job specifications, and project monitoring. Minutes of meetings indicate horizontal information-sharing, such as between an LIO and several nearby watershed groups and a salmon Lead Entity group.

LIOs compete for grants to accomplish actions. In 2016 the United States Environmental Protection Agency's (USEPA) National Estuary Program, working with the PSP, allocated $100,000 for each LIO to fund local projects. In addition, the PSP recommends which LIO projects to fund towards regional goals, and guidelines indicate that the closer a grant proposal matches PSP goals, the more likely it is to receive funding. LIO meeting minutes indicate strategic positioning to frame their local priority actions in terms of PSP goals to increase funding chances.

In addition to funding through the PSP, LIOs seek funding from a variety of sources and help others seek funding for projects that align with LIO priorities. For example, the Snohomish Camano Eco Net organization funded by PSP notes that as Eco Net program funding phases out, they are considering how to integrate with a LIO in the region for funding. They foresee opportunities to partner with LIOs to apply for funding from the USEPA National Estuary Program to implement strategic plan initiatives, as the USEPA funding process shifts away from funding through the PSP and towards more funding directly to LIOs (Snohomish Camano 2015).

Overall, at the operational level, LIOs use information and resources to incentivize others to conduct ecosystem restoration activities. This parallels the PSP's use of information and resources to incentivize the LIOs to develop compatible Ecosystem Recovery Plans at the collective choice level. Unlike the PSP, LIOs also conduct activities on the ground to restore ecosystem functions.

5.3.4 Summing up: Authority, Information, and Resources across Levels

In the Puget Sound case, the PSP develops an overarching mission and priorities for the broader region and cooperates with LIOs to encourage the creation and implementation of locally relevant plans to address these regional priorities. This cooperative approach involves authority, information, and resources across constitutional, collective choice, and operational levels.

Authority to act in Puget Sound restoration efforts is shared across multiple centres in the region. The existence of multiple jurisdictions (local, state, and federal) and problems (water pollution, water quantity, endangered species, hydroelectric power) means no single centre can command compliance. At the constitutional level, the PSP constituted nine LIOs to comprise local actors representing diverse interests and organizations. The creation of LIOs was based not on authoritative coercion, but on incentives from grant funding. At the collective choice level, LIOs held the authority to develop their own plans to reflect local circumstances, but were incentivized through information and funding to follow PSP guidelines. At the operational level, LIOs lacked authority to compel others to carry out actions, but LIOs themselves carried out some restoration activities or incentivized others through grant funding recommendations.

Information flow differs across levels of analysis. At the collective choice level, LIOs engaged in ecosystem recovery planning using information shared horizontally among the organizations of their diverse membership, as well as vertically from the PSP. The influence of the PSP is particularly evident in comparing across the nine plans, which were similar in format and content, and which drew largely on the same three technical reports suggested by the PSP. At the operational level, LIOs gathered time- and place-specific information to carry out restoration activities. This information was routinely shared horizontally with other entities, but vertical information-sharing was less prevalent; LIOs did not rely much on PSP as a source of information for conducting operational level activities.

Resources have been vital to encourage cooperation at all levels. At the constitutional level, the LIOs were established by approval of the PSP, which is funded by the State of Washington and two federal agencies, USEPA and the NOAA. The PSP developed criteria, issued calls for proposals and awarded certain proposed LIOs funding to hire a coordinator. At the collective choice level, LIOs received funds from the PSP to develop an Ecosystem Recovery Plan, as well as additional funds to hire consultants, collect data, and analyse data. These funds were crucial to planning efforts. At the operational level, funding from the PSP and other sources is critical for carrying out actions.

Incentives for cooperation in this case stem largely from resources. LIOs produce locally relevant ecosystem restoration plans that are in sync with PSP goals and priorities, because they receive funding and training to do so. Moreover, LIOs whose proposed actions match PSP priorities have a better chance to receive funding from the USEPA. However, some LIO participants have been discouraged because more funding is not available for the projects they have planned and prioritized, feeling that it is no longer worth their while to continue participating (LIO 1 2016).

5.3.5 Performance

Governance systems can be assessed on a variety of performance criteria. Public policy scholars have long been interested in performance measures such as efficacy, efficiency, coherence, and accountability. Polycentricity and collaboration scholars have examined these and additional performance measures, including representation, social learning, adaptability and network building. These performance measures are described in more detail in Chapter 8, which synthesizes Part II, and are applied to the PSP case below.

Efficacy is a measure of the degree to which an effort achieves desired outcomes. This is perhaps the most important performance measure, and also the most challenging to obtain. Its measurement requires baseline data, the ability to control for confounding factors, and long-time horizons for social and ecological processes that unfold over time (Koontz and Thomas 2006). For the PSP, while a number of restoration projects have been completed, it is too early to tell whether and how much the PSP's efforts in cooperation with LIO plans and actions caused the Puget Sound recovery. The most recent biannual progress report from the Puget Sound Partnership (2017), the *State of the Sound 2017*, finds that thousands of restoration projects have been completed since the agency's establishment. Nevertheless, it is unlikely that most of the PSP's twenty five ambitious human and environmental recovery goals set for 2020 will be met (Cochrane 2017). To date, there have been gains in estuary, floodplain, riparian and shoreline habitat, but forest habitat continues to be lost. Populations of orcas, Chinook salmon and herring continue to decline. Shellfish harvest areas have increased but overall water quality continues to decline. The economic health of natural resource-based industries remains strong. Overall, this is a mixed record of success compared to baseline values when the agency began, with some system components improving, others declining, and many remaining steady.

Cooperation in a polycentric system is characterized by the potential for high transaction costs, reducing efficiency. Compared to a centrally controlled governance structure, cooperation can occur both horizontally and vertically, which gives actors greater possibilities. This can increase search costs and take time to unfold, as actors navigate myriad sources of authority, information, and resources. It can duplicate collaborative interactions, when multiple forums are present to provide the same function in the same location. For example LIO 2 includes representatives from several organizations that are themselves collaborative forums. And it can reduce efficient use of resources and may lead to a zero-sum game of taking resources away from other collaborative forums (Scott 2016; Scott and Thomas 2015).

Although such cooperation can reduce efficiency, on the other hand it can foster adaptability and persistence of efforts in the system. One reason is that the absence of funding from one source does not necessarily lead to collapse of the effort, but rather entrepreneurial groups can seek cooperation with other entities. Minutes of LIO meetings indicate inter-actions with a wide range of stakeholders and outside organizations to help the LIOs accomplish their goals, adapting strategies and partners to pursue opportunities. This is in line with the Koontz and Sen (2013) finding that collaborative groups may persist beyond the end-of-programme funding by seeking to align with other funding sources. Another benefit of bringing multiple decision makers together is that, although duplication of effort may occur, adaptability can increase as participants return to their home jurisdiction with different understandings (Korfmacher 1998), and they can find opportunities to work together with other jurisdictions as needs arise (Koontz and Newig 2014). The trade-off between economic efficiency and adaptability in systems has been highlighted by resilience scholars (Korhonen and Seager 2008; Walker 1992), who point out that having duplicate efforts in a system is not economically efficient but does provide redundancy in the face of system shocks. Cooperation in polycentric governance systems such as the Puget Sound recovery efforts exhibits this trade-off.

Although cooperation can be effective in encouraging action, it requires the government to give up control. Unlike in a hierarchical structure, where higher level authorities can demand compliance, a polycentric system involves different amounts of action across the landscape. This is a benefit in terms of allowing localities to tailor actions to local circum-stances, and a drawback in that it can raise questions of accountability for failure to achieve system-wide goals. Moreover, some localities will not take effective actions to solve the problems, or may export harm to other localities. Local control without cooperation is also known as fragmenta-tion, where individual entities do not take each other into account. For collective goods such as clean water and habitat, fragmentation runs the risk of not solving such problems. In contrast, cooperation in a polycentric system allows the possibility of coordination across spatial scales to bring coherence in addressing problems that are interconnected across localities. This is the function that the PSP attempts to fill by bridging the overall Puget Sound restoration efforts (Action Agenda) with local priorities for actions on a smaller spatial scale. Such bridging is not always successful, and different goals between the PSP and localities make an imperfect alignment. But cooperation as structured by the PSP does bring in infor-mation that is incorporated into plans to help align local actions with system-wide needs, increasing coherence across levels.

An important consideration for measuring the performance of cooper-ation is the representation of diverse interests at the collaborative table.

Most collaboration scholars have found that including diverse stakeholders in a cooperative effort can bring more complete information for consideration, encourage stakeholders to support the plan, increase social learning, and build social capital that may be used for tackling other societal problems. At the same time, inclusion of more diverse interests can reduce process efficiency, lead to 'lowest common denominator' recommendations that are agreeable to all but not dramatic enough to be effective, and delay action in the face of urgent problems. In the Puget Sound recovery efforts, the PSP worked with LIOs to create diverse representation. Most LIOs had at least a dozen members representing a wide range of organizations such as county elected officials, tribes, environmental non-profit organizations, county public health departments, county natural resource departments, conservation districts, marine resources committees, salmon recovery Lead Entities, university researchers, WRIAs, and municipal officials. This diverse representation was fostered by the PSP's authority to provide resources to LIOs that agreed to include diverse representation.

Another performance measure for cooperation is social learning. Cooperation by its very nature features interactions among different stakeholders, and when these stakeholders work together to develop plans and take actions they are expected to learn about ecological, social, political, and process realities (Koontz 2014; Muro and Jeffrey 2012). This learning depends on information-sharing, which is done vertically and horizontally in the Puget Sound system. Unfortunately, learning data have not been collected for this case, so the level of social learning is not known.

Cooperation in polycentric governance in a given action arena, such as Puget Sound ecosystem restoration, is likely to exist alongside multiple jurisdictions, some of which may not be polycentric. In other words, the authority structure in these jurisdictions may be very different and this difference may affect interactions within the given jurisdiction. For example, much of the clean-water efforts in the Puget Sound initially stemmed from an existing coercive governance authority for species protection under the Endangered Species Act (ESA). The listing of salmon and threat of additional listings in the future under the ESA spurred state-level efforts to encourage local cooperation. The ESA is a hierarchical structure where an agency, backed by the courts, has the power to unilaterally prohibit state, local, and private actions that would harm a listed species. This co-existing jurisdiction can catalyze cooperation, as it has in the Puget Sound, by creating a less desirable (in the minds of participants) alternative to cooperation.

The overlapping decision centres can also affect network building. Scholars in the ecology of games have examined the relationship between old and new networks of individuals in a crowded field of network opportunities (Berardo and Scholz 2010; Henry et al. 2011; Lubell et al. 2010; Prell et al. 2009). A study of Puget Sound organizations collaborating through the PSP indicated that such participation enhances network ties between organizations, but such enhancement diminishes for those organizations already interacting with each other in other collaborative venues (Scott and Thomas 2015). An implication for polycentricity is that the existence of multiple overlapping decision centres shapes cooperation, as polycentric systems presumably feature more interactions in multiple venues than do other kinds of systems. This likely leads to diminishing returns, where investment in new collaborative forums yields smaller returns when there are pre-existing collaborative forums and cooperative relationships. In fact, members in one LIO have recently proposed to dissolve their LIO and instead allow their work to continue in alternate decision centres, in order to avoid duplication and burnout (LIO 1, 2016).

The performance measures discussed are shown in Table 5.1, which also summarizes the degree to which these measures were affected by authority, information, and resources. Results from preliminary data suggest the PSP has performed well on most, but not all, of these measures.

5.4 Conclusion

This chapter has described how cooperation plays out in polycentric governance systems, focusing specifically on authority, information, and resources. Using the example of Puget Sound ecosystem restoration efforts, particularly the PSP and LIOs, this chapter has examined constitutional, collective choice, and operational levels of action and discussed performance measures.

The PSP constituted nine LIOs to match local with basin-wide priorities, as a way to integrate restoration actions across scales. In order to promote restoration efforts that would be effective at local and basin scales, the PSP encouraged local planning tied to PSP priorities. Thus a polycentric governance system allowed dispersed authority to be steered by information and funding via cooperative interactions. Results thus far indicate that LIOs have created locally relevant Ecosystem Recovery Plans tied to PSP's Action Agenda priorities, although it is too early to tell whether these plans will eventually translate into effective outcomes.

Table 5.1 *Measuring performance of cooperative interactions in the Puget Sound Case*

Measure	Link to authority, information and resources	Results[a]
Efficacy	Authority to coerce is weak, but resources are available to incentivize some actions.	Mixed results to date
Efficiency	Resource use is subject to duplication and transaction costs.	Low
Coherence	Information leads to alignment between local actions and system-wide recovery goals.	High
Accountability	Weak authority to coerce means it is hard to hold a centre accountable.	Low
Representation	Constitutional level PSP authority to decide who gets resources.	High
Social learning	Learning depends on information-sharing.	No data
Adaptability	Multiple sources of resources promotes ability of centres to pursue goals in the face of resource reductions from a given source.	High
Network building	Information-sharing across LIOs and resources given to local organizations increases networks for some centres, but little network building for centres with large existing networks.	High for centres with few existing network ties, low for other centres

[a] Rated as high, low, or mixed from the available case evidence (e.g. reports, meeting minutes, plans, and published studies).

Examining the performance of cooperation in polycentric governance systems highlights several theoretical insights. First, cooperation is a means to navigate the complex array of decision centres to find appropriate information and resources, but it can incur high transaction costs, which are likely to increase in pursuit of diverse interest representation. At the same time, cooperation can provide adaptability in the face of change. In addition, cooperation is well-suited to certain biophysical contexts, such as nonpoint-source pollution, where biophysical systems do not align with political boundaries, and where coercion is politically infeasible. Also, cooperation entails government steering rather than controlling, which can raise questions about accountability. Such steering includes the possibility that local efforts can be steered into alignment with system-wide goals.

The presence of multiple overlapping decision centres affects cooperation in polycentric governance systems, both positively and negatively. In the Puget Sound, the hierarchical authority of the ESA sparked collaborative efforts, and multiple grant opportunities were available to fund restoration through federal, state and local programmes. However, the existence of additional collaborative efforts outside the PSP reduced the network gains achieved among stakeholders participating in LIOs.

Policy makers seeking to reach goals via collaboration should consider the advantages and disadvantages of funding existing versus new local organizations. The PSP decided to include both types of groups. Funding an existing group to take on the LIO role could benefit the PSP by having existing organizations up and running more quickly (Sabatier et al. 2005), but a potential downside is that the existing organizations may not embrace the PSP's mission fully because they have pre-existing missions (e.g. Bidwell and Ryan 2006).

Measuring performance of cooperation in a polycentric system should include attention to multiple dimensions. These dimensions include some relevant for all forms of interactions in polycentric governance systems, and others particular to cooperation (as opposed to conflict and conflict resolution, and competition). Understanding how authority, information and resources affect actions and performance, and the trade-offs among performance measures, will better position policy makers to make decisions about which policy strategies to use in which circumstances.

Cooperation is likely to be more prominent in polycentric governance systems than in monocentric or decentralized systems because the shared authority and interconnectedness across multiple scales opens up more potential partners – both horizontal and vertical. In monocentric systems, cooperation is likely to be reduced due to fewer horizontal power centres and their tendency to compete with each other (Wegerich 2007). In decentralized systems, fragmentation may reduce opportunities for interactions conducive to cooperation. Polycentric governance systems occupy a middle ground, where both vertical and horizontal power centres exist, and these centres frequently interact with each other. Of course, polycentric governance systems are not just about cooperation. Often, they involve conflict and conflict resolution, and competition. It is to these types of interaction we turn to in the following chapters.

6

Conflict and Conflict Resolution in Polycentric Governance Systems

Tanya Heikkila

6.1 Introduction

Polycentric governance systems not only create opportunities for actors to compete and collaborate in the provision or management of public goods, they also can lead to conflictual interactions or disputes. While conflicts that go unresolved can undermine the performance and quality of any governance system, opportunities for resolving conflicts in a polycentric system are also possible. It is through both conflict and conflict resolution that actors may learn and adapt the institutional arrangements that structure their interactions in polycentric governance (Anderies, Janssen, and E. Ostrom 2004; Dietz, E. Ostrom, and Stern 2003; E. Ostrom 2005a).

The goal of this chapter is to examine conflictual interactions in polycentric governance systems, the factors that shape these interactions, and how conflicts are resolved. The research context for this chapter is a comparison of the governance of hydraulic fracturing and shale development in two US states. Advancements in hydraulic fracturing and horizontal drilling technologies made it easier to access oil and gas in shale formations starting around 2008, resulting in a boom in US fossil-fuel production. However, with the boom came governance challenges, particularly with externalities associated with the production process, such as air or water pollution from drilling, noise, dust, and road traffic. The rapid expansion of shale development also exposed many communities that previously had not experienced oil and gas development to these externalities. Shale oil and gas development also involves important questions around water use. First, water is the primary ingredient in the process of hydraulic fracturing, which is used to crack open shale formations. The drilling process also has the potential to affect groundwater supplies (i.e. if well integrity is compromized), and substantial volumes of wastewater are produced through drilling, which then must be disposed, or treated and reused. The governance mechanisms related to shale development, therefore, have important implications for water resources.

Similar to the companion chapters in Part II of this book, which explore competitive and collaborative interactions, this chapter draws attention to the authority of actors in the system, their resources, and information. It also considers the performance of polycentric governance systems, particularly by examining the degree to which conflicts are resolved and evidence of learning and institutional adaptation for conflict management.

6.2 Conflict and Conflict Resolution

In any governance system, conflict can be defined as a dispute or disagreement among actors over how to provide a good or service, or over the rules, policies or institutions for addressing a governance issue (Weible and Heikkila 2017). Governance conflicts often manifest as actions or behaviours, such as trying to compel other actors to take action (i.e. through court cases), or influencing the general public (i.e. framing information in the media) or public officials (i.e. lobbying). Conflicts may occur within specific action situations or venues, or they may play out across the broader governance system. They can also vary in duration and intensity, in terms of the number of actors involved and the degree of divergence in their positions or their conflict activities (Heikkila and Weible 2017; Weible and Heikkila 2017). With natural resources governance, different types of conflicts can arise, including those dealing with the supply or demand for public goods provision, those associated with externalities from the use of common-pool resources, or those dealing with questions of equity in the distribution of resources (Heikkila and Schlager 2012). Conflict resolution, on the other hand, involves an agreement or decision where actors or decision units no longer have the incentives to engage in conflictual behaviours, or where they are willing to compromise on an issue. Both conflict and conflict resolution in polycentric governance systems are ways that actors take each other into account in their interactions (Ostrom, Tiebout, and Warren 1961).

Conflict occurs in polycentric governance systems, in part, because the decision units within polycentric systems often have competing interests or goals with respect to governance choices (Ostrom, Tiebout, and Warren 1961). For instance, if public goods are required (i.e. regulation to control pollution crossing multiple jurisdictions) at a scale that exceeds the authority of a single jurisdiction, then conflict can ensue. Alternatively, conflict may occur if jurisdictions disagree on the need for public goods, on the means for achieving shared public goods, or if one jurisdiction attempts to free-ride off the public goods provision of another. Likewise, disputes may ensue over questions about who has appropriate authority to make governance decisions when authorities overlap. Scholars of federalism have made similar arguments, suggesting that the authority and scope of governments in a federal system can lead to conflict dynamics, as well as opportunities to negotiate conflict (Bednar 2011; Christin and Hug 2012; Rodriguez 2014; Wibbels 2005). This disagreement may then result in perceptions that actors with divergent positions are threatening, and result in an unwillingness to compromise on collective rules or strategies for addressing shared issues (Weible and Heikkila 2017). At the same time, actors' resources and information can shape how conflicts arise because actors can use their resources to pursue their conflict aims in different venues or can frame conflicts around particular types of information sources.

Whether and how actors in a polycentric governance system are incentivized to resolve conflict depends on a variety of factors. For instance, as conflict-resolution scholars recognize the design of institutional rules and venues matters (Emerson et al. 2009; Weller and Wolff 2005;). In particular, opportunities for fair and open contestation, dialogue, and engagement by relevant actors, with recognized authority to participate in a given venue, can affect the performance of conflict-resolution outcomes (Susskind and Cruikshank 1987). At the same time the incentives for actors to engage successfully in such resolution processes may depend upon the resources that actors possess, the information they have accessible, and how information is exchanged (Emerson et al. 2009).

6.3 Methods

This study compares how conflict and conflict-resolution interactions unfold in two different polycentric systems related to the governance of shale oil and gas in two US states – Colorado and New York – which have both experienced conflicts over shale but have different conflict-resolution outcomes. Similar to the cooperation and competition cases, this chapter presents a descriptive analysis of how conflict has emerged in these two polycentric systems using guidance from the IAD framework to compare interactions at constitutional, collective choice, and operational levels. It also uses the concepts of authority, incentives, resources, and information to help understand differences across these two systems, and to shed light on the performance of conflict-related interactions.

Data on the conflicts and conflict-resolution interactions in these systems come from document analyses and interviews (twelve in Colorado and fifteen in New York), collected between 2012 and 2016 in these two states. Additionally, results from surveys, conducted by the author and her colleagues, in Colorado (2013 and 2015) and New York (2014) provide supplementary evidence of the underlying nature of the conflicts (i.e. positions of different actors), their resources, and information, as well as on performance criteria (Heikkila et al. 2014b; Heikkila and Weible 2015; Pierce et al. 2013). The assessments of performance criteria, described in this chapter, were made qualitatively, based on evidence from surveys, interviews and primary documents. Additionally, the analysis draws upon secondary literature published on the politics of hydraulic fracturing in these states to support the analyses (Arnold and Robert 2014; Davis 2012; Heikkila et al. 2014a; Rinfret, Cook, and Pautz 2014; Weible and Heikkila 2016).

6.4 Case Background

6.4.1 Polycentric Governance of Shale Development in the United States

Overlapping and semi-autonomous units of decision-making – or linked action situations – involved in regulating, monitoring, and enforcing the various aspects of shale development in the US states have maintained much of the legal and administrative purview over permitting of wells, creating standards for well siting and construction, pollution control and drilling safety. States may distribute that authority in different ways. Most oil- and gas-producing states have statutes that enable an agency to hold responsibility for regulating and permitting oil and gas activities. Other state agencies may also have statutory authority to regulate issues such as air emissions from wells or monitor drinking water quality near oil and gas spills. States set rules for financial assurances of well closure and remediation of well sites, and fees or taxes for compensating local communities that need to mitigate externalities associated with oil and gas development. States also work together in oil and gas governance. For example, the Susquehanna River Basin Commission has rules for water withdrawals before shale gas can be produced in the basin, which runs across three states. Most oil- and gas-producing states are also members of the

Interstate Oil and Gas Compact Commission, which assists member states in identifying regulatory practices and in sharing information on the industry.

The federal government plays a more limited role in oil and gas governance.[1] For federally owned oil and gas mineral rights, the Bureau of Land Management (BLM), under the Department of Interior, maintains authority over mineral leases and permitting. BLM further permits access to private oil and gas mineral rights underlying federal lands.[2] Another avenue for federal involvement in oil and gas management is through the Environmental Protection Agency (EPA), which has authority over regulating air quality under the Clean Air Act. Through that authority, the EPA has passed rules that affect the release of methane from oil and gas operations.

In addition, local governments may hold authority over land-use policies that can affect the location of oil and gas drilling and other surface-level impacts of oil and gas. In Texas, for instance, local governments often use ordinances or zoning rules to restrict how or where drilling occurs, provided the rules do not conflict with state regulations.

Other centres of decision-making authority include courts, which may arbitrate conflicts over the interpretation of policies and regulations related to oil and gas management. Some government agencies provide mechanisms for citizens or other private actors to engage in governance advisory committees or similar venues. Interested actors – whether governmental or non-governmental – can also express their positions on conflict or seek out conflict resolution through state legislatures, state ballot initiatives, participation in regulatory or policy-making processes and hearings.

6.4.2 Polycentric Governance in Colorado

In Colorado, the authority for conventional and unconventional oil and gas development is set largely under the state statutes and regulations. Specifically, the Oil and Gas Conservation Act grants the Colorado Oil and

---

[1] One way that federal authority has been limited is through the Energy Policy Act of 2005, which exempted fracking fluids from the Safe Drinking Water Act's underground injection-well requirements. The exemption became known as the Halliburton Loophole. Additionally, the 2005 Energy Policy Act emphasized that the states maintain jurisdiction over the oil and gas industry.

[2] BLM has recently attempted to pass rules on the regulation of fracking on public lands, but they have been blocked by a federal court decision that found the Interior Department lacked authority from Congress to issue the regulation (Davenport 2016).

Gas Conservation Commission (COGCC) the authority to regulate oil and gas and to protect public health safety, and the environment 'taking into consideration cost-effectiveness and technical feasibility' (§34-60-106(2) (d)). COGCC regulations include rules for pollution prevention, permitting, well integrity, hydraulic fracturing, large-scale planning, and surface owner notification and protections. The COGCC also handles the drilling permit process, monitoring, and enforcement of regulations. While the COGCC holds primary authority for the action situations of oil and gas drilling and operations, another actor with regulatory, monitoring, and enforcement authority is the Colorado Department of Health and Environment, through its Air Quality Control Commission and Water Quality Control Commission. This authority is granted through Colorado's Air Pollution and Prevention Control Act and Water Quality Control Act. Local governments have some authority for the siting action arenas around oil and gas, but hold very limited authority within regulatory, monitoring, or enforcement action situations. Citizens, industry, non-profits, and interest groups engage in action situations related to oil and gas governance by providing input into regulatory and legislative processes, proposing ballot initiatives, serving on advisory groups and task forces, and filing lawsuits. As a result, courts play an important role in Colorado in hearing and resolving conflicts.

Oil and gas development is not new in Colorado, but the advent of high-volume hydraulic fracturing resulted in a rapid expansion of shale development. Since 2001, Colorado's natural gas production nearly doubled, and since 2010 Colorado's oil production nearly tripled (U.S. Energy Information Administration 2018). Although new drilling began to slow in 2015 as the result of low oil and gas prices, development started to increase again in 2017. Much of the shale development has occurred in the Denver-Julesberg Basin in northeast Colorado (U.S. Energy Information Administration 2018), which is close to many of Colorado's urban centres.

Conflicts, and attempts to resolve these conflicts, have emerged both within and between different centres of authority related to shale development in Colorado. Involved in these types of conflicts are dozens of governmental and non-governmental actors, on issues related to both whether and how development should occur and who has authority to make such decisions (Heikkila and Weible 2016). Survey research on the actors involved indicate wide variance in policy positions among both governmental and non-governmental actors (Heikkila and Weible 2015; Pierce et al. 2013). While industry groups and industry associations have held policy positions that are strongly supportive of the industry, and environmental and citizens' groups have largely opposed hydraulic fracturing, actors representing government entities, especially local government, take a diversity of positions.

6.4.3 Polycentric Governance in New York

Part of New York State overlies the Marcellus shale formation, which is the source of neighbouring Pennsylvania's shale gas boom. Unlike its neighbour, the state has not allowed the use of hydraulic fracturing to develop these shale resources and after six years of a de facto moratorium on the practice, the Cuomo administration instituted a state-wide ban in 2014 (Kaplan 2014). Yet, the authority to make these decisions was afforded under an institutional setting that has notable similarities with Colorado. That is, the state legislature has established rules and authorities for oil and gas under the State's Environmental Conservation Law (Article 23 – the Oil and Gas Solution and Mining Law). The state granted authority to the New York Department of Environmental Conservation (DEC) to regulate, permit, monitor, and enforce oil and gas drilling through its Bureau of Oil and Gas Regulation and its Division of Mineral Resources. In 2008, when initial requests for permitting hydraulically fractured wells in New York were presented to the DEC, this triggered a review under the State Environmental Quality Review Act. During this review process, questions about the health impacts further brought in authority from the New York Department of Health, creating a new action situation for monitoring. In addition, like Colorado, the New York Constitution affords local governments relatively broad authority to adopt local laws. Unlike Colorado, local governments have exercised these rights extensively in the case of hydraulic fracturing, especially during the time prior to the state-wide ban in 2014 when the state was conducting its environmental and health reviews (Simonelli 2014). Thus, numerous local-level action situations that focus on deciding whether to allow hydraulic fracturing have occurred in New York, alongside state-level action situations.

The governance decisions that restricted shale development in New York were controversial, and various conflictual interactions emerged among different levels and units of government, industry, environmental and citizens' groups. Additionally, anti-shale development groups, and several pro-shale development groups formed in the five years prior to the 2014 ban and their efforts were targeted largely at local government decision-making (Arnold, Le Anh, and Gottlieb 2017). A survey of 129 of the actors involved in these debates, conducted in 2014 (Heikkila et al.

2014a; Weible and Heikkila 2016), interviews, and document analyses (Heikkila, Weible and Pierce 2014) provide ample evidence of the conflictual nature of these interactions. Policy and governance positions were highly polarized among various actors during this time, and different actors employed a range of political strategies across various venues to shape policy and governance outcomes to achieve their goals. Yet, there is evidence that actors used various venues to address these conflicts and sometimes collaborated even when they had divergent policy positions (Heikkila et al. 2014a).

6.5 Conflict and Conflict Resolution in Colorado's Oil and Gas Governance

6.5.1 Constitutional Level

Constitutional-level decisions play an important role in shaping authority, and thus, they also can influence conflicts over authority. In Colorado, the state constitution does not provide language specific to the governance of oil and gas, but it does establish 'home rule' authority for local governments, and conditions where state pre-emption of that authority may arise.

The extent of local authority to govern oil and gas has been a source of contention in Colorado. Local governments passed bans or moratoria on hydraulic fracturing, and the oil and gas industry has sued local governments.[3] The state regulatory agency, the COGCC, also opposed local bans, arguing that they pre-empt state authority (COGCC Rule 201 allows local governments to regulate land use related to oil and gas operations, but only when it is not in conflict with COGCC regulations.) In 2014 and early 2015, Colorado's Governor Hickenlooper created a new collective choice venue, called the Governor's Task Force, designed to mitigate the ongoing conflicts over the authority of local governments related to hydraulic fracturing.

While the Task Force was a short-term venue to address questions of local authority, debates in the courts continued. In May of 2016, the Colorado Supreme Court ruled that the city of Longmont's ban on fracking

---

[3] These suits include: *Gunnison County* v. *SG Interests* in 2011–12 for local regulations; *Longmont* v. *COGA and COGCC* in 2012 for local regulations; *Longmont* v. *COGA* in 2013 for a local ban; *Lafayette* v. *COGA* in 2014 for a ban; *Broomfield* v. *Sovereign* and then against COGA in 2014 for a local ban; Colorado Springs citizens against the city in 2013 to allow vote on a ban; and *Fort Collins* v. *COGA* in 2013 for a local ban.

(approved by voters in 2012) was pre-empted by state law, and the Court further invalidated a moratorium on fracking that had been passed by the city of Fort Collins (Colorado Supreme Court 2016). Other local governments including Boulder, Boulder County, and Broomfield had moratoria, which were affected by these decisions. In response, opponents of shale development tried to propose ballot initiatives in 2016 that would have given local governments more authority, but none achieved enough signatures to reach the November ballot.

In Colorado, 'softer' forms of local authority exist. For instance, local governments can engage in Memoranda of Understanding with oil and gas companies to ensure that firms meet certain requirements that are above and beyond state laws (i.e. noise-reduction mechanisms, pollution reduction, monitoring) (Golten, Ward, and Mutz 2016). They have also used city ordinances to achieve similar outcomes by allowing for expedited permitting, for instance, if oil and gas companies meet certain requirements.

In addition to the authority of state versus local governments, constitutional-level questions have emerged in Colorado over the authority and composition of the COGCC, which is the commission that regulates oil and gas. In 2008, the Colorado legislature changed the structure of the COGCC to bring in more environmental and public health interests to the commission, in response to criticisms over the domination of the commission by oil and gas.

6.5.2 Collective Choice Level

Conflicts, and conflict resolution, also appear at the collective choice level. For instance, since 2008, the COGCC's rule-making processes have addressed several contentious issues, such as the disclosure of hydraulic fracturing fluids, setbacks, well monitoring, and notice to local governments of large, multi-well development related to unconventional drilling. Similarly, the Colorado Department of Public Health and Environment engaged in rule-making to reduce methane emissions from oil and gas wells. Information played different roles throughout these processes. For instance, limited information was available on the public health impacts of oil and gas development to inform decisions about setbacks. In fact, many stakeholders disagreed on the effectiveness of the setback rule-making process (Pierce et al. 2013) and the issue remains conflictual. Conversely, in the collective choice decision over methane/air quality regulations in Colorado, recent data on air quality impacts were a key tool for the collective choice processes and actors were relatively satisfied with that regulatory process and the quality of those regulations. Thus, better access to information or information-sharing in the process may have made it easier for conflict resolution to occur.

Local-level actors played an important role in informing these collective choice decisions, through their participation in the policy process at the state level, but local governments' resources, in terms of who can influence the process, can vary widely (Heikkila et al. 2014b). The Colorado Task Force created by Governor Hickenlooper in 2014 involved several months of information-gathering from relevant stakeholders and recommendations from the Task Force on new regulations for planning for large-scale multi-use wells. The COGCC then adopted rules based on these recommendations in early 2016. The effectiveness of the Task Force and the resultant rules in resolving the conflict have continued to be contested, however (Glick, Ray, and Wood 2016; Heikkila and Weible 2015). This suggests that opportunities for information-sharing do not necessarily mitigate conflicts, if the underlying debates over authority remain.

Resources and information have influenced the collective choice processes, especially when conflicts appear at the local level. Garfield County Colorado, for instance, in response to some concerns over the effects of oil and gas drilling in the early 2000s, created an Energy Advisory Board to help the Board of County Commissioners analyse these potential impacts (Rada 2007). The County also funded a two-year air quality monitoring study across the county to generate more information (Rada 2007).

6.5.3 Operational Level

In Colorado, operational-level decisions related to shale development are ongoing, and these decisions and actions by governments, oil and gas operators, and other actors can be contentious. Often community concern is raised when operators propose new well sites within residential areas of a local jurisdiction, or even in a neighbouring jurisdiction, as communities feel that they have no recourse against well-funded industries with recognized private property rights (or authority) to access subsurface oil and gas resources (Glick, Ray, and Wood 2016). Other concerns arise over the ability of the state's access to resources for monitoring and enforcing oil and gas regulations (Pierce et al. 2013). Individuals in these communities have attempted to shape the authority structure of decision-making to bring more local-level control over operational activities (e.g. through regulatory processes, or ballot initiatives), although many of these efforts have been blocked by court decisions on constitutional grounds. Local governments have had more success in shaping operational activities using Memoranda of Understanding (MOUs), through which industry operators agree to certain changes in operations to mitigate risks or concerns by using best management practices (Golten, Ward, and Mutz 2016). However, state-level officials have argued that the MOU process comes with operational-level challenges. Namely, these agreements imply enforcement authority by the state on issues that the state has not agreed to, and the state may lack both the authority and the resources it needs to engage in such enforcement (Golten, Ward, and Mutz 2016; Shaffer, Zilliox, and Smith 2014).

The state of Colorado has sought to mitigate disputes and concerns at the operational level before they move to collective choice processes by providing a resource for local communities to interface with the state – through local government liaisons under the COGCC. Regulations passed in 2016 by the COGCC (a collective choice action) also expanded information and input by local governments in the operational process of siting/permitting decisions when wells are proposed in urban areas. However, the quality of that process, again, has been questioned (Glick, Ray, and Wood 2016).

6.6 Conflict and Conflict Resolution in New York's Oil and Gas Governance

6.6.1 Constitutional Level

Similar to Colorado, New York State's Constitution provides home-rule authority to local governments. Some conflicts in New York over oil and gas have arisen around local government authority, but not with the same intensity as in Colorado. Over a period of a few years, dozens of New York municipalities proposed, or passed, bans on hydraulic fracturing, while several others passed ordinances that stated their support for the practice (FrackTracker 2018). The authority of municipal governments to ban the practice was contested by the industry, but the New York State Court of Appeals, the state's highest court, ruled in 2014 that the state law does not pre-empt local ordinances that ban hydraulic fracturing (*Wallach v. Town of Dryden*). Of course, New York's decision at the state level to ban hydraulic fracturing eventually gave local governments no authority over whether to support oil and gas development. Yet, this decision has not emerged as a major source of conflict.

6.6.2 Collective Choice Level

Relative to constitutional-level decisions, collective choice processes have been a source for more intense conflict, but also an opportunity to mitigate conflict in New York around oil and gas development. Unlike Colorado, the focus of collective choice decisions were on 'whether' high-volume hydraulic fracturing should be permitted. At the state level, the locus of these decisions rested with the DEC and Governor Cuomo's administration. Information was critical in New York to the state-level collective choice decisions that eventually restricted unconventional oil and gas development. During the 2009 and 2011 public comment periods for the review process for the Supplemental Environmental Impact Statement, conducted by DEC, interested citizens and communities raised concerns over both the potential impacts and the transparency of the review process (Rinfret, Cook, and Pautz 2014). The first comment period yielded 66,000 responses; a second round, ending on 12 January 2013, resulted in 204,000. In 2011, former Governor Patterson issued Executive Order 41, which put a moratorium on horizontal fracking, mandating that horizontal drilling would not be allowed until the completion of a final SGEIS. The review process itself was controversial. In the fall of 2012, when the DEC was prepared to release the environmental impact statement, which could have set the stage for moving ahead with permitting hydraulically fractured wells, Governor Cuomo ordered that the New York Department of Health review the potential health impacts of hydraulic fracturing (Hakim 2012). Ultimately, this information was used to make a final policy decision to impose a state-wide ban in 2014.

While the state-level collective choice decisions on this issue were under-way between 2008 and 2014, decisions on whether hydraulic fracturing would be allowed also were debated by many municipal governments. In addressing local-level debates, policy entrepreneurs in New York provided substantial resources that helped shape the conflicts emerging at the collective choice at the local level (Arnold, Le Anh, and Gottlieb 2017). For example, according to interviewees in New York, representatives from grassroots organizations, 'big green organizations', and activist lawyers collaborated to diffuse the idea of bans across local jurisdictions and to provide information to local jurisdictions on how to pass these bans (Anonymous Interviews 2014).

6.6.3 Operational Level

New York offers a notable contrast to Colorado with respect to operational-level conflicts and conflict resolution. Due to the 2014 state-level ban on hydraulic fracturing in New York, and the previous de facto moratorium, operational activities including the permitting of drilling of hydraulically fractured wells, and the ensuing operations, monitoring, and enforcement, have not occurred in New York. The incentives for interested actors, including industry and local governments in support of shale development, to push back against this lack of authority and to continue the conflict, were curtailed, in part, due to low energy prices and the relatively pro-environmental political climate in the state (Heikkila and Weible 2015). In other words, the low value of the resource, and the political conditions surrounding the governance system, have contributed to dampening the available resources for those who want to see oil and gas development move forward in New York.

6.7 Performance in Polycentric Oil and Gas Governance

One of the primary criteria for assessing the performance of polycentric systems where conflict occurs is the efficacy of conflict resolution. How-ever, conflict resolution can take time and is not necessarily a single-shot game. Therefore, other factors, such as the efficiency of the process, the degree to which the outcomes improve coherence in the governance system are also important outcome measures. At the same time, there are important process measures for how either conflicts unfold or how a conflict-resolution process works, which can be used to assess performance around these interactions. As discussed in Chapter 5, which focuses on collaboration, such outcomes include accountability of those with author-ity to diverse interests, representation of diverse actors, social learning among the actors involved, adaptation of policies or processes to manage conflict; and network building. (See Table 6.1 for a summary of the performance measures related to conflict and conflict-resolution inter-actions.) Additionally, this section will consider how the authority, infor-mation, and resources of actors may shape these performance outcomes.

In Colorado, it is not clear that conflict resolution has been effective – particularly about the role of local and state governments in making decisions over oil and gas development. The pervasiveness of disputes in Colorado may be due to the lack of satisfaction with the conflict-resolution

Table 6.1 *Measuring performance of conflict/conflict-resolution interactions in oil and gas governance[a]*

Measure	Colorado: Links to authority, information, and resources	Colorado: Results[a]	New York: Links to authority, information, and resources	New York: Results[a]
Efficacy	Authority and information contested, and conflicts over who makes governance decisions is ongoing.	Low	Conflicts resolved through state's authority to ban fracking. Information-gathering used to justify the ban. But efficacy can depend on perspective of actors.	Mixed
Efficiency	Actors with resources sought different sources of authority to resolve conflicts and information is contested.	Low	Actors with resources sought different sources of authority to resolve conflicts and information-gathering was slow.	Low
Coherence	Efforts to align policy positions across levels of authority have occurred, but are imperfect.	Mixed	Compatibility in decisions across levels of authority is unclear.	Mixed
Accountability	Information-gathering processes have improved accountability, but limits on local authority constrain accountability.	Mixed	Information-gathering processes have improved accountability, but opaque processes can hinder accountability.	Mixed
Representation of diverse interests	Limits to local authority can challenge representation, but actors with resources have opportunities in state venues.	Mixed	Access to authority and information at the state level by diverse interests was limited.	Low
Social learning	Efforts to resolve conflicts, gather information and share resources enhances learning.	Higher	Limited social learning evident during conflict resolution across actors.	Low
Adaptability	Contribution of resources by decision centres to institutional change.	High	Contribution of resources by decision centres to institutional change.	High
Network building	Resources and information facilitate network-building across actors.	High	Network-building among actors with similar types of authority, but more limited across levels and actor types.	Mixed

[a] Rated as high, low, or mixed from the available case evidence (e.g. reports, meeting minutes, plans, and published studies).

mechanisms. As noted by one interviewee: 'The Task Force process was not very effective. Only industry was satisfied.' The lack of satisfaction is further evidenced by efforts to get new proposals for expanding local authority on the 2016 state-wide ballot, which failed, and by ongoing complaints that the new rules are not addressing local concerns – or coherence of aligning local actions with system-wide needs. Fundamentally, this seems to stem from deep disagreements over the nature of local authority. According to one of the Colorado interviewees: 'We need more ability for locational decisions... We need someone to look at long term health issues and with the current regulations, this is not happening' (Anonymous Interview 2015). Still, while conflict remains, it is not necessarily widespread across all actors in the governance system. One interviewee in Colorado stated: 'Most communities have a good relationship with the state. The state has ceded some control to local government (as much as they can do without having a patchwork of regulations) and locals are working pretty well with the state' (Anonymous Interview, 2015). This may suggest that the incentives for some actors, at least, may be shifting to move towards dispute resolution, but information and authority constraints may still be limiting progress.

In contrast to Colorado, one could argue that the conflicts among units of decision-making in New York have been resolved, since the state used its authority to impose the 2014 state-wide ban. While those opposed to oil and gas development may perceive this to be efficacious, actors who were in favour of oil and gas development, including some of the local governments, could have a different perspective.

While efficacy differs, low levels of efficiency of conflict and conflict resolution appear in both cases. In Colorado, disputes about local control have appeared in multiple venues (e.g. ballot measures, the Task Force, city councils) and ultimately before the Colorado Supreme Court. In part, limited efficiency may stem from fundamental disagreements in Colorado about authority. At the same time, they may have to do with the challenges of acquiring information on the health and environmental effects of hydraulic fracturing, which was also the case in New York. Information-gathering ultimately took five years, which reduced the efficiency of the process for the state to come to a decision in New York. Also, in both states, when actors have resources for venue shopping across levels or decision centres in polycentric governance systems, conflicts are more likely to be regularly revisited, which may limit efficiency.

Coherence across both systems is mixed. In Colorado, the state passed new regulations, recommended through the Task Force, to improve coherence between local authority and state authority and to encourage more communication between local governments and industry. These improvements in coherence largely relate to how authority is structured (or restructured) within the polycentric systems. In New York, the state-wide ban was compatible with many of the local-level bans that had passed during the moratorium. However, a number of local governments remained supportive of hydraulic fracturing and shale development, suggesting inconsistencies in coherence.

With respect to the process measures of performance, we find mixed results across the two cases. First, accountability to diverse communities is difficult to assess. In both cases, constraints on local authority (e.g. after the state-wide ban in New York; and due to limits on local control in Colorado) can make it difficult for local jurisdictions to be accountable to their citizens. Yet, in both cases, information-gathering efforts also enhanced accountability. For instance, in Colorado, the Task Force aimed to improve accountability by tackling the concerns of local governments and making recommendations to the Governor on policy changes that would mitigate conflict. In New York, accountability was made possible through information-gathering in the public comment period of the Environmental Impact/Review and in the authority that was available to various local government venues prior to the ban.

The question of accountability is closely tied with representation. Although representation has been an issue for some forms of interactions within different venues in Colorado (e.g. more elite actors involved in regulatory interactions), the system overall has had more opportunities for a wider diversity of actors to have a represented voice in different conflict and conflict-resolution processes. Actors may also have had more resources to engage in Colorado and sustain more diverse forms of representation. Conversely, across state-level action situations in New York, some actors complained about not having adequate representation in decisions on the fracking ban and with the state-level process for public health and environmental review. These decision-making processes were effectively closed and the governor prevented the state agencies from communicating during the process. One interviewee stated: 'There is a complete absence of dialogue and this is a big problem' (Anonymous Interview 2014). In other words, both authority and information was limited.

Social learning is another area where there are differences in the performance between New York and Colorado. In Colorado, there is evidence of higher levels of social learning, especially where resources have been put into creating new venues to facilitate interactions across actors. An interviewee from western Colorado noted: 'We have an oil and gas forum that the COGCC, federal agencies, etc. attend once a quarter and a public comment period. The university has produced a water initiative about reusing water. The community hotline routes directly to the producer in the area. We have learned a few things along the way' (Anonymous Interview 2015). While the information-gathering efforts in New York to study the health and environmental impacts arguably led to some learning and agreement among select state-level actors, little evidence exists of learning across actors on different sides of the issues, based on the surveys and interviews conducted prior to the state-wide ban.

Arguably, conflict and conflict-resolution interactions also lead to adaptability of both of the polycentric governance systems, as new policies and new venues, and institutional processes have been created. Colorado passed over a dozen new regulations and passed multiple pieces of legislation, while also creating new venues for dialogue and interaction following the introduction of hydraulically fractured wells. These changes required, however, investment of resources by the decision units involved, alongside the private and non-governmental actors who had adequate representation or authority to participate and contribute to decision-making. Similarly, in New York, local governments passed various policy decisions related to fracking in New York and the state engaged in the health and environmental review process.

Adaptability of the governance system may be related to network building in both governance systems. In both states, this took the form of networking within like-minded groups of actors (e.g. national level non-profits, local community groups, and local governments opposed to fracking or industry and pro-fracking governments working together). However, network building across the competing coalitions involved in the conflict were lower in New York than in Colorado (Heikkila and Weible 2016). Arguably, network building requires some dedicated resources, alongside information-sharing.

6.8 Conclusion

Overall, despite similarities in the basic structure of their polycentric systems for oil and gas governance, there are differences in how conflicts over unconventional oil and gas governance have emerged and how they have been resolved across Colorado and New York. These differences can be explained in part by the authority, incentives, information and resources of the actors.

In both states, administrative agencies at the state-level have held a large portion of authority. However, differences in how they exercise that authority have emerged. In New York, local governments held the right to make local decisions on whether to allow hydraulic fracturing to go forward for several years, at least until 2014 when the state ultimately decided to ban permits on hydraulic fracturing. In Colorado, local governments have been restricted in their authority over whether hydraulic fracturing and shale development more generally occurs, but have some limited authority over how it happens, while different state agencies are largely responsible for permitting, regulating, monitoring and enforcement. In Colorado, some collaborative groups also have formed to inform decision-making (i.e. the Garfield County Advisory Body). Still, the distribution of authority, and the lack of clarity on authority at the local government level, has contributed to conflicts in Colorado. The prohibition of local jurisdictions from banning hydraulic fracturing gave incentives for conflicting sides to ramp-up their political activities, which may be an indicator of more conflict, but also potentially more adaptation and learning.

Information and resources also are essential in enabling both conflict and conflict resolution. In both states, information has been lacking on many of the impacts of shale development, yet resources have been invested in the search for information to inform conflict resolution and policy processes in both states. State actors in Colorado used information for state regulations on air quality, which were generally supported, but information was less readily available to inform policy choices over setbacks, where conflicts remained. Similarly, resources available to particular decision-making units make it more or less possible for actors to pursue their interests and to engage in conflictual strategies or behaviours. In New York, the state used information on health and environmental effects to ban fracking while anti-fracking groups diffused information about how to enact local bans.

In examining the ways in which authority, information, and resources shape conflict and conflict resolution, this chapter also explored questions of performance of the two polycentric governance system. How these factors matter for performance depend on one's performance criterion. For instance, access to resources that allow for venue shopping, for instance, may have helped to extend conflicts and reduce the efficiency of conflict-resolution processes in both states. At the same time, resources help facilitate networks and collaboration with other types of actors (e.g. NGOs, industry, mineral rights owners), which can make conflict resolution easier. Finally, although authority, information and resources are critical, we also cannot ignore the broader community and biophysical context that constrains and enables the nature of interactions among actors and the performance of these interactions. Therefore, we recommend continued exploration of the complex array of factors that condition conflict and conflict resolution in polycentric governance systems, and careful attention to appropriate criteria for assessing performance of these processes by which actors take each other into account.

Competition in Polycentric Governance Systems

Dustin E. Garrick and Sergio Villamayor-Tomás

7.1 Introduction

Competition is a distinctive feature of polycentric governance systems. Theories of polycentric governance acknowledge that competition among decision-making authorities to deliver public goods 'may produce desirable self-regulating tendencies similar in effect to the "invisible hand" of the market' (Ostrom, Tiebout, and Warren 1961). Competition, however, can also result in 'races to the bottom' and/or conflict (da Silveira and Richards 2013; Poteete, Ostrom, and Janssen 2010).

Different jurisdictions compete for citizens through the public goods and services they provide (Ostrom, Tiebout and Warren 1961). Resource users compete in the appropriation of common-pool resources. This competition may arise as a natural effect of resource scarcity, or by markets and market-like institutional arrangements. These two forms of competition – the production of public goods and the appropriation of common-pool resources – are governed, in turn, by an overarching set of rules and cooperative efforts to resolve conflicts between decision-making centres and between actors.

Water-resource allocation illustrates the nature and dynamics of competitive interactions in polycentric governance arrangements. Intensified competition for water is part of a global trend leading to increases in water scarcity, pollution and impacts of climate change on common-pool water resources, particularly in arid, semi-arid and rapidly urbanising regions. Such competition can aggravate upstream–downstream externalities and environmental degradation, leading to conflict. However, competition can also spur water-use efficiency (i.e. the economic productivity generated per unit of water consumed), and lead to cooperative efforts to enhance the social and ecological resilience of shared river basins and groundwater systems. These interactions often depend on the evolution and performance of polycentric governance arrangements.

Governance actors in freshwater basins have pursued institutional reforms to facilitate market-like reallocation as an adaptation, or response, to scarcity and climate-related shocks. These allocation institutions involve polycentric governance arrangements to establish diversion limits, tradable water rights and associated administrative and conflict management mechanisms to enable the reallocation of water-use rights and facilitate risk reduction (Copes 1986; Garrick 2015). Such approaches can address trade-offs across uses (Garrido 2007). The performance of market-like arrangements in polycentric systems varies depending on the authority of actors in the system, their resources, information and incentives.

In this chapter, we identify different types of competitive interactions in polycentric governance systems, examine factors that shape these interactions, and explore the implications for performance. We compare the governance of water-resource allocation and reallocation in the US portion of the Columbia river basin and the Ebro river basin (Spain). This analysis supports an overarching argument that competition is conditioned by collective choice processes, including the accompanying conflict resolution and cooperation.

7.2 Competition in Polycentric Systems

Polycentric governance theory challenged the prescriptions that competition between public agencies was inefficient or leads to poor performance according to other criteria. A polycentric system has been described as creating the conditions for 'emergent order to occur via a bottom-up competitive process', by establishing an overarching set of norms and rules (Aligica and Tarko 2012).

Competition can be considered in all action situations within polycentric governance systems. Three action situations are relevant to empirical analysis of competition: appropriation of common-pool resources (CPRs), provision of CPRs or public goods and production of public goods. Individuals compete for access and withdrawal of CPRs, such as water, fisheries and pasture. Traditional economic theory and policy analyses long predicted the destruction or exhaustion of CPRs, in recognition of such competition. As community-based natural resource management (CBNRM) scholars later began to question this hypothesis, attention turned to exploring the conditions under which groups of users can successfully channel such competition via the imposition of rules and adherence to norms.

Competition also occurs in the provision of CPRs and public goods when jurisdictions compete with one another for citizens. The origins of polycentricity – and public choice – more generally, can be traced back to this observation. Ostrom, Tiebout, and Warren (1961) note that 'competition can generate self-organizing tendencies in metropolitan areas as municipalities are forced to compete for residents through their mix of public goods and services on offer, and as producers of public goods and services compete for the business of municipalities'. This initial definition can be associated with the notion of citizens voting with their feet, as a means of spurring competitive pressures (Ostrom et al. 1961), as well as with the understanding of political elections as electoral markets.

Finally, competition in public goods delivery arises due to duplication and overlapping services. This notion was put forward by Schneider (1989), among others, in noting that polycentric competition. . . simulates a market for public goods. A similar take is reflected in Carlisle and Gruby (2017: pg 9.), who point out that 'municipalities may compete for residents through the provision of cleaner water or more green spaces. Additionally, NGOs may have to compete against one another for the right to lead or influence an environmental initiative undertaken by a political jurisdiction' (2017, 14).

All three forms of competition above are inextricably related to cooperation and conflict resolution (Carlisle and Gruby 2017). These interactions will be examined in two contrasting constitutional settings: the use of market-oriented, water-allocation institutions to allocate CPRs (Spain) and to restore environmental flows for salmon fisheries in the Northwest USA, providing a public good through market-based reallocation of water rights from irrigation to environmental purposes. These contrasting examples of market-based water allocation illustrate the types and dynamics of competition in polycentric systems and some implications for performance.

7.3 Methodology

Drawing on the institutional analysis and development framework, this chapter examines and compares two case studies of market-based water allocation in the Columbia River[1] (US portion) and the Ebro River of Spain. This analysis

---

[1] The Columbia River Basin is shared by 7 states in the US and one province in Canada.

focuses on the authority, information and resources that affect competitive interactions, contrasting the relatively decentralized arrangements in the USA with the relatively centralized arrangements in Spain. Our analysis of authority structures examines the roles and responsibilities of different actors in water allocation decisions, drawing on an institutional mapping of the different decision-making centres involved. The analysis of resources and information focus on the human, technical and institutional capacities and knowledge that actors use in competitive interaction, highlighting in particular the transaction costs, barriers and strategies employed by actors.

The data draw on multi-method, long-term research in the two study sites, involving review of archival data (documentary evidence related to laws and rules), semi-structured interviews with governance actors participating in market-based water reforms, and different techniques for examining institutional change and performance (including process tracing). Detailed descriptions of the data and analytical techniques are described in the relevant work led by the authors (including Garrick 2015; Garrick and Aylward 2012; Villamayor 2014).

The analysis spans multiple levels of action – operational, collective choice and constitutional – in contrasting settings. First, it examines the constitutional arrangements distributing authority over water allocation within and across levels and sectors in Spain and the USA. Second, it traces the diverse collective choice processes used to plan and finance market-based water reallocation, illustrating the interdependency and tension between competition, cooperation, and conflict resolution. Finally, it examines the operational-level rules governing competition. By contrasting two river basins with market-oriented water allocation, the analysis generates insights about the nature of competition and its implications for the performance of polycentric governance systems within and across different constitutional settings.

7.4 The Polycentricity Context in Spain-Ebro-Aragon

Much of the current water governance system in Spain finds its origins in the organization of water supply and allocation for irrigation development more than a century ago. By the end of the nineteenth century, industrial and urban uses were only nascent and, in a context of colonial dismantlement, irrigation was portrayed as the main economic engine of the country. In this vein, the Water Act of 1879 declared the public ownership of all surface waters and prescribed its management at the basin level, via autonomous basin authorities (RBOs). The main goal of the RBOs at that time was to set a water-use rights system and plan for big storage and conveyance infrastructure that could supply new irrigated land, and secondarily other uses. This new 'hydro-agricultural policy' found unconditional support in the farming sector. The hydropower lobby, in turn, provided the necessary economic resources to construct the reservoirs in exchange for electricity production concessions (Perez Picazo and Lemeunier 2000). The law prescribed a completely decentralized system for irrigation management. Farmers would be allocated collective use rights and would need to self-organize into water user associations (WUAs) to manage them.

The transition to democracy and regional and local decentralization process in the 1980s, the growth of the cities and industrial poles, the boom of tourism and emergence of new recreational water uses, concerns about environmental flows, and social contestation against new dam building in the 1980s and 1990s, all led to a dramatic increase in the diversity of interests and competition around water resources. This, along with European prescriptions about conservation of environmental flows resulted in the approval of new Water Laws in 1986 and 2001 and a number of subsequent reforms.

Currently, the basin authorities maintain their authority over the water-use right concessions, large infrastructure planning and conflict resolution. The regional governments, in turn, have exclusive powers over environmental policy, which includes water quality and protection, and agricultural policy (e.g. irrigated agriculture). Local governments have authority over drinking water, including infrastructure planning and financing, water allocation, the management of the sewage system and the treatment of waste water. In rural areas, the WUAs frequently include industrial users and small local governments, as they all share the same infrastructure and water sources (MIMA 2001).

The regional government, irrigation and industrial users and hydropower organizations all enjoy voting rights in the General Assembly, Executive Board, Reservoir Management Board, Water Council and sub-basin management committees of the basin authorities. Local governments sit in the Water Council. All venues are used to make decisions about water allocation and infrastructure maintenance and operations, and for general accountability purposes.

7.4.1 Competition in Spain: Dealing with Resource Allocation via Market Competition

A common trend involves competition for water between traditionally dominant irrigation water uses on the one hand, and the growing urban, recreational and touristic uses and, secondarily, environmental uses, on the other. As a way to channel competition over scarce resources, the regulatory framework has allowed water markets as an allocation mechanism since 1999. Water leases can occur both across user groups and within user groups, within and across basins.

Water leases have been limited since the approval of the reform (Palomo-Hierro, Gómez-Limón, and Riesgo 2015). At best (i.e. in 2007), leases have reached less than 1 per cent of all water used. Irrigation to urban transfers across basins have ranked first in volume of water transferred; irrigation to irrigation transfers within basins have been dominant in numbers of transactions. All have tended to concentrate during droughts (i.e. 2005–2008) and in the Southwest of Spain (Palomo-Hierro, Gómez-Limón, and Riesgo 2015).

Despite the constraints on formal water markets, there is a diversity of informal market experiences that do not entirely fit the conditions specified by law. Many of these leases have occurred between WUAs and urban users, and among WUAs, to cope with punctuated water-scarcity situations; they can involve both surface, ground and recycled water; and not always involve economic compensation (Hernández-Mora and De Stefano 2013). Significant among these are water transfers between farmers within and across WUAs. These are not monetarized, but they still respond to the logic of competition (Villamayor-Tomás 2014b). The case of the Riegos del Alto Aragon irrigation (RAA) project, in the Ebro river basin is a paradigmatic example of transfers across WUAs that do not involve a market per se, but do follow the logic of allocative efficiency. Although water deficits are not structural in the Ebro basin (not as severe as in the south-west), farmers have still been confronted with an increasing pressure over resources due to both the expansion of irrigation, the growth of cities, and the periodic recurrence of droughts (Villamayor-Tomás 2014a). This has coupled with a process of farm concentration and agricultural intensification due to rural depopulation and the globalization of markets (CESA 2012). The RAA project encompasses 50 WUAs, more than 120,000 hectares of irrigated land and close to 10,000 irrigators. The 'Comunidad General de Riegos del Alto Aragon' (CGRAA) is responsible for coordinating the delivery of a collective use right across the 50 WUAs. In a context of recurrent droughts, the GCRAA promoted the implementation of a transferable quota policy, according to which each WUA is allocated a share of the collective water-use right. The rights, in turn, can be transferred across WUAs.

A look at the constitutional, collective choice and operational rules operating in the country and the Ebro basin help to characterize and understand: (1) the shape taken by water leases in the country, and (2) the success of the RAA project in the Ebro valley.

7.4.2 Constitutional Level

Important constitutional provisions help to understand the allocation of authority for water use and water transfers. According to the water law, there is an important distinction between 'private' and 'collective' concessions. Private concessions are conditional on a specific use, be it industrial, hydropower, urban or irrigation, and most commonly granted to individual entities for a renewable period of seventy-five years. Collective concessions are those granted to irrigation systems that fulfil a public interest (i.e. most of current irrigation systems). Here, the concession is granted conditional on the collective request of the majority of farmers in the system and the organization of farmers into WUAs. All the concessions can be revised and cancelled without compensation if the water is not used in the specified purpose or quantity (MIMA 2001). The water law only allowed markets for 'private' concessions; however, the country wide drought of 2005 motivated a Royal Decree to temporally authorize markets for 'collective' rights too (BOE 2005).

The law grants basin authorities with the power to revise concessions; however, this has rarely been the case, even if it is known that water rights allocated (not necessarily used) to the irrigation sector exceed the amount of water available in a number of basins (Embid 2013; Palomo-Hierro, Gómez-Limón, and Riesgo 2015). The costs of monitoring actual use add to the fear of basin authorities of the contestation of users, mostly irrigators (Embid 2013). In some basins, like the Ebro river basin, and inner regions, like Aragon, such contestation would be particularly strong, given the historical perception among some political elites and the farming sector that irrigation has not developed as much as it should (Aranda-Martín 2009).

The rigidity of the water-use right system contrasts with the constitutional discourse promoting the need to transition from a water policy based on supply works to a policy based on demand measures (Garrido and Llamas 2009). This discourse materialized for the first time in the Water Law of 1985 and inspired the reform that would introduce water markets later on. The discourse translated into strong subsidy programmes for irrigation efficiency and infrastructure improvements, but only very timid efforts to rationalize the water-use concession system. Paradoxically enough, losing water-use rights if these are not used (i.e. due to efficiency improvements or just overestimation) is still possible in theory, and undermines the willingness of farmers to engage in markets (Hernandez Garcia 2014).

There are several requirements to participate in water markets in Spain that conflict with the attempt to make the water-rights system more flexible (Garrido 2007). Water-use rights holders can only lease their rights to other holders with equivalent or higher priority in the order of preference established by law. According to the law, domestic and urban uses have priority over all other uses (irrigation, hydropower, aquiculture, recreational uses, and others). Secondly, holders of non-consumptive water-use rights (i.e. hydrological uses) cannot sell their rights to holders of consumptive water-use rights (i.e. irrigation). The law also foresees the exceptional use of water banks (i.e. public purchase and reallocation of water rights) during severe water-scarcity periods by water authorities.

7.4.3 Collective Choice Level

The irrigation sector is the biggest water-use rights holder and one that could benefit the most from water leases both as a buyer and a seller (i.e. to urban users). Several collective choice aspects constrain such development. First, basin authorities are to approve river management plans every ten years, which can introduce modifications in the ranking of uses, thus affecting the viability of existing leases. Also, leases within basins need to be approved by the basin authority and those across basins by the Department of the Environment. Additionally, in the case of irrigation rights leases, operations have to be approved by the regional authority and the Department of Agriculture. The duration of the lease contracts is set by the buyer and the seller, and should fit the average volume used by the seller during the five years prior to signing the formal lease contract. There are, however, no mechanisms that provide water-use information publicly at the basin level by default. Indeed, information about potential water prices, volumes transferred or agents willing to participate in the market is for the most part lacking (Palomo-Hierro, Gómez-Limón, and Riesgo 2015).

More importantly, in the context of WUAs, the lease of water-use rights is subject to approval by the majority of farmers of the WUAs, as the rights are held collectively. WUAs are organized into General Assemblies and decisions usually made according to the one farmer, one vote rule vote. Heterogeneity of interests is likely to make decisions rather complex and controversial, particularly during periods of drought. Recent investments in irrigation efficiency should have liberated water rights and eased the process; however, the opposite has tended to occur,

as those investing in improvements within WUAs have, in turn, intensified production and expanded irrigation (Berbel et al. 2015; Lecina et al.
2010).

The basin authorities have authority to reallocate water-use rights
during exceptional scarcity conditions. As illustrated during the
2005–2008 drought, this is accomplished by reducing proportionally all
non-domestic/non-urban uses, making necessary the leasing of rights from
irrigation to urban users. In the Ebro basin, for example, negotiations took
place between WUAs and the river basin authority (RBO) officials at the
sub-basin level. Supply to the RAA project was finally reduced by 60 per
cent (Villamayor-Tomás 2014b).

The decision to implement a transferable quota policy by the WUAs in
the RAA project was relatively smooth, given all formal challenges highlighted above. A consensus about the protocol to follow during droughts had
been previously reached at the GCRAA level among representatives of all
WUAs. According to the agreement, the activation of the drought protocol
and thus the possibility of inter-WUA transfers is decided by the GCRAA
and WUAs before the beginning of the irrigation campaign. They use, for
this purpose, information provided by the RBO on water stored in the dams
that serve the system and snow pack. This meeting parallels meetings
between the GCRAA and RBO authorities to coordinate potential restrictions of rights. Also according to the agreement, each irrigation system is
allocated a quota on irrigated land and historical water consumption. This
rule satisfies both the interests of WUAs dominated by large landholdings
with very efficient irrigation technologies, and WUAs dominated by small
farms and traditional irrigation techniques. Each WUA is, in turn, responsible for allocating the quota among its membership. Some WUAs decided
to replicate the quota system; some others relied on other protocols. All
agreed, however, that farmers can transfer water from one system to another
if cultivating land in both. The quota of the WUAs involved in transfers
needs to be updated accordingly. Finally, the decision to apply, or not, the
transferable quotas is made before the seeding campaign so farmers can plan
accordingly (Villamayor-Tomás 2014b).

7.4.4 Operational Level

At the operational level, the effective implementation of lease contracts
requires conveyance infrastructure. If the infrastructure does not exist, it

has to be financed by the contract parties after the approval of the works by basin authorities. This makes water leases economically viable only to users who are already connected by a shared infrastructure (i.e. within basins and large irrigation projects like the RAA project), or among users willing to transfer large volumes of water (permanent leases are not formally possible). Also, regulations are unclear about who is responsible for monitoring the leases, which adds uncertainty to the process. Water banks make monitoring more amenable than spot markets; however, the use of public bids for the large-scale acquisition of water-use rights require significant public resources (Palomo-Hierro, Gómez-Limón, and Riesgo 2015).

In the RAA project, a number of operational rules ease the implementation of the transferable quotas. The GCRAA regularly collects data on water delivered to each WUA and has also regular access to updates on water availability by the RBO. This eases the collective decision by WUAs of whether to apply the drought protocol, and the calculation of the quotas. If the quotas are implemented, farmers who want to transfer their rights from one system to another need to notify the affected WUAs and the GCRAA at the beginning of the irrigation campaign. The transfers of rights hold for the entire campaign. Thus, water does not need to be first delivered to the systems and then transferred across the systems, but just distributed to the systems according to the updated quotas. Information and monitoring are crucial in the process to both update the quotas and keep track of their use. The GCRAA maintains a registry of the water delivered to WUAs and most WUAs, in turn, keep a registry of the water used by farmers (Villamayor-Tomás 2014b).

7.4.5 Concluding Remarks about Performance

The scarcity of formal water-market experiences at the national level in Spain, contrast with the rather successful experiences in the Ebro river basin and RAA project illustrated, shedding light on the importance of competition in polycentric systems. At the national level, the pervasive imbalance between water rights issued and actual use of water, particularly in the irrigation sector, constitutes a disincentive for farmers to sell water to other users or among themselves. Getting leases of irrigation rights first approved by WUAs and then by the water authorities is costly at best and uncertain at worst. Finally, there is a lack of mechanisms for users to reveal their preferences, as well as monitoring and publicizing the fulfilment of contracts.

The bulk of formal water leases has involved transfers for more than 1hm^3 per lease on average, and revealed a trend to transfer water from the inner basins to the Mediterranean basins. The willingness of users in the Mediterranean basins to sometimes pay quite expensive prices for water can be used to indicate that water allocative efficiency has taken place (Palomo-Hierro, Gómez-Limón, and Riesgo 2015); however, there is also evidence that, due to the lack of information and proper assessments, environmental externalities may have taken place (Hernández-Mora and Del Moral 2015). Water banks have been mostly used by the government to guarantee environmental flows and protect the environment, although also at considerable monetary cost (Palomo-Hierro, Gómez-Limón, and Riesgo 2015). Informal markets fulfil an important role at the more local level, to the extent that they are tailored to the specific needs of local users; however, informal markets also raise concerns about impact. The agreements are not monitored by public authorities and thus their potential impact on the environment or third parties are rather unknown. In general, the fact that leases have occurred mostly during droughts indicates that they are viewed as an ad hoc instrument to cope with the lack of water, rather than as a means to increase allocative efficiency.

The case of the transferable quota system and polycentric competition in the RAA project illustrates a middle-ground solution between the strict requirements of formal markets and the ad hoc nature of informal markets. Water transfers during the 2005–2008 drought in the project not only effectively allowed farmers to allocate water to the most productive plots, but also buffered water management in some WUAs from the risk of uncooperative behaviour due to the reduced water availability (Villa-mayor-Tomás 2014b). Here, the clear division of *authority* between RBO, GCRAA and WUAs, and *information* that fits the purpose helps to understand the success of the experience. Division of labour is indeed coherent within a long-standing governance system that provides GCRAA and WUAs with sufficient physical and human resources to manage cross-WUA and within-WUA reallocations, respectively. Information-sharing and meetings can be intense; however, the transferable quota system is only used during droughts, which increases its efficiency. Although the mechanism was the result of a collective agreement across all WUAs in the RAA project, reallocations themselves are not part of collective decisions, information about them is centralized at the WUAs and GCRAA, and available only on a request basis and just for transfers across WUAs. These features undermine the representativeness, social-learning, adaptability and network-building nature of polycentric competition.

The middle-ground solution in the Ebro river basin illustrates how polycentric governance systems address competition in the appropriation of water resources using market-oriented water allocation systems that blend formal and informal, local and cross-district institutions.

7.5 The Polycentricity Context in the US-Columbia Basin

Water allocation institutions in the USA have evolved from common law over the past 200 years (Tarlock 2001). In water-scarce regions of the Western USA, allocation institutions developed through a laissez faire system of 'prior appropriation' (first in time, first in right), which predated the establishment of states in many regions. As with Spain, these institutions developed as part of a vision for irrigation as a path to rural and regional development, underpinned by growing public investment after private irrigation systems failed. The distribution of authority for water allocation has evolved over time to establish a polycentric system of water governance with multiple, formally independent, but functionally interdependent, decision-making centres: state governments, water user associations, the federal government and tribal nations play important roles, while municipal governments and interest groups have a growing influence.

Authority over water allocation is vested in the state government, where agencies or courts administer permit systems and adjudicate water rights, respectively. The precise approach varies from state to state. Local and national jurisdictions are also involved in key aspects of water allocation. Local water users associations and utilities (irrigation districts and municipal water supply) have substantial authority for water allocation within their boundaries, while the national government provides funding and operates storage and distribution infrastructure with operational rules that affect water allocation. Indigenous nations have been recognized as sovereign entities, with independent authority to allocate water within their territory and granted high-priority water rights in relation to other water users, who arrived after the nations' establishment. Coordination institutions have developed to manage competition, facilitate cooperation and resolve conflicts within and between these decision-making centres and the water users with them. Unlike Spain, where river basin authorities are an extension of the national government, basin-wide coordination in the Western USA relies on different forms of interstate venues, often governed by an intergovernmental agreement known as a Compact and sanctioned by the Commerce Clause of the US Constitution. The resulting Compact Commissions and related institutions implement these agreements to apportion water between states sharing rivers.

The Columbia Basin is an international river basin shared by the USA and Canada (671,000 km^2). It is an iconic example of a 'polycentric' river basin governance system with seven states in the USA, one province in Canada, fifteen indigenous nations and a number of municipal water providers and irrigation districts (Cosens et al. 2018). A nested set of watershed or catchment organizations has emerged in response to coordination challenges among these different jurisdictions, sectors and interests. These organizations range from volunteer and state-organized watershed organizations to interstate or basin-wide organizations. Although an international treaty governs the sharing of flood control and hydropower benefits between the USA and Canada, there is neither an international, nor interstate agreement governing allocation of water between the states. Coordination of water allocation and planning between states is limited to indirect influences from governance regimes created to address other problems, principally related to hydropower and salmon conservation: the Northwest Power and Conservation Council and the Bonneville Power Administration, both of which have a role in energy policy.

7.5.1 Competition: Irrigation versus Environmental Water Uses in the Columbia Basin

The Columbia Basin has over 400 dams and contributed 44 per cent of the total hydroelectric generation in the USA in 2012. The Basin also supports 5.1 million acres of irrigated agriculture, concentrated along the semi-arid tributaries, where the peak irrigation water use coincides with the natural low flow in the hydrograph, reducing stream flows. The combined effect of hydropower and irrigation development has endangered migratory salmon fisheries. This hydropower system has led to the fragmentation of salmon habitat, restricting migration and reproduction, while irrigation has reduced instream habitat. The Endangered Species Act requires the Federal Columbia Basin Power System (FCBPS) to mitigate its impact on salmon fisheries. This mitigation requirement has created incentives for farmers to participate in a mitigation programme, established by the Bonneville Power Administration (BPA) to offset the impacts of hydropower development, by restoring stream flows in dewatered tributaries. BPA established a fish and wildlife programme and works with partner organizations to implement a range of restoration and conservation activities. As one component of these mitigation activities, market-based transactions have been used to reallocate water from irrigation to environmental purposes in dewatered tributaries needed for salmon reproduction (Garrick and Aylward 2012).

State governments administer and distribute water rights and have the primary authority to review river restoration projects that reallocate water rights from irrigation to environmental water uses. A polycentric governance arrangement facilitates water transactions, involving decision-making centres associated with each of the parties to the transaction: the sellers (irrigators and irrigation districts), the buyers (non-profit or state governments), the regulators (state governments), third parties (irrigation districts, municipalities, and other interest groups), and the financing sources (primarily, but not exclusively, the federal government). The Columbia Basin Water Transactions Programme (CBWTP) was established in 2002 as a public–private partnership of the BPA and the National Fish and Wildlife Foundation, a non-profit entity authorized by the US Congress. The CBWTP serves as an umbrella organization and coordinates financing and capacity building among eleven 'Qualified Local Entities' authorized to implement water transactions in priority sites. The QLEs include state government agencies (water resources departments) and different types of non-profit organizations (state-wide and place-based) implementing water transactions.

Water transactions address competition between irrigation and environmental water uses by reallocating water-use rights from irrigation to environmental flows (with the character of a public good). The parties to the transaction compete for water, but also cooperate. The premise of market-based river restoration is to enable the state and non-profit agencies to enter the market on behalf of the environment. State agencies and non-profit organizations receive funding from the CBWTP and other sources to acquire water rights for restoration purposes. As of 2016, the programme had 224 active transactions and had protected almost 1,000 cubic feet per second since 2003 (CBWTP 2017).

In most tributary regions, there is one implementing organization, limiting the duplication of service delivery and constraining competition among environmental water 'buyers'. However, state-wide (agencies and non-profit) entities and place-based (non-profit) organizations overlap in some circumstances. Limited *information* and asymmetries of information influence the types and effectiveness of different implementing organizations. Water rights are administered according to a priority system and require that water users 'use or lose' their rights, requiring information about the local history of water use to ensure the validity of water rights before acquisition.

In this context, competition involves three forms: competition between irrigation and environmental water users (CPR appropriation); competition between implementing organizations for financing (public goods provision); and competition between implementing organizations to deliver reallocation projects in specific geographies (public goods production). The patterns of competition are shaped by constitutional, collective choice and operational levels of action.

7.5.2 Constitutional Level

The distribution of *authority* between local, state and federal entities is governed by constitutional-level rules. The four main states in the US portion of the Columbia Basin – Idaho, Montana, Oregon and Washington – share the same system of water rights, but vary in their legal and regulatory approaches to instream (environmental) water rights and the agencies and actors authorized to play different roles in acquisition and administration (Loehman and Charney 2011).

Constitutional rules influence the roles and responsibilities of the public and private actors in the collective choice processes shaping market-oriented institutional reforms. The state government owns the water resources and administers water permits based on laws and policies enacted by the state legislature. Market-based water-rights reforms include efforts to recognize environmental and instream flows as legitimate water uses, enact trading rules to regulate leasing and acquisition and stipulate requirements for conflict resolution, monitoring and enforcement. These constitutional rules determine which state agencies and private entities can participate in collective choice processes involving planning, rule-making, financing decisions, negotiation of prices and conflict management.

The four states share a prior appropriation system of water rights but differ in their approach to these constitutional-level rules. The state of Montana has authorized private (and non-profit) entities to hold leases to water for instream flow purposes, while the other three states have restricted private entities to participation in collective choice processes associated with watershed and water allocation planning. There has been a steady call for allowing environmental non-profit groups to hold and administer the water rights reallocated for river restoration, which gives these groups standing in the collective choice processes and operational decisions related to water delivery. Despite these formal restrictions, non-profit groups have been included in collective choice processes related to rule-making and have influenced the administrative review process to streamline efforts, illustrating the scope for informal arrangements and coordination efforts between decision-making centres.

7.5.3 Collective Choice Level

Collective choice rules affect competition through planning efforts, rule-making and participatory decision-making regarding reallocation, particularly regarding the social and legal safeguards in place to address 'third party effects': the externalities associated with reallocation, principally associated with the changing patterns of 'return flows' as environmental water transactions affect the reliability of water rights downstream. Collective choice rules enable or constrain participation of water buyers, sellers and regulators in the design of market-based acquisition programmes and the implementation and approval of water transactions. A water transaction must pass through multiple layers of collective choice: financing decisions, administrative decisions by state governments and approvals by water users associations. Implementing organizations often contribute to rule-making (e.g. trading rules) and the development of wider institutional arrangements (such as water banking and water budgets) to facilitate and streamline their implementation efforts. The most successful experiences with market-based river restoration have involved implementing organizations that combine competitive roles (securing water from irrigated agriculture and striving to out-perform other agencies involved in water acquisition) with participation in collaborative processes and capacity building. For example, the Deschutes River Conservancy has implemented water reallocation projects and also invested in efforts to build or strengthen venues for collective choices, including water planning efforts, water banks and partnerships with irrigation districts.

Like the Spanish case, collective choice rules also determine how irrigation districts make decisions in relation to water markets and the implementation of market-based environmental water-acquisition projects. Many irrigation districts impose restrictions on water leaving their borders and require voting or board decisions to authorize the lease or transfer of water for environmental purposes. These restrictions, which guard against too much water leaving the district, have led to cooperative interactions and partnership agreements between implementing organizations and districts. These cooperatives pursue reallocation projects that confer environmental benefits, while maintaining irrigation productivity and ensuring cost-recovery to underwrite the costs of operations and maintenance of the infrastructure system (Kendy et al. 2018).

7.5.4 Operational Level

The operational rules and actions involve the search, negotiation and enforcement of water transactions. Transactions include temporary agreements (leases), permanent acquisition (purchases) and novel arrangements that involve reduced irrigation seasons, reallocation of water saved through water-use efficiency projects and agreements for multiple water users to maintain minimum instream flows by reducing water use proportionally.

Competitive markets involve many buyers and sellers with limited or no influence on price. The water transactions in the Columbia Basin are marked by few buyers and, often, a limited number of sellers. As a result, the search for willing sellers can require substantial resources to identify water-rights owners who can deliver the intended environmental benefits. The market power of both the buyers and sellers has required price discovery efforts, resolution of valuation disputes and efforts to address the social and economic costs of the reallocation incurred by the surrounding water users and community. As a result, competitive interactions between the relevant decision-making centres and actors are inextricably linked with cooperative interactions. Implementation of water transactions has been associated with increasing efforts to structure negotiations as a form of partnership-building, rather than purely independent responses to market and price signals.

7.5.5 Concluding Remarks about Performance

The performance of market-based river restoration can be assessed across multiple criteria – efficiency, accountability and representation of diverse interests, among others. These criteria cannot be maximized simultaneously (Garrick and O'Donnell 2016). In short, there are trade-offs, particularly between efficiency and other measures. For example, there are trade-offs between efforts to enhance efficiency and ensure representation of diverse interests, particularly over the short term. At the operational level, competitive interactions between conservation buyers and irrigation water sellers are embedded within cooperative efforts to forge partnerships and balance restoration objectives with rural community and economic development. Polycentric governance arrangements facilitate these diverse interests and multiple goals at the expense of efficiency. At the collective choice level, market transactions have relied on sustained efforts to adapt institutional arrangements to enable and regulate reallocation. The efficacy of market-based reallocation is therefore conditioned by the coherence, representation and adaptability of the polycentric governance arrangements in place. The Columbia Basin is noteworthy for demonstrating that local institutions and small-scale polycentric governance arrangements are potentially necessary, but, on their own, insufficient. Institutional linkages have proven important for coordinating decision-making centres involved in more operational-level action arenas with the state-wide and even national decision-making centres involved in collective choice processes.

7.6 Discussion and Conclusion

The Spanish and USA experiences with market-oriented water reallocation illustrate several key themes. First, there are multiple forms of competition. Competition for water involves multiple appropriators pursuing a scarce, common-pool resource. However, competition also involves delivery of the public goods underpinning the CPR. In Spain, irrigators compete with each other, and, increasingly, other sectors for water; at the same time, multiple water users associations have been created to maintain the CPR with different rules for managing competitive interactions. In the Western USA, competition between irrigation and environmental water uses illustrates the complex interplay of competition between appropriative water users (irrigators) with different entities operating on behalf of the environment.

Second, competition is inextricably linked with cooperation and conflict resolution at all levels – constitutional, collective choice and operational. Cooperation at the constitutional level entails efforts to coordinate the multiple, partially overlapping, but formally independent spheres of authority governing water allocation. This is particularly relevant in Spain and the Western USA, as the institutional arrangements governing water allocation were devised in a period of two dominant, and mostly complementary, water uses – irrigation and hydropower – but today face a diverse array of interests and associated governance arrangements and authorities.

Both countries have experimented with coordination institutions, such as basin authorities (Spain) and interstate compacts and more ad hoc efforts (USA). The evolution and form of these coordination institutions is shaped by the wider constitutional arrangements and overarching set of rules in the two countries, which vary in terms of their levels of centralization.

Cooperation and conflict resolution also govern the institutional reform process leading to the establishment of water markets and market-like arrangements for reallocation. Collective choice processes have guided the development of laws and policies, including the 1999 Spanish Water Law and the series of state-wide instream water-rights statutes across the four main states in the US portion of the Columbia Basin. These collective choice processes are not restricted to formal rules, or state-wide or national initiatives. Instead, they involve also local and informal arrangements, including water users associations or the integration of public–private partnerships that link water users associations with environmental organizations. In Spain, informal markets have relied on the internal governance and rules devised by water users associations. In the Western USA, water users associations have internal rules and decision-making procedures to review reallocation projects; increasingly, these irrigation organizations are part of local collective choice venues, such as watershed organizations or water banking arrangements that structure competitive interactions. Even at the operational level, these markets are thin and shaped by market power, which leads to cooperation and conflict resolution associated with bargaining and enforcement efforts. The capacity to reallocate water through market-like transactions, paradoxically hinges on the capacity and effectiveness of polycentric governance arrangements to foster representation of diverse interests, accountability, social learning and adaptability.

Finally, the performance of polycentric governance arrangements governing competitive interactions involves multiple criteria balancing efficiency with other objectives. These multiple criteria cannot be maximized simultaneously, which means that efficiency alone is insufficient for evaluating the performance of markets governed by polycentric governance arrangements. Table 7.1 contrasts the two cases relative to one another, according to a set of criteria identified at the beginning of this chapter. The comparison is insightful by illustrating how efficiency comes at the expense of accountability and representation, and vice versa. The balance between efficiency and other criteria is influenced by matters of institutional design (authority) and capacity (information and resources), which vary across the two settings. In Spain, authority is more clearly defined across different actors, and nested in hierarchical structures, with

Table 7.1 *Measuring performance of competitive interactions in the Ebro and Columbia Basins[a]*

Measure		Ebro Basin[a]		Columbia Basin[a]
	Links with Authority, Information and Resources.		Links with Authority, Information and Resources.	
Efficacy	Clear roles, but limited information and resources.	Higher	Fragmented roles and authority, compounded by high information burden and capacity constraints.	Lower
Efficiency	Informal markets facilitate efficient reallocation.	Higher	Public goods nature of environmental flows involves administrative frictions.	Lower
Coherence	Coherence across irrigation decision-making and districts.	Higher	Coherence varies based on coordination between federal, state and local initiatives.	Lower
Accountability	Limited accountability and attention to the public interest.	Lower	Institutional safeguards prioritize accountability.	Higher
Representation of diverse interests	Representation restricted primarily to irrigation communities.	Lower	Multi-stakeholder groups and partnerships facilitate representation.	Higher
Social learning	Social learning constrained by path dependencies	Lower	Emphasis on governance and monitoring enables learning in parts of the Basin.	Higher
Adaptability	Vested interests limit adaptability.	Lower	Experimental approaches to leasing allow adjustment.	Higher
Network building	Lack of stakeholder venues limits links.	Lower	Representation fosters networks.	Higher

[a] Rated as high, low, or mixed from the available case evidence (e.g. reports, meeting minutes, plans, and published studies).

rules devised to cope with limited information (climate variability) and resources (informal arrangements). The informal markets of the Ebro river basin are effective in facilitating improvements in irrigation performance during droughts and highly efficient in reallocating water with a coherent and coordinated multi-layered system of decisions by irrigators, water users associations and central entities; this comes at the expense of accountability, representation and social learning due to the exclusion of broader public interests in the design and performance of the markets. By contrast, the USA is marked by fragmented authority and a substantial information and resource burden in allocation decisions. The Columbia Basin has experienced more limited progress in delivering water for environmental restoration outcomes using market-based reallocation. The balance of private irrigation interests and public environmental benefits has meant that markets are thin and subject to substantial regulation to protect third parties; the institutional fragmentation of allocation authority inhibits the levels of coherence observed in the relatively centralized Spanish system. In other words, the higher degrees of polycentricity in allocation decision-making in the USA reduces the efficiency of market-based programmes. The relative inefficiency of market-based reallocation in the USA stems, in part, from the added institutional safeguards and participatory decision-making processes occurring at local and basin-wide levels to enhance accountability, representation of diverse interests and the social learning needed for long-range progress.

This comparative analysis illustrates how competition takes many forms, governed by polycentric arrangements across multiple levels of action. It also illustrates how polycentric governance arrangements vary in terms of authority, information, incentives and resources to shape the patterns of competitive interactions and the role of cooperation and conflict resolution in facilitating the development of market-like resource-allocation institutions. The contrasting experience in Spain and the Western USA show how the efficiency must be balanced with a broader range of performance criteria to understand and evaluate the evolution and performance of polycentric governance arrangements.

The next chapter will build on Chapters 5–7 and draw overarching comparative conclusions in regard to the performance of these different types of interactions.

8

Assessing Performance of Polycentric Governance System Interactions

Tomas M. Koontz, Tanya Heikkila, Dustin E. Garrick, and Sergio Villamayor-Tomás

8.1 The Roles of Authority, Information, Resources for Incentivizing Interaction Types

By comparing across the three types of interactions described in our cases (cooperation, conflict and conflict resolution, competition), we can examine how authority, information, and resources create different incentives by type of interaction. Recall that cooperative interactions are those where multiple centres choose to work together to advance shared goals. To do so, they communicate, coordinate, and/or share resources with each other. In conflictual interactions actors disagree about how to provide a good or service, or over the rules, policies or institutions for addressing a governance issue. Conflict resolution involves an agreement or decision where actors no longer engage in conflictual behaviours, or where they are willing to compromise on an issue. Competitive interactions feature a market logic where decision units are pressured to respond to client demands for goods or services.

In the case study on cooperation, we found that key decision centres (the Puget Sound Partnership [PSP] and Local Integrating Organizations [LIOs]) within the focal action situation (restoring the Puget Sound) lack authority to coerce. Authority outside the focal action situation related to compelling actors to provide clean water and species protection does exist in adjacent action situations, and the actors overlap with actors in the focal action situation. Moreover, such authority in adjacent action situations provides incentives for actors within the focal action situation to come together, seeking to cooperate rather than face coercive authority (e.g. to avoid listing of salmon under the Endangered Species Act).

In the Puget Sound case, we found that information flows horizontally among members of independent centres (LIOs), as well as vertically from the independent centre incentivizing actors (the Puget Sound Partnership) to the other independent centres (LIOs).

Resources are a key element for the success of cooperative interactions in the Puget Sound case. Resources are shared at every level to motivate action in line with the resource provider's priorities, from the PSP establishing LIOs in accordance with the PSP goals and then incentivizing LIOs to plan in alignment with the PSP priorities, to LIOs incentivizing local actors to carry out plan recommendations. In the PSP, funds flowed from government agencies to the PSP to LIOs to local actors carrying out actions.

The importance of resources to incentivize action depends, in part, on how actors view their odds in adjacent action situations. Many actors in the Puget Sound case believed cooperation via the PSP would yield greater resources than other ways of interacting, although after several years some of the local groups were questioning this belief.

Our examination of cases of conflict and conflict resolution highlighted that the source of conflict in a polycentric system often stems from both distributed authority and a lack of clarity, or agreement, on who has authority on specific issues. For instance, in the case of oil and gas conflicts, many disputes have centred around questions of whether actors at lower levels of government can extend their authority on certain issues to a state-wide scale. In the context of the oil and gas system, certain actors also have high incentives to engage in conflict due to the economic value of the industry, as well as the potential impacts associated with the industry. In other words, the distribution of potential benefits and costs of the good being managed may be important in understanding the different incentives leading to conflict and conflict resolution.

Approaches to mitigate, or resolve disputes over authority, in the oil and gas example were facilitated by the creation of action situations that encouraged conflict resolution. For example, in Colorado, actors created a Task Force of diverse stakeholders to identify policy options that would give local governments more voice in siting decisions. The Task Force process resulted in the state regulatory commission adopting new rules that expanded local government advice and consent for drilling proposed in urban areas. In other words, actors in Colorado distributed authority among a wider range of interests as a means to resolve conflicts. In the process, information from the different interests could be exchanged more openly. However, it was difficult to sustain information-sharing during the conflict-resolution processes. This may have been due the fact that the underlying issues driving the conflict persisted, despite conflict-resolution efforts. Conversely, in New York, information was seen as key to bringing the conflict to resolution. That is, state actors spent years doing environmental and health impact assessments, which led to the decision to ban fracking.

Our analysis of the cases of competition in polycentric systems in Spain and the USA illustrate how information and resources affect the patterns of competition and outcomes in two settings with different levels of centralization and distinct approaches for distributing authority among independent centres: water allocation among irrigation districts in the Ebro river basin (Spain) and water reallocation from irrigation to environmental purposes in the Columbia Basin (USA). In both cases, the distribution of authority in water allocation decisions creates a dynamic tension and issues of potential conflict between decentralized self-governance by irrigators and local water users, on the one hand, and institutions to address sectoral competition and the redistribution of water across jurisdictions, on the other.

In the Spanish irrigation project case, a nested governance structure addresses competition for water among irrigators during drought at two levels – within districts (self-governed Water User Associations, i.e. WUAs) and between them (via a project-level second-order organization). Information and resource asymmetries justify the devolution of authority from the river basin organization (RBO) to the second-order organization to generate and disseminate information about water use and demand, and provide mechanisms to reallocate water on a competitive basis, as well as resolve conflicts between farmers and districts.

In the US portion of the Columbia Basin, market-based river restoration involves two interrelated forms of competition: (1) competition among appropriators (water users) and between sectors (irrigation and environmental uses) and (2) competition for resources (funding) by the organizations implementing water acquisition projects to reallocate water from irrigation to environmental purposes. Implementing organizations therefore compete with independent decision-making centres (irrigation districts) for water and with each other for external resources. Both cases illustrate the potential for market mechanisms to address resource competition within local districts.

Across the three case studies in Part II, the elements of authority, information, and resources create different incentives for the three types of interactions (see Table 8.1). For example, in the cooperation case the lack of authority to command compliance led to other elements, such as funding resources, coming to the fore, while in the conflict case the lack of clarity on who has authority slowed conflict resolution. Information

Table 8.1 *Effects of authority, information, and resources across the cases*

	Cooperation in Puget Sound	Conflict and conflict resolution in NY and CO fracking	Competition in the Ebro and Columbia river basins
Authority	Lack of coercive authority led PSP to use information and resources to guide LIO behaviour. Coercive authority in other action arenas, especially endangered species, encouraged some actors to seek cooperation.	Distributed authority and a lack of clarity on who has authority on specific issues challenges timely conflict resolution.	Ebro: Management autonomy of WUAs allows them to reallocate water within the district on a competitive basis. Columbia: Authority over water allocation formally vested in state governments. Irrigation districts control allocation decisions within their boundaries.
Information	Flowed vertically from PSP to LIOs and also horizontally among LIOs. Information was critical in shaping cooperative actions.	Created venues that allow for more open exchange of information can mitigate conflict, but the influence of information on conflict was slow and conditioned by other factors.	Ebro: second-order organization mediated information-sharing between WUAs and RBO, thus facilitating the organization of water reallocations within the project. Columbia: information asymmetries plagued efforts to reallocate water from agricultural to environmental purposes.
Resources	Flowed vertically from PSP to LIOs, and then LIOs further distributed some funds. Resources were a key element in shaping cooperative actions.	Neutral centres of decision-making provided resources for convening conflict resolution dialogue or producing information; but resources were also used strategically to further conflict.	Ebro: WUAs funded the maintenance of canals that connect the districts, guaranteeing physical feasibility of water reallocations. Columbia: Federal and state funding for environmental water acquisitions were channelled to 'qualified local entities' with responsibility for implementation.

flow varied across the cases: in the cooperation case it flowed vertically and horizontally; in the Colorado fracking case it flowed from many directions in the venues created for open exchanges; in the Spanish competition case it flowed through a key second-order organization.

Recall as well that within each case, authority, information, and resources interacted with each other. For example, Chapter 5 [cooperation], described how lack of authority within the focal action arena led the Puget Sound Partnership to turn to information and funding resources, which together provided incentives for actors at the local level to create ecosystem recovery plans that fit with regional priorities. As described in Chapter 6 [conflict], new forms of authority to address conflict were created, which also ensured resources were available to facilitate information-gathering in the conflict-resolution processes. At the same time, resources were used to further conflict by enabling key actors to engage in conflict strategies. As described in Chapter 7 [competition], a clear understanding of the division of labour and thus authority at different levels of decision-making (from the basin down to the local levels) facilitated the dissemination of information and articulation of resources to effectively reallocate water rights.

8.2 Performance Criteria across Types of Interactions

Scholars of polycentricity, and governance more generally, have identified a wide range of performance criteria (McGinnis 2011). These can be grouped by outcome and process measures. The primary outcome measure is based on a fundamental question: what results did the system produce? A related outcome measure is whether the results were achieved with efficient use of resources. For some interaction types, we can also ask whether results were coherent across system levels. Several process measures of performance focus on how decisions were made and actions were taken. Was the decision-making process accountable and representative to those affected? Did the process generate opportunities for learning, adapting, and growing networks for future interactions?

To analyse performance in polycentric governance systems, we recommend attention to the basic building block: interactions. The previous chapters of Part II described how interactions can be grouped into three general types: cooperation, conflict and conflict resolution, and competition. In fact Ostrom, Tiebout, and Warren (1961, 838) argued 'The performance of a polycentric political system can only be understood and evaluated by reference to the patterns of cooperation, competition, and conflict that may exist among its various units.' Appropriate performance measures may differ depending on the type of interaction, as we illustrate in our case studies. It is important to note that not all performance criteria are relevant for every situation. Moreover, when analysts desire multiple criteria, the relative importance of one criterion compared to another is not self-evident. This is especially true when trade-offs exist among different criteria which cannot simultaneously be maximized.

8.2.1   Outcome Performance Measures

One set of performance measures relates to outcomes. These include efficacy, efficiency, and coherence.

8.2.1.1   Efficacy

Efficacy suggests achievement of, or movement towards, a desired goal. Measuring this in complex social-ecological systems is challenging. It requires baseline data, the ability to control for confounding factors, and long horizons for social and ecological processes that unfold over time (Koontz and Thomas 2006). Aside from these data challenges, what constitutes a 'desired goal' depends on one's perspective. For some, it may mean sustainability of a system to provide long-term societal and environmental benefits. For others, it may mean achieving individual gains. Polycentricity scholars have suggested additional goals, such as maintenance of self-governance habits that allow citizens to avoid tyranny (Marshall 2015; Ostrom, Tiebout, and Warren 1961) and matching citizens' preferences with goods and services provided (Oakerson 1999).

Efficacy in cooperation can be measured in terms of movement towards goals shared by participants. Were the participants able to find common ground and make progress towards achieving it? While participants retain their individual preferences over goals, efficacy means the action or decision makes progress on the subset of preferences that overlaps with other participants. For example, LIOs in Puget Sound ecosystem recovery created ecosystem recovery plans that identified priority areas for action that the participants agreed upon, suggesting that the plan as an output achieved some degree of efficacy. But it is too early to tell whether the plans are efficacious in achieving as outcomes these agreed-upon priorities in practice.

In the case of conflict, the measure of efficacy will point in different directions, as two or more stakeholders have conflicting goals. For example, disputes over the appropriate level of government to decide limits to oil and gas development led to different results in New York and Colorado. In New York, the state's ability to ban fracking was praised by environmentalists but disliked by the oil and gas industry. In Colorado, several state-level policy decisions on how to mitigate risks of fracking were agreed upon and forums were created to allow disputing actors to discuss their different positions. However, on one of the hotly disputed issues, that of the local authority to ban fracking, the state Supreme Court ruled against local governments. This decision was satisfactory to the industry but many citizen and environmental groups disliked this decision. By definition, conflict resolution means that disputing parties come to some agreement, or that an accepted conflict-resolution venue makes a decision on the issue. While the outcome may not match either party's preferred position, it could still be efficacious if the outcome or dispute resolution process is accepted by the parties. It also may be more favourable than the status quo (dispute). However, in a polycentric system, actors with resources and sufficient authority (or standing) may be incentivized by one decision to move the dispute to another venue if the actors are dissatisfied with the outcome. That appears to be the case in Colorado, at least, with the issue of local authority.

Efficacy in competition can be measured as the provision of valued goods or services in the right quantity, quality and timing, i.e. as demanded by users of the good (economists refer to this concept as allocative efficiency). For example, in the case of the Ebro River, competition among irrigation districts served to reallocate water to users who would need it the most and/or make the most valuable use of it in a context of severe scarcity. What 'most valuable' use means has been hotly debated by farmers regarding the decision of whether to allocate water on a per hectare or per volume basis. WUAs where farmers cannot afford high-irrigation-efficiency technologies ('traditional') favour the former, while 'modernized' WUAs favour the latter. In the Columbia Basin, competition between agricultural and environmental needs spurred reallocation through market-based water transactions, and this reallocation is assumed to have moved the resource to higher-valued uses, at least in terms of paying users.

Ecological economists argue that the demands of paying users are not the only appropriate consideration for efficacy. Rather, non-priced goods such as environmental quality and other ecosystem services should be considered (Garrick et al. 2009; Postel and Carpenter 1997; Pahl-Wostl et al. 2013). In the Columbia Basin, water acquisition programmes have established flow targets to determine the quantities and timing of water needed for environmental flows. In this case, evaluators judged that the water allocation and timing in the Columbia Basin provided insufficient resources to restore environmental quality. Measuring efficacy in terms of environmental quality is challenging because restoration outcomes are influenced by multiple factors, which means efficacy must account for the complex causal chains linking competition with system-level outcomes. As with conflict and conflict resolution, competition limits consensus on the goods and services being delivered. What one actor views as the right quantity, quality, or timing might be disputed by another actor. For example, a river restoration project may be perceived as effective for environmental flows, yet ineffective from the perspective of rural livelihoods and sustainable agriculture. Thus, efficacy is a difficult performance criterion to apply to competition.

8.2.1.2 Efficiency

In simple terms efficiency, or cost-effectiveness, refers to the minimum amount of resources needed to achieve a given result. Efficiency has long been a performance criterion for the provision of goods and services. In the private sector, free market exchanges can increase efficiency if certain conditions are met. In the public sector, polycentric governance systems can bolster efficiency when citizens compare results across different centres and demand efficient use of their tax dollars (Ostrom, Tiebout, and Warren 1961). Polycentric systems also allow centres to enter into agreements with each other to provide goods and services at the most efficient scale (Ostrom et al. 1993). Efficiency is reduced to the extent that actors incur the transaction costs of searching, negotiating, and enforcing agreements.

Cooperation in a polycentric system is characterized by the potential for high transaction costs, reducing efficiency. Compared to a centrally controlled governance structure, cooperation can occur both horizontally and vertically, which gives actors greater possibilities. This can increase search costs and take time to unfold, as actors navigate myriad sources of authority, information, and resources. It can duplicate collaborative interactions, when multiple forums are present to provide the same function in the same location. For example, in the Puget Sound ecosystem recovery case, one of the LIOs includes representatives from several organizations that are themselves collaborative forums. Cooperation can reduce efficient use of resources and may lead to a zero-sum game of taking resources away from other collaborative forums, as it has done to some extent in Puget Sound recovery efforts (Scott and Thomas 2015).

Conflictual interactions are likely to be inefficient, to the degree that participants expend resources in seeking to prevail. For example, in both the New York and Colorado fracking cases, disputes lasted for several years; moved across multiple decision-making units, including the highest courts in each state; and involved dozens of local government actors, private sector actors, and several state agencies. Of course, given the intense nature of the fracking debate, it is questionable as to whether the inefficiencies observed are generalizable to other types of disputes that may arise in a polycentric system.

Competition is a key means by which centres in a polycentric governance system are pressured to provide public goods and services efficiently (economists refer to this concept as productive efficiency). In the case of the Columbia River, competition between environmental water buyers for funding resources spurred more rigorous due diligence to ensure that reallocation projects delivered maximum value for money; however, it also raised the search costs and reporting requirements, creating uncertain consequences for efficiency. In the Ebro River case, the introduction of competition partially led to the concentration of water in the WUAs, where irrigation technologies are more efficient, and in farms where soil conditions, size and business models make the water most productive. The possibility to reallocate water across districts has also made water accounting within the project more complex; however, the added costs are relatively minor, given that the accounting system was already in place.

8.2.1.3 Coherence across Levels of the System

In a system of multiple centres, the decisions and actions of some centres may export harm to others, or achieve ends that are detrimental to the system as a whole. The potential for scale mismatches between decision makers and affected actors was described by Ostrom, Tiebout, and Warren (1961) as a rationale for public organizations to reconstitute themselves or interact with other decision centres. Thus, performance measures should include whether the interactions lead to coherence across system levels and decision units.

A foundational premise of cooperation is that centres working together can achieve results that extend beyond the boundaries of an individual centre, to a higher level of the system. This logic has been described by Ostrom (1990) and other polycentricity scholars as 'nestedness'. With nestedness, centres at lower levels of a system come together to undertake actions at higher levels, such as coordinating work and designing institutions. In the case of cooperation for Puget Sound ecosystem recovery, the PSP cooperates with LIOs in an attempt to bridge the overall Puget Sound restoration efforts with local priorities for actions on a smaller spatial scale. Such bridging is not always successful, and different goals between the PSP and localities make an imperfect alignment. But cooperation as structured by the PSP does bring in information that is incorporated into plans to help align local actions with system-wide needs.

In the fracking cases, conflict and conflict-resolution interactions have occurred at multiple levels within the polycentric systems. In the case of New York, many local jurisdictions banned fracking, although some passed resolutions in support. When the state-level actors ultimately banned fracking, there was coherence with those lower-level jurisdictions that imposed bans, but not with those in support. In Colorado, the Task Force recommendations led the state regulatory commission to pass new rules that expanded some of the local government authority for consultation in oil-and-gas permitting decisions, which arguably mitigates the likelihood that state-level decisions may potentially harm local governments. At the same time, state court decisions clarified how the limits to local decisions (i.e. bans) that state government argued could harm their interests. Despite these examples, some of the actors in the system still express concerns about coherence. Perhaps to some degree in a polycentric system, it is unreasonable to expect perfect coherence across a system. Moreover, some incoherence or diversity may be beneficial to the functioning of the system. Yet, if authority of some centres is impinged upon, then such lack of coherence may be detrimental. It can also mean that conflicts fester, especially if authority is constrained.

In competitive interactions, competition can be enabled and regulated at multiple levels nested within cooperative and other coordination structures. This creates cross-level interactions in two ways. First, competition at lower levels depends intrinsically on an overarching set of rules and the availability of conflict-resolution mechanisms when dispute arise. For example, water planning, regulations and trading rules have all predated efforts to use market-based water transactions to address competition between agricultural and environmental water needs. Second, competition at lower levels may lead to incoherence at higher levels due to externalities. For example, in both the Ebro River and Columbia River cases, local jurisdictions established robust market mechanisms for reallocation within their boundaries, maximizing water productivity. These local approaches created spillover effects in the form of land abandonment and polarization of socio-economic profiles of farmers within and across districts (Ebro), and across geographic zones (Columbia) when accounting for the 'third party effects' of water reallocation. This concern about externalities has led to rigorous monitoring and reporting processes in the case of the Columbia Basin (McCoy and Holmes 2018).

Outcome performance measures across interaction types are summarized in Table 8.2.

8.2.2 Process Performance Measures

In addition to outcome performance measures, we can also consider process performance. These measures include accountability, representation, social learning, adaptability, and network building.

8.2.2.1 Accountability

Accountability is the ability of those affected to hold a decision centre to account for its actions (Acar et al. 2012). Whenever a centre makes a decision or takes action on behalf of others (e.g. citizens of a jurisdiction), accountability comes into play.

Although cooperation can be effective in encouraging action, it requires the government to give up control. Unlike in a hierarchical structure, where higher-level authorities can demand compliance, a polycentric system involves different amounts of action across the landscape. This is a benefit in terms of allowing localities to tailor actions to their local circumstances, and a drawback in that it can raise questions of accountability for failure to achieve system-wide goals. Cooperative efforts for Puget Sound ecosystem restoration involve fiduciary accountability when resources, such as funds, are shared from the Puget Sound Partnership to the Local Implementing Organizations, but the attainment of system-wide goals lacks clear accountability mechanisms because authority is so diffuse.

Resolving conflicts can be done with more or less accountability. For example, in New York and Colorado, certain constraints on local authority can make it difficult for local jurisdictions to be accountable to their citizens. However, some conflict-resolution efforts in both instances (i.e. through the Governor's Task Force in Colorado, or through the public comment period of the Environmental Impact/Review process in New York, and in various local government venues in New York prior to the state-wide ban), demonstrated how accountability to diverse constituencies can be encouraged.

Table 8.2 *Outcome performance measures across interaction types*

Performance measure	Cooperation	Conflict and conflict resolution	Competition
Efficacy	Centres achieved some movement towards shared goals.	Decisions were made on some disputed issues (i.e. local authority question in CO and ban in NY) but disagreements persist. Perceived efficacy of decisions depends on actors' goals/interests.	A valued good/service (water) was provided and allocated in qualities/quantity/timing that satisfies demand to some degree. However, perceived efficacy depends on actors' goals/interests, and it is difficult to determine for non-priced goods and services such as environmental quality.
Efficiency	High transaction costs and duplication of functions reduced efficiency.	High transaction costs of dispute resolution across scales and venues reduced efficiency.	Competition for funding spurred delivery of maximum value for the costs.
Coherence across system levels/ decision centres	Cooperation led to local level plans that fit with broader system aims	Variable coherence in NY, as state-wide fracking ban matched local bans enacted in some places but not others. Coherence in CO improved through new rule adoption	Competition between implementing organizations in specific geographies limited coherence

In competitive interactions, accountability requires that competition operates within the boundaries established by rules and norms governing markets and provision of public services, based on the public interest. In the context of public service provision, accountability entails mechanisms to foster competition in public-service industries to give citizens options. In the context of resource appropriation (common-pool resources), accountability involves steps to redress information asymmetries. In the Ebro case, water reallocations across the WUAs rely on an integrated system of water accounting, which restrains the immediateness of transfers, but also prevents water speculation. In the case of the Ebro and Columbia River basins, accountability involves adherence to the 'no harm' principle for identifying and responding to negative third-party effects of water reallocation.

8.2.2.2 Representation

Representation refers to the degree to which those making decisions can be said to 'speak for' affected parties who are not participating in the decision-making. As the number of individuals affected by a particular issue increases, at some point it becomes untenable to directly engage all affected interests in decision-making. Instead, it is expected that their interests will be represented by others. The assurance of representation, along with accountability, helps to ensure a process is viewed as fair and legitimate.

An important consideration for measuring the representation in cooperation is the diversity of interests represented at the collaborative table. Most collaboration scholars have found that including diverse stakeholders in a cooperative effort can bring more complete information for consideration, encourage stakeholders to support agreements, increase social learning, and build social capital that may be used for tackling other societal problems. Ethically, those affected by a process should have the right to be represented in that process. At the same time, inclusion of more diverse interests can reduce process efficiency, lead to 'lowest common denominator' recommendations that are agreeable to all but not dramatic enough to be effective, and delay action in the face of urgent problems. In the Puget Sound recovery efforts, the PSP worked with LIOs to create diverse representation. Most LIOs had at least a dozen members representing a wide range of organizations, such as county elected officials, tribes, environmental non-profit organizations, county public health departments, county natural resource departments, conservation districts, marine resources committees, salmon recovery Lead Entities, university researchers, Water Resource Inventory Areas, and municipal officials. This diverse representation was fostered by the PSP's power to provide resources to LIOs contingent on the inclusion of diverse representation. Thus, decisions about who is to be included in decision-making, a constitutional-level action, are important.

In conflict and conflict resolution, not everyone with a stake is represented in interactions; however, diverse opportunities exist for actors to be represented depending on the conflict-resolution venue or forum. In New York, there were complaints against the state when actors did not feel represented in the decision-making process that ultimately resulted in the administration banning fracking. Such complaints even came from actors who agreed with the final outcome, because they were dissatisfied with their voice in the process of reaching that decision. Representation has been an issue for some forms of interactions within different venues in Colorado (e.g. more elite actors involved in regulatory interactions), but overall the openness of the system has brought opportunities for many diverse actors to have a represented voice in the process of debating and addressing the issue.

In competitive interactions, mutually beneficial exchanges are agreed upon by parties to a transaction. When these exchanges have spillover effects, affected third parties are not represented in those decisions. In the Ebro Basin, spillover effects across WUAs were partly addressed by restraining water reallocations to farmers with land in more than one WUA. Also, decisions of whether allowing water reallocations at a given year, or implementing any reforms to the mechanism, are collectively taken by all farmers in the project, regardless of whether they will feature any reallocation or not. Decisions about potential reforms to the mechanism are made only during periods of normal water availability to favour consensus. In the Columbia Basin, spillover effects were regulated carefully by state water laws and agencies; they were also addressed proactively and conservatively by implementing organizations working closely with affected agricultural communities to identify and offset the impacts of water reallocation.

8.2.2.3 Social learning

Through the process of interacting, participants can gain information and insights that increase their knowledge of the system. Such social learning allows for mutual adjustment and adaptation.

Previous collaborative watershed management studies have highlighted the importance of social learning (Ison et al. 2013; Koontz 2014; Muro and Jeffrey 2012; Pahl-Wostl and Hare 2004). Cooperation by its very nature features interactions among different stakeholders, and when these stakeholders work together to develop plans and take actions they are expected to learn about ecological, social, political, and process realities (Koontz 2014). Cooperative interactions can be structured so as to provide more or less social learning, depending on who participates and how exchanges are structured. In Puget Sound ecosystem recovery cooperative efforts, performance data have not been collected regarding what participants learned.

Social learning is also an important performance measure in conflict and conflict-resolution interactions. This is because conflictual interactions can bring divergent perspectives on issues into public venues or into forums for decision-making. Learning is possible where people have adequate levels of trust in information being shared in these forums. In the case of fracking, this has occurred on some issues. In Colorado, on the issue of chemical disclosure of fracking fluids or on reducing air pollution from drilling operations, actors worked through rule-making processes to come to some agreement on the nature of the problems and feasible solutions. In New York, efforts to study the health and environmental impacts arguably led to some learning and agreement among select state-level actors. However, when trust among actors is low or questions arise over basic questions of authority, social learning can be impeded.

Competition may structure social learning as centres seek to address appropriation and provision challenges. In the Ebro case, droughts and the exploration of ways to adapt (including water reallocations) triggered debates about distributional effects across WUAs. The centralization of said debates in the second-order organization allowed the formation of a common understanding about the existence of 'modernized' and 'traditional' WUAs, and the need to accommodate the stakes of both types. In the Columbia Basin, monitoring protocols and reporting requirements ensured information was gathered, and social learning has varied across the Basin. Social learning has required effective linkages between monitoring and decision-making by multi-stakeholder groups and place-based initiatives engaged in the acquisition of water for the environment.

8.2.2.4 Adaptability

Adaptability refers to the ability of a system to adjust to change in a manner that continues to provide desired functions (Engle and Lemos

2010). If interactions fail to adjust over time in a dynamic system, their utility decreases.

Cooperative interactions can boost adaptability to the extent that centres are connected to multiple sources of funding and information. The loss of one centre or connection does not mean a loss of function if a centre can turn to cooperation with other entities. For example, in the Puget Sound ecosystem recovery effort, one centre worked to integrate with an LIO in the face of reduced funding. Minutes of LIO meetings indicate interactions with a wide range of stakeholders and outside organizations to help the LIOs accomplish their goals, adapting strategies and partners to pursue opportunities. This is in line with the Koontz and Sen (2013) finding that collaborative groups can persist beyond the end-of-programme funding by seeking to align with other funding sources. The trade-off between economic efficiency and adaptability in systems has been highlighted by resilience scholars (Korhonen and Seager 2008; Walker 1992), who point out that having duplicate efforts in a system is not economically efficient but does provide redundancy in the face of a system shock. Cooperation in polycentric governance systems such as the Puget Sound recovery efforts exhibits this trade-off.

Conflict and conflict-resolution interactions in the fracking cases are highly adaptive. Efforts to resolve conflicts have led to numerous policy changes, reinterpretation of authorities, and the creation of new venues. This may not be efficient, but it does indicate the ability to be responsive to differences in positions among the actors in the system.

Competitive interactions promote innovation and risk-taking behaviour by the public service industry (provision) and resource users (appropriators). Hence, competitive interactions among centres can allow centres to adjust to changing information but cannot guarantee they will be adaptive. In the Ebro case, the possibility to transfer water from other WUAs constitutes an incentive for farmers to invest in drought adaptations (i.e. irrigation-efficient technologies). It is unclear, however, whether competition encourages an unhealthy specialization in certain adaptations by individuals (i.e. irrigation efficiency and intensification), which foreclose other types of adaptations in the system. In the Columbia Basin, adaptation involves efforts by implementing organizations to adjust trading rules and create institutional mechanisms to facilitate water banking and groundwater mitigation. It also involves capacity building processes for drawing on implementation experience, and transferring lessons across tributaries in the basin.

8.2.2.5 Network building

Finally, network building – connections among actors – may emerge from interactions. Strengthening existing networks and creating new networks can generate greater resources and channels to achieve collective aims (Margerum 2011). This performance measure is especially relevant for cooperative interactions, where multiple stakeholders come together to share information and resources. In the Puget Sound ecosystem recovery case, cooperation did not uniformly build networks. Rather, network building was inversely correlated with existing networks (Scott and Thomas 2015). That is, centres with many pre-existing networks exhibited little network building, while those with few pre-existing networks gained considerable network ties.

Network building is apparent in the conflict and conflict-resolution interactions, largely because actors started to build coalitions with other like-minded actors in an attempt to shape governance outcomes in support of their positions. At this same time, this may increase the level of cross-coalition polarization, as we have seen in the fracking cases. Still, research on the actors and their network relationships in both of the fracking cases we have explored has shown that the actors do engage in network relationships across competing coalitions (Heikkila and Weible 2016). This is especially true as actors interact with each other across diverse types of venues. These cross-coalition networks were stronger in Colorado than in New York.

Network building is possible for competitive interactions. In the Ebro case, water reallocations across the same WUAs tend to repeat over time, strengthening interactions among subsets of WUAs. In the Columbia Basin, market transactions are embedded in informal networks and collaborative governance processes, although the success in strengthening networks varied tremendously across the Basin.

Process performance measures across interaction types are summarized in Table 8.3.

8.2.3 Trade-offs among Performance Measures

There is no single performance measure for all polycentric interactions. A range of process and outcome measures may be appropriate for different types of interactions, and these measures cannot all be simultaneously optimized. The trade-offs and conflicts among desired criteria in

Table 8.3 *Process performance measures across interaction types*

Performance measure	Cooperation	Conflict and conflict resolution	Competition
Accountability	Diffuse authority reduced accountability for meeting system-wide goals.	Increased through Task Force (CO) and Environmental Impact process (NY).	In the Ebro case, the nested authority serves as the basis for a sophisticated accountability system. In the Columbia Basin case, monitoring and evaluation protocols ensure compliance and 'value for money.'
Representation	PSP gave resources to LIOs who included diverse stakeholders, thus increasing representation.	Some constraints in CO and NY, but opportunities emerged in different conflict resolution venues for representation in both cases.	There is a nested and inclusive system of elected representatives that guarantees minimal consensus over the conditions for competition. Involvement of local collective choice arrangements in planning and rule-making addressed third-party effects of reallocation.
Social learning	Interactions may have provided opportunities for social learning but data have not been collected to measure this.	Evidence of social learning through rule-making processes (CO) and studies of health and environmental impacts (NY). Depends on trust and information availability.	In the Ebro case, the authority and centralization of information by the second-order organization counter-acts the effects that competition may have on social learning.

Adaptability	Multiple sources of funding and information enhanced the adaptability of the system.	Both cases were adaptable, as efforts to resolve conflicts led to numerous policy changes and creation of new venues.	Monitoring protocols and reporting requirements may have provided opportunities for social learning but data have not been collected to measure this. In the Ebro case, water reallocations may be driving specialization in irrigation efficiency and a particular farm business model, which may hurt system adaptability over time. In the Columbia Basin, different transaction tools have been developed to create flexibility for reallocation.
Network building	Interactions built some new networks where existing networks were sparse.	Interactions built networks by building coalitions, but sometimes they become more polarized in their networks. Actors in the CO case built more cross-coalition networks than did actors in the NY case.	In the Ebro case, water reallocations have given visibility to a network of highly efficient farmers and WUAs within the project. Repeated reallocations strengthen interactions among subsets of WUAs. In the Columbia River case, networks connecting agricultural communities, state and local environmental NGOs, and regulatory agencies are present and essential for market exchanges.

polycentric governance were recognized by Ostrom, Tiebout and Warren (1961) and many scholars since. We compare likely performance trade-offs within cooperation, conflict and conflict resolution, and competition.

Cooperation is a means to navigate the complex array of decision centres to find appropriate information and resources, but it can incur high transaction costs. These transaction costs can be increased in pursuit of diverse interest representation. At the same time, cooperation can provide adaptability in the face of change. Also, cooperation entails government steering rather than controlling, which can raise questions about accountability; without a central controller with agreed-upon authority and responsibility, it is not clear who to hold to account for system performance. Such steering includes the possibility that local efforts can be steered into alignment with system-wide goals. Cooperation that builds networks in the focal action arena may do so at the expense of pre-existing networks in adjacent action arenas.

In conflictual interactions, at least two opposing stakeholders contest an action or decision. This makes measuring efficacy challenging, as different stakeholders have different desired results. One measure of efficacy in conflictual interactions is whether opposing stakeholders are able to reach an agreement. In addition, efficiency of resource use is of interest as disputants expend resources in seeking to prevail or in finding common ground for an agreement. Of course, what makes sense for parties to a dispute does not necessarily promote coherence across system levels or centres, so agreement may come at the expense of system coherence. Besides agreements reached, the process of working through conflicts and conflict resolution can generate social learning and adaptability. In fact, reaching an agreement more efficiently may reduce the social learning and adaptability benefits that come from prolonged searching for common ground, creating an inverse relationship between these process and outcome measures.

Competition is typically measured in terms of whether a valued good or service is provided, and the efficiency with which it is provided. But achieving greater efficiency can come at the expense of coherence. As illustrated in the Ebro case, such trade-offs can be partially addressed via representation of all affected interests in the design of the competition rules. However, such representation, along with the need to provide accountability, makes the system less adaptable to cope with swift changes in water availability. In the Columbia Basin, the cooperative efforts by environmental groups and state governments purchasing or leasing water from irrigators led to a reduction in efficiency and overall efficacy in order to enhance accountability, representation of diverse interests and social learning.

8.3 Conclusion

This chapter set out to synthesize findings across Chapters 5–7 regarding cooperation, conflict and conflict resolution, and competition interactions. Our cases indicate that authority, information, and resources create different incentives by type of interaction. In the cooperative case of ecosystem restoration in the Puget Sound, resources and information were the most important factors affecting how the interactions performed. In the conflict and conflict resolution cases of fracking in Colorado and New York, distribution of authority and lack of shared understanding about authority spurred conflicts that were resolved in one case (New York) largely from information. In the competition case of water management in the Ebro Basin and Columbia Basin, information and resource asymmetries affected interactions, regardless of the distribution of authority.

We examined the performance of our cases on several outcome and process criteria. On the outcome criteria of efficacy, results were mixed across all three interaction types. Efficiency in the cooperation and conflict and conflict-resolution cases was limited by high transaction costs. Coherence was high in the cooperative case, mixed in the conflict cases, and low in the competition case. For process criteria, accountability was low in the cooperation case, increased for the conflict cases, and high for the competition cases. Representation was generally high in the cooperation case, in certain venues within the conflict cases, and in the competition cases. Social learning was evidenced in the conflict cases (depending on trust and information availability), but is unclear for the competition cases, and cooperative cases. Adaptability was high in the cooperation and conflict cases, while it was uneven in the competition cases, due to varying success embedding markets within collaborative governance structures. Network building was mixed in the cooperation case, higher in the Colorado than the New York conflict case, and high in the competition case. Overall, no case performed well across all performance criteria, and no performance criterion scored well in every case.

It is important to note that the many performance measures exhibit trade-offs. Higher levels of performance based on one measure may mean lower levels on another, as was evident across our cases. For example, the many connections present in the cooperation case promote high levels of adaptability, coherence and efficacy but at the expense of accountability and efficiency. In the conflict and conflict-resolution cases, working through the conflicts generated social learning and adaptability benefits, but also decreased efficiency. In the competition cases, allowing water-right reallocations favoured efficiency but may result in lack of coherence at higher levels of the system.

Although we treated the three types of interactions (cooperation, conflict/resolution, competition) as distinct for purposes of analysis, in reality a polycentric governance system includes all three types of interactions. Existence of multiple centres tied together under a common set of overarching rules provides many opportunities for all three kinds of interactions to occur. Centres in generally cooperative relationships are likely to compete with each other for resources such as grants; centres in conflict attempt to resolve the conflict by creating cooperative interactions; centres in competition that do not act coherently (align local actions with system-wide needs) encourage other centres to create mechanisms for coordination and conflict resolution. These dynamics were all present across our case studies.

Further research is warranted to test our findings in other contexts. This will require attention to different types of polycentric interactions, which may be analysed distinctly, even while recognizing that they occur simultaneously and interact.

Building on the in-depth understandings of polycentric governance, its dimensions, determinants and change in Part I and its operation and performance in Part II, Part III will address determinants and change of polycentric governance arrangements at a deeper level, before it ends on insights on how polycentric governance could be put into practice.

Constituting Polycentric Governance

Graham Marshall and Andreas Thiel

OVERVIEW

Part I of Governing Complexity provided readers with a basic understanding of the concepts, it introduced 'thinking polycentrically' as a mode of inquiry and it connected the operation and change of polycentric governance to the theoretical underpinnings of the Bloomington School of Political Economy. Part II analysed the operation of polycentric governance focusing on the interactions of cooperation, conflict and conflict resolution and competition, in particular water and natural-resource-management-related cases. Further, it explored ways to assess the performance of polycentric governance. Based on these preliminaries, Part III deepens our understanding of polycentric governance in a conceptual, research-oriented, and a practice-oriented manner. First, Chapters 9 and 10 deepen our conceptual understanding of polycentric governance and that way expand the research agenda. Chapter 9 specifically adopts a micro-level perspective. It addresses the way (polycentric) governance depends upon and shapes individuals' motivations and values in relation to governance. In doing so, to some extent it also clarifies the deep-down normative reasonings that underpin polycentric governance according to the Bloomington School of Political Economy. The conceptual points are illustrated in reference to examples of water governance, for example in Western Australia. In contrast, Chapter 10 adopts a macro-level perspective. It illustrates how the Faustian bargain underlying the institution of the state can be kept in check and what problems emerge when, at the constitutional level, institutions need to be adapted to changing circumstances. These issues are illustrated in the way constitutions are instituted and changed in the context of state-building initiatives in former Somalia and water governance in the state of New York. Finally, Chapter 11 addresses practitioners and practice that seeks inspiration from polycentric governance for improving natural resource management. It describes tools that can be used to assess governance constellations, and it introduces pathways and conceptions to furthering initiative and self-organization in natural resource management.

Polycentricity and Citizenship in Environmental Governance

Graham R. Marshall and Anas Malik

9.1 Introduction

Citizenship in conserving the environment and natural resources has become a topic of increasing interest to policy makers and scholars, as the capacities of governments to meet the escalating conservation challenges of the Anthropocene become increasingly stretched (Chen et al. 2009). In much of the world since the late nineteenth century, the role of citizens in democratic societies has been understood conventionally through the paradigm of 'political modernism'. This paradigm viewed centralized modes of governance (wherein all significant public policy decisions are made by central governments and then implemented through a bureaucratic chain of command) as ideal, and the appropriate involvement of citizens in these processes as therefore limited to voting periodically in elections for political representatives (V. Ostrom 1991).

The interest in citizenship as a means of helping to solve contemporary conservation problems stems from critiques that political modernism is ill-fitted to the complexity of these problems (Marshall 2010) and recognition of a need to augment centralized efforts to solve them by strengthening the motivation (civic virtue) and means (civic capacity) for citizens to willingly 'co-produce' solutions (E. Ostrom 1990). The 'environmental citizenship' (Dobson 2007) or 'ecological citizenship' (Wolf, Brown, and Conway 2009) invoked in such discussions accords with Heater's (2004, 182) argument that '[h]e who has no sense of a civic bond with his fellows or of some responsibility for civic welfare is not a true citizen whatever his legal status', and with V. Ostrom's (1991, 256) emphasis on the importance for sustaining democracy of 'the willingness of people to cope with problematical situations instead of presuming that someone else has responsibility for them'.

This interest has led to research efforts across multiple disciplines (e.g. Dobson and Bell 2005) seeking to better understand the antecedents of environmental citizenship so that steps might be taken to strengthen, or at least not weaken, this phenomenon in particular conservation settings. Our concern in this chapter is with that portion of those efforts concerned with relationships between governance arrangements and environmental citizenship, and with the challenges of establishing and sustaining governance conducive to this citizenship.

9.1.1 Investing in Environmental Citizenship: An Illustrative Case

The significance of this concern, and the difficulty of these challenges, can be illustrated by an ambitious 'experiment' in Australia with governance arrangements seeking to promote citizenship (typically referred to in this context as 'self-help' or 'self-reliance') among rural landholders in natural resources conservation that has been underway since the 1980s (Curtis et al. 2014). This citizenship can manifest in multiple ways within this context, including: voluntary adoption of conservation practices; exerting peer pressure on neighbours to adopt such practices; supporting establishment of a local natural resource management (NRM) group; serving on the committee of such a group; coordinating the activities of such a group with those of neighbouring groups; contributing skills, labour and/or equipment to group activities (e.g. controlling weeds in adjoining public lands); and sharing knowledge of local issues with governments (Marshall 2011).

The Australian Government sought to catalyze this process in the 1990s by investing public funds in supporting the formation and facilitation of 'Landcare' and related groups (Curtis et al. 2014). These groups were established predominantly at the neighbourhood level, typically with membership of a few dozen farming families. About one-third of Australian farming families became involved in more than 6,000 Landcare-type groups (Campbell 2016). The essence of the Landcare initiative has been described as 'landholders working in their own local social group to solve their own local land conservation problems in their own way' (Poussard 1992) and 'promoting sustainable environmental and natural resources management through voluntary collective action at a neighbourhood or district level' (Campbell 2016).

In the early 2000s the Australian Government introduced what became known as the 'regional delivery model', under which its funding of on-ground NRM activities would be channelled through new organizations established for fifty-six NRM regions it had newly delineated across the nation. Choosing to establish this governance at the regional level was justified by claims that this level was best suited not only for integrating local NRM actions by Landcare and other groups, but also for engaging the community in NRM (Council of Australian Governments 2000).

Community engagement was, nevertheless, soon identified as a major challenge for the regional NRM organizations. Most of these organizations saw their roles less as building on the Landcare initiative's successes in promoting local self-reliance, than using public funds more strategically and professionally to externally motivate landholders to act on NRM issues determined from the top down as national priorities (Campbell 2016). The large sizes of the regions also made community engagement difficult, with many local NRM groups viewing the regional NRM organizations as remote from the communities with which they actually identified (Regional Implementation Working Group of the NRM Ministerial Council 2005).

Landcare groups are now struggling across much of Australia. Some of this decline in environmental citizenship has been attributed to those responsible for developing the regional delivery model 'fail[ing] to articulate how the regional framework should relate to voluntarism and, as a result, undermin[ing] it. ... The tendency for the regional NRM policy reform to displace and undermine rather than augment community Landcare was a grave error' (Campbell 2016).

Box 9.1 Vignette: Polycentricity and citizenship in environmental watering – Australia's Murray-Darling Basin

Efforts at policy reform to achieve environmentally sustainable water use in the Murray-Darling Basin (MDB) commenced in the early 1990s as a cooperative-federalist initiative of the Commonwealth and state/territory governments. Progress in implementing the agreed water policy reforms was slow, however. In the depths of a prolonged drought, when Australia's most important river system was claimed to be in crisis, the Commonwealth intervened through the Water Act 2007 to take control of the reform agenda (Garrick 2015).

The Murray-Darling Basin Authority (MDBA) was established under the Water Act 2007 to develop and implement a Basin Plan. Legislated in 2012, this Plan provides for a reduction in surface water use of about 20 per cent from pre-existing levels. The Commonwealth Environmental Water Holder (CEWH) was also appointed under this Act to manage the Commonwealth's holdings of 'environmental water' entitlements acquired through an AUD$13 billion water recovery programme.

The Basin Plan has been described as 'one of Australia's most controversial water policies ever implemented' (Wheeler et al. 2017, 253). The preceding Guide to the Basin Plan brought to a head mounting criticism of what had become widely characterized as a centralized, technocentric approach to developing the Plan. The strength of the irrigation lobby's negative reaction to the Guide led the Commonwealth to disavow 'a key principle under which the MDBA had operated, namely that environmental sustainability was a binding requirement for the Plan' (Quiggin 2011, 53).

Byron (2011, 389) observed that the centralized approach to developing the Basin Plan had left local people with 'little commitment to the strategy. Without their commitment, the strategy will lack the necessary cooperation at the grassroots level.... [T]he key [to turning this around] is to start with the knowledge and energy of the people on the ground ...'. Similarly, Horne and O'Donnell (2014, 129) identified subsidiarity – 'devolving the maximum work and decision-making to the lowest level possible, while still retaining the capacity for Basin-wide environmental watering outcomes' – as vital for strengthening citizenship in MDB environmental water management. They argued that the increased autonomy granted to local organizations through subsidiarity would enable these organizations to gain greater trust from their constituents. Nesting these local organizations, and indeed organizations at higher levels, within the larger governance system in ways that preserve their essential autonomy would, moreover, enable 'trust at the local level to filter up so that trust extends from local communities up to Basin-wide agencies' (2014, 129).

O'Donnell and Garrick (2017) observed that the CEWH's early focus on efficiency and effectiveness in environmental water management had not been sufficient to gain trust from local communities, and noted that this entity had sought more recently to build this trust by nesting local arrangements within its broader strategy for managing environmental water. In 2012, for instance, the CEWH formalized a partnership agreement with a non-government organization (NGO), Nature Foundation South Australia, under which it would make available 10 gigalitres of water each year to use in wetlands located in that state. This NGO became accountable to the CEWH for managing the delivery of this water, including through engaging local communities in deciding where, when and how the water should be used.

The incumbent in the CEWH position until early 2018 identified the value of such partnerships in gaining trust and cooperation from private landholders and other community members. He observed that these partnerships 'sort of grow organically, if they're working, and so far they are. ... I just see these things, with appropriate limitations imposed by legislative responsibilities and resourcing implications, growing in spread and value. ... My understanding is evolving with my experience of it; so I'm seeing it already being more powerful than I thought it could be. ... I think the system that will work is one that's built around a realistic understanding of who's best suited to do what' (David Papps interviewed in Marshall 2017, 199, 200, 209).

9.1.2 Focus of This Chapter

In pursuing our concern with relationships between governance and citizenship in the environmental policy domain, and the challenges of establishing and sustaining governance conducive to this citizenship, we take our lead from a line of thinking about polycentric governance that was developed at length by Vincent Ostrom but often overlooked by other analysts of this form of governance. This line of thinking drew from insights drawn by Alexis de Tocqueville (2003) in the early nineteenth century from his analysis of the American democratic experiment. Tocqueville warned that the social basis of democratic order could be undermined by erosion of the citizenship that had enabled this experiment to take root and flourish. Ostrom's (1997) final book-length work was subtitled *A Response to Tocqueville's Challenge*. To the extent that the scope of scholarship within the Bloomington School of Political Economy is adequately captured by the name of the academic group from which this school took its lead – the Workshop in Political Theory and Policy Analysis – Vincent's work exemplified the 'political theory' tradition within this scholarship.

Ostrom, V. (1991, 8) identified 'the way people think and relate to one another' as fundamentally significant for achieving and sustaining polycentric governance supportive of citizenship and vice versa. He viewed polycentric governance as both contributing to and depending on the self-governing capacities of citizens. His concern with how citizens think and relate to one another pertains to what is understood in the Bloomington School's 'policy analysis' tradition of scholarship, and particularly through its Institutional Analysis and Development (IAD) framework, as the meta-constitutional level of analysis. This rarely analysed level of the IAD Framework (Ostrom 2005a) 'encompasses long-lasting and often subtle constraints on the forms of constitutional, collective, or operational choice processes that are considered legitimate within an existing culture' (McGinnis 2011a).

Key insights drawn from the American democratic experiment by Vincent Ostrom (1991) regarding the metaconstitutional conditions required for establishing and sustaining forms of polycentric governance conducive to promoting citizenship are considered in Section 9.2, as they suggest areas for continuing research into the viability of self-governing polycentric orders. One way to think about this is in terms of Douglass North's (2005, 1) suggestion that social change is driven by at least three components: beliefs, the stock of knowledge, and institutions. Our beliefs about reality, imperfect as they necessarily are, form part of the stock of knowledge. Vincent Ostrom's emphasis on metaconstitutional conditions touches on both beliefs and institutions. The metaconstitutional level raises questions of inter-subjectivity that extend beyond the academic discipline of psychology into such areas as ontology, epistemology, metaphysics, hermeneutic keys, and starting points generally. Examining these issues often requires an interdisciplinary openness, which can sometimes be difficult for social scientists. Yet they are important in the Bloomington school perspective as articulated by Vincent Ostrom, in particular, and are areas for ongoing research.

Recognizing that the metaconstitutional conditions upon which American democracy was founded had weakened considerably under the pervasive influence of political modernism, Ostrom subsequently proposed that alternatives to this paradigm should be founded on the theory of collective action in public goods provision: 'When the central problem in public administration is viewed as the provision of public goods and services, alternative forms of organization may be available for the performance of these functions apart from the extension and perfection of bureaucratic structures' (V. Ostrom 2008a). This proposal was acted on in the 'policy analysis' tradition of the Bloomington School scholarship; most notably by Elinor Ostrom who in her book *Governing the Commons: The Evolution of Institutions for Collective Action* (E. Ostrom 1990) laid out a far-reaching agenda for empirical research into how institutions of state, common and individual property interact with one another and other attributes of action situations to influence provision of common-pool resources. In Section 9.3, we document the progress achieved in implementing this agenda in respect of understanding relationships between polycentric governance and citizenship in the environmental policy domain. The chapter concludes in Section 9.4 with suggestions for further research.

9.2 Insights from the 'American Democratic Experiment'

The metaconstitutional conditions for citizenship that are conducive to polycentric governance can be found in diverse settings around the world. These metaconstitutional conditions are not exclusive or unique to the United States of America. The American experience includes a historical lineage of self-governing townships of Anglo–American settlers, with a relative equality of social condition, and a departure from an aristocratic social context. The prominent role of civic engagement in shaping the rules governing local communities attracted the attention of Alexis de Tocqueville, who also argued that the American case was part of a geographically and historically broader millennium-long trend towards social equality and democracy. Investigations of the American experience can help inform understandings of potentials and vulnerabilities of self-governing poly-centric orders in the United States of America and elsewhere.

For V. Ostrom (1991) the concept of democracy 'implies that people govern'. He concluded from his analysis of the American democratic experiment that a particular constitutional order – polycentric govern-ance – is of basic importance for understanding how the citizenship required for a self-governing society might be achieved and maintained. He understood polycentric governance as generalizing the concept of federalism, which had come to be defined narrowly as a governance arrangement where authority is exercised concurrently by a national and state (or provincial) governments. For him '[t]he crucial issue is that the concept of federalism enables people to break out of the conceptual trap inherent in a theory of sovereignty that presumes there must exist some single centre of supreme authority that rules over society' (V. Ostrom 1991).

V. Ostrom (1991) asserted that people necessarily proceed from meta-physical assumptions – even unacknowledged or implicit ones – in pro-viding meaningful starting points from which to work together in attempting to solve their own problems. He observed that a shared under-standing of these metaphysical assumptions is crucial to these attempts, and that such a shared understanding – particularly in respect of the value of federalism grounded in covenantal practices – in the case of the Ameri-can democratic experiment was made possible by the religious beliefs of the Pilgrims of New England, who sowed the seeds of this experiment.

He noted that that the word 'federalism' is derived from the Latin term for 'covenant', and that the Pilgrims adhered to federal theology which was at the time 'a covenantal theology ... developed by some Protestants to conceive a system of church governance ...' (V. Ostrom 1991). Covenant can be defined as 'a foundational affirmation of open-ended mutual obli-gation that is difficult to break even if it is not consistently reciprocated' (Malik 2017, 111). A 'proper covenantal order' was defined by V. Ostrom (1991, 61–62) as 'one in which a covenanting people chooses to act in a way that is consistent with a transcendent order, "which it is that men call God", and with their idea of one another as a people who are faithful to their covenant with God and respectful of God's creation'. He observed that in the Mayflower Compact the Pilgrims effectively covenanted them-selves to a federal (or polycentric) system of governance. It was federal in the original linguistic sense, and also federal/polycentric in the broader sense as the local self-governing units interacted with each other and formed multiple layers of relationships.

Ostrom emphasized the potential of 'Golden Rule' covenants to provide a normative anchor for a polycentric constitutional order. The Golden Rule refers to wanting for others what one wants for oneself, and is grounded in a metaphysical supposition that all people are created equal. Versions of the Golden Rule have a prominent position in the Abrahamic traditions, inter-religious collaboration initiatives, and ethical teachings from other contexts (Malik 2013; 2017, 2018). V. Ostrom (1991, 54) argued that conceiving the Golden Rule as a method of normative inquiry 'opens the way to a community of understanding, to the development of just laws, and to drawing upon the resources of others to enhance our own understanding of ourselves and the world in which we live. It is these elements as they are bound together in covenantal relationships that give meaning to American federalism as a public philosophy – a metaphysics for citizenship in self-governing societies' V. Ostrom (1991, 54). The self-governing habits that provide the building blocks of a polycentric order rest on civic commitments to devise and revise rules which are appropriate for particular contexts, yet consider and take into account the interests and perspectives of others.

Since the Golden Rule 'is surprisingly devoid of moral content' (V. Ostrom 1991, 54), such a method of normative inquiry by any group of individuals will lead to a covenantal order consistent with their shared moral precepts. Hence it may, at least in initial rounds of its application, lead members of a particular group within society (e.g. upstream irrigators) to covenant (e.g. in respect of their permissible levels of water extraction) in ways considered to be morally deficient by other groups (e.g. downstream irrigators or environmentalists). Applied at a higher (e.g. river basin) level, however, the method offers the prospect of a mutually agreed normative basis for resolving such conflicts. In pursuing this prospect, V. Ostrom (1991, 54) argued, 'it is possible for human beings to strive for an understanding of universals applicable to nature as God's creation and, as a result, to achieve some rudimentary appreciation of how human beings might best relate themselves to one another and to God (that which is eternal)'. This raises the ongoing research question of what set of intersubjective understandings beyond the Golden Rule promote conflict-resolution processes and entrepreneurial efforts to identify and build upon complementarities to promote collectively desirable outcomes.

Eventual extension of the notion of citizenship to the national level in America was made possible, V. Ostrom (1991) argued, by metaconstitutional conditions conducive to growing federalism grounded in covenantal practices incrementally upwards from the local level. The English colonial mode in the American colonies happened to be favourable for the emergence of self-governing townships. Thus, the early emigrants 'continually exercised the rights of sovereignty . . . as if their allegiance was due only to God', and there was a freedom from political prejudices which enabled them to experiment freely with political principles, laws and other institutions (Tocqueville 2003, 28). Tocqueville regarded this early history as pivotal to democracy because 'town meetings are to liberty what primary schools are to science; they bring it within people's reach, they teach men how to use and enjoy it' (in V. Ostrom 1991, 213). He noted that this practical education in citizenship was complemented by the high value placed by the early emigrants on public education.

These early local-level experiences served as a foundation upon which successive generations of Americans would come to build in extending their citizenship as far as enabling them ultimately to constitute a self-governing society at the national level. Vincent Ostrom (1991) observed accordingly how:

[T]he federal system of 1787 emerged from some 167 years of experience in fashioning civil bodies politic by covenanting and combining together to form local units of government and colonial charters. With this cultural heritage, people were able to undertake the American Revolution, the formulation of state constitutions, the organisation of Continental Congresses, the Articles of Confederation, and the Constitution of the United States. People looked to one another in constituting associations that exercised the prerogatives of government.

Vincent Ostrom (1991) observed that this heritage of the American people containing certain metaconstitutional conditions, which had enabled them to come to govern themselves polycentrically as a nation, found itself undermined from the late nineteenth century onwards by the advent of political modernism. In place of the shared community of understanding that had underpinned a bottom-up covenantal method of citizens governing themselves polycentrically, political modernism sought to substitute the understanding that citizens are governed more effectively the more that governance is centralized towards a single decision-making centre. This paradigm steadily gained influence not only in the USA, but internationally, reaching its zenith in the 1960s and 1970s when considerable faith existed in the capacity of strong, national governments to solve all public problems through top-down interventions (Marshall 2005; E Ostrom 2005a).

Far from being unique to the American context, the metaconstitutional conditions comparable to Golden Rule covenants are found in numerous contexts. Daniel Elazar (1998) described notions of covenant in the

Jewish context, and Malik (2018) has argued that the Islamic tradition includes covenantal thinking as well as other elements conducive to polycentric order. Vincent Ostrom (1997) argued that covenant-like understandings existed in Confucian, Islamic, and other contexts. Indeed, it is arguable that versions of Golden Rule covenant-like orientations can be found in many ethical systems in the world. The American experience provides a cautionary and still-evolving tale about the vulnerabilities of polycentric governance to strategies of dominance or control which, coupled with loss of the habits of self-governance, lead to increasingly monocentric decision-making.

9.3 Collective Action and Civic Virtue

The premise of political modernism that citizens are incapable of self-organizing effective solutions to the problems they share was given intellectual credence in the mid-twentieth century by non-cooperative game theory (particularly the Prisoner's Dilemma game) and the conventional theory of collective action. In his seminal contribution to this theory, Mancur Olson (1965, 2) concluded that 'unless the number of individuals in a group is quite small, or unless there is coercion or some other special device to make individuals act in their common interest, rational, self-interested individuals will not act to achieve their common or group interests'.

This inability of individuals to act collectively (except in small groups) in solving their shared problems is posited in this theory to follow from an irresistible temptation to 'free-ride' on others' efforts which prevents them from volunteering their own contributions. On the basis of non-cooperative game theory, moreover, it became conventionally accepted among scholars that individuals faced with collective-action problems cannot use communication as a way of making credible commitments to one another to resist temptations to free-ride. All such communication, including of the covenantal kind, thus became viewed as mere 'cheap talk' (E. Ostrom 1998). Elinor Ostrom (2010, 248) observed upon being co-awarded the Nobel Memorial Prize for Economic Sciences how this conventional theory of collective action corroborated the political-modernist assumption 'that the momentum for change [towards realising collective action] must come from outside the situation rather than from the self-reflection and creativity of those within a situation to restructure their own patterns of interaction'.

The influence of the conventional theory of collective action on shared community understanding of the role of citizens in their own governance was amplified by publication of Garrett Hardin's (1968) 'The tragedy of the commons', which made similar predictions regarding the capacity of individuals to solve their problems of collective action (or more specifically the subset of these known as 'commons dilemmas'). Hardin predicted that users of any common-pool resource will, in the absence of external intervention, be trapped in over-using and ultimately destroying the resource. This article captured the attention of policy makers and scholars worldwide, and spurred an immense theoretical and empirical research effort of particular relevance to environmental citizenship, given the common-pool characteristics of many environmental and natural resource systems.

9.3.1 Developments in a Behavioural Theory of Collective Action

The Bloomington School research effort started with case studies that identified numerous contemporary examples across many nations, where tragedies of the commons had been avoided through self-organized collective action. However, '[n]o single case study was conclusive; each could be dismissed as an anomaly' (Poteete, Janssen, and E. Ostrom 2010, 32). Adoption of a standard framework for analysis – based on the IAD Framework – made it easier to compare cases and identify patterns across them. Moreover, experiments performed in the laboratory and field in numerous cultural settings around the world have confirmed that in controlled replicable situations self-organized solutions to commons dilemmas can emerge more often than predicted by the conventional theory of collective action.

Of particular relevance to Vincent Ostrom's identification of covenantal practices as foundational to the American people's achievements in establishing a self-governing society, experimental studies have consistently demonstrated the important role of face-to-face communication in enabling self-organized solutions to commons dilemmas – even where promises made as a result of this communication cannot be enforced (E. Ostrom 2010).

Malik (2017) argued that the moral psychology of covenant distinguishes the Bloomington School from other schools of public choice such as the Austrian approach. A question for ongoing research concerns the nature of covenant or functionally similar understandings in different cultural settings. Vincent Ostrom suggested several possibilities in the Jewish, Islamic, and Confucian contexts (V. Ostrom 1997), while Malik

(2018) has described covenant-like understandings and other religio-cultural practices consonant with polycentricity in the Islamic tradition. Shivakumar (2005) suggests that covenant-like understandings can be found in most or all cultures. A related research question is the degree to which covenant-like understandings are specific to polycentric governance rather than political orders more generally.

From this cumulative research effort spurred by the 'tragedy of the commons' prediction, a behavioural theory of collective action is emerging which 'views humans as adaptive creatures who attempt to do well given the constraints and opportunities of the situations in which they find themselves (or which they seek out). Humans learn norms, heuristics, and full analytical strategies from one another, from feedback from the world, and from their capacity to engage in self-reflection and imagine a differently structured world' (Poteete, Janssen, and E. Ostrom 2010, 222).

This behavioural theory recognises that human motivations in responding to collective-action problems are more diverse than the rational egoism assumed as universally applicable in the conventional theory. Whereas rational egoists contribute to collective action only when motivated to do so by externally implemented incentives, the behavioural theory of collective action has been developed from experimental evidence that contributions by at least some individuals are motivated by internalized social norms; e.g. relating to reciprocity, trustworthiness and fairness. Individuals with such internalized motivations may respond to collective-action problems as conditional co-operators (contributing to joint efforts depending on their assessments that other beneficiaries can be trusted to reciprocate), and thereby become motivated to initiate efforts in solving these problems. Increasing numbers of others may come to reciprocate these efforts over time as a result of mutually reinforcing feedbacks between cooperation level, trust, reputation for trustworthiness, and reciprocity (E. Ostrom 1998; 2000).

A cautionary note is appropriate here: reciprocity and collective action are not universally desirable from the point of view of society. Reciprocity among a tight circle of similar individuals can, for instance, lead to discrimination against people of a different religion or ethnicity. And '[i]t is everyone else's interest that some [collective-action problems] are *not* resolved, such as those involved in monopolies and cartel formation, and those that countervene basic moral standards and legal relationships, and those that restrict the opportunities for an open society and expanding economy' (E. Ostrom 1998, 17–18, original emphasis). Polycentric arrangements are vulnerable to strategies of dominance. An important research question in this context is whether the Golden Rule needs to be accompanied by a norm of non-dominance to promote well-functioning polycentric governance.

The mutually reinforcing feedbacks between trust in others, the investments others make in trustworthy reputations, and the propensities to follow reciprocity norms are at the core of the behavioural theory of collective action. Whether these feedbacks serve in a particular setting to strengthen or weaken cooperation in contributing to collective action depends on a diverse array of structural variables. E. Ostrom (1998) called for research into the effects of different structural variables on the likelihood of people organizing successfully for collective action, and highlighted in particular a need for research into how institutions enhance or detract from the building of mutual trust, reciprocity and reputations. Of particular relevance to this call, Frey and Jegen (2001, 604) observed:

Civic virtue (a particular manifestation of intrinsic motivation) is bolstered if the public laws convey the notion that citizens are to be trusted. Such trust is reflected in extensive rights and participation possibilities. . . . The basic notion enshrined in the constitution that citizens are on average, and in general, reasonable human beings thus generates a crowding-in effect of civic virtue. In contrast, a constitution implying a fundamental distrust of its citizens, and seeking to discipline them, tends to crowd out civic virtue and undermines the support which citizens are prepared to give towards the basic law.

We turn now to considering the potential for polycentric constitutional orders, predicated on trust that citizens are capable of governing themselves, to crowd-in the civic virtue required (along with civic capacity) for this capability to be realized.

9.3.2 Civic Virtue: Insights from Self-Determination Theory

The foregoing observation from Frey and Jegen was informed by a body of research by behavioural economists in the tradition of Motivation Crowding Theory (MCT) (Frey 1997, 2012). MCT took its lead from early work by social psychologists in developing Self-Determination Theory (SDT) (Deci 1971, 1975). According to SDT, individuals are most likely to optimize satisfaction of their psychological needs, and thus experience well-being, when they feel autonomous. Ryan and Deci (2011, 59–60) observed that 'when people act autonomously, rather than being controlled or amotivated, they act with a sense of choice, are more mindful, think flexibly, and express their values and interests'. Intentional actions are regarded as autonomous in this tradition only to the extent that they are experienced as fully volitional.

SDT distinguishes types of motivation based on their relative autonomy (Ryan and Deci 2011). The most general distinction is between intrinsic and extrinsic motivation. Intrinsic motivation arises from the inherent satisfaction an individual experiences from an action; that is, from enjoying an activity for its own sake. Although intrinsic motivation is an important impetus for action in many circumstances, it is not normally the most important determinant of behaviour: much of human behaviour is motivated, initially at least, by factors external to the self. SDT distinguishes between four main types of external (extrinsic) motivation that vary in the degree to which behavioural regulations are internalized. Two of these motivation types involve a high degree of internalization and volition, so SDT scholars have grouped them with intrinsic motivation into a more general motivational category called autonomous motivation (Ryan and Deci 2011). Civic virtue can be understood as a manifestation of this type of motivation.

Important insights into the civic virtue dimension of environmental citizenship are offered by SDT. This theory offers a psychological explanation of how behavioural changes that arise initially from externally induced motivations can become permanently internalized, as socially endorsed values, identities and institutions become more fully integrated to the self. It proposes that the potential for internalization of behaviour changes that were motivated at first externally can be realized to the extent that the values, identities and institutions are transmitted to individuals in a manner that they perceive supports their autonomy, rather than seeks to control them. Both proximal and distal contextual influences on whether the manner in which transmission occurs is perceived as autonomy supportive or controlling are recognized as relevant by SDT (Ryan and Deci 2011). Proximal contextual influences include parents and peers who interact regularly with an individual, while distal influences include the mass media and governments (Pelletier, Baxter, and Huta 2011).

E. Ostrom (2000, 13) referred to findings from both MCT and SDT in observing that 'much of contemporary policy analysis and the policies adopted in many modern democracies crowd out citizenship', while E. Ostrom (2005a, 245-55) did likewise in arguing that 'instead of relying on the state as the central, top-down substitute for all public problem solving, it is necessary to design complex, polycentric orders that involve both public governance mechanisms and private market and community institutions that complement each other. . . . Reliance primarily on national governments crowds out public and private problem solving at regional and local levels . . .' .

However, the advantages of polycentric governance for developing and sustaining the civic virtue dimension of citizenship were not clearly articulated on the basis of these theories. The advantages of this kind of governance for citizenship were more clearly identified in terms of its civic capacity dimension; i.e. 'the capacity of citizens to experiment with diverse ways of coping with multiple problems and to learn from this experimentation over time' (E. Ostrom 2005a, 270). Such advantages for civic capacity are illustrated by the enhanced opportunities for practical education in covenanting as a basis for self-governance that Vincent Ostrom (1991) identified as having flowed from evolution of the polycentric structure of the American democratic experiment from the bottom up. More recent illustrations of the advantages of polycentric governance for growing and sustaining civic capacity include Blomquist's (1992) study of groundwater governance in southern California, and Acheson's (2003) analysis of lobster industry governance in Maine. While suggestive, these cases do not provide conclusive evidence of the advantages of polycentric governance for growing and sustaining civic capacity due to lack of comparison with counter-factual (non-polycentric) cases. Future research designed to fill this gap would make a significant contribution to the literature on this form of governance.

9.4 Subsidiarity, Community-based Governance, and Civic Virtue

Marshall, Hine, and East (2017) argued within an SDT framework that the advantages of polycentric governance in respect of the civic virtue, or autonomous motivation, dimension of environmental citizenship can be expected to accrue to the extent that this governance is organized in accordance with the principle of subsidiarity. This principle proposes that governance be structured such that decision-making in respect of any matter be assigned to the level closest to the individual where it can be exercised competently. Higher levels of governance are understood accordingly as subsidiary to lower-level ones (and ultimately to the individual), not the reverse as has conventionally come to be presumed (Marshall and Stafford Smith 2010).

Governance of this kind is polycentric, but the definition of polycentric governance does not require it to be consistent with the subsidiarity principle. While this definition requires that all decision-making centres encompassed by this constitutional order be formally independent of one another (V. Ostrom, Tiebout, and Wagner 1961), formal independence is no guarantee of de facto decision-making autonomy (Carlisle and Gruby

2017; Marshall 2015), and the level of such autonomy experienced by individuals and their proximate groupings under polycentric governance may be less than that entailed by the subsidiarity principle. V. Ostrom (1991, 270) was concerned, for instance, that despite the polycentric (or federal) constitutional order of American democracy, there had been an erosion of the shared community understanding which had enabled this order to become established, which had led in turn to a drift towards 'democratic despotism' as rule-making in practice became increasingly relegated to central authorities. He observed: 'Federalism is a sham if covenants become mere words on paper' (V. Ostrom 1991, 272).

9.4.1 Community-Based Governance

Polycentric governance arrangements organized in accordance with the subsidiarity principle have been described as community-based (Marshall 2009; Marshall et al. 2016). A community-based approach to polycentric governance is consistent with Andersson and E. Ostrom (2008) observing that the polycentric approach to institutional analysis assumes that the self-governing capabilities of citizens and their associations should be the foundation for higher-level governance arrangements. The characterization of community-based governance as polycentric governance structured in accordance with the subsidiarity principle is consistent with Berkes (2005, 34) using the term community-based governance as 'shorthand for governance that starts from the ground up but deals with cross-scale interactions', and with Berkes' (2005, 15–193) description of such governance in the conservation context as 'extend[ing] beyond communities to include institutional linkages and multiple levels of organization that impact and shape institutions at the local level'. Berkes (2007, 2017) was concerned to remedy the common misapprehension that community-*based* governance is limited to community-*level* governance. The concept of community based polycentric governance is implicit in Tocqueville's (2003, 30) depiction of the township as the starting unit of political organization in the establishment of American democracy, with 'the township ... organized before the county, the county before the State, and State before the Union'.[1]

The significance for community-based environmental governance of E. Ostrom's (1990) eighth design principle for robust governance of

---

[1] The 'Union' refers here to the confederal and federal arrangements that underlie the United States of America.

common-pool resources was highlighted by Marshall (2005, 2008). This 'nesting principle' requires inter alia that governance of such resources be 'organised in multiple layers of nested enterprises' (Marshall 2008, 90). Community-based environmental governance can accordingly be characterized as the 'result of larger, more inclusive organizational units emerging from, and then "nesting" – in the sense of complementing rather than absorbing or side-lining – smaller, more exclusive units that manage to self-organize sooner. Smaller organizations thus become a part of a more inclusive system without giving up their essential autonomy' (Marshall 2005, 47).

Marshall (2008, 2005, 2009) proposed that the value of nesting lower-level governance structures, rather than supplanting or side-lining them, follows from the 'vertical' problems of collective action that arise as 'higher' levels of governance are introduced. Adding a higher-level structure was argued to augment efforts by lower-level actors to self-organize remedies to their 'horizontal' problems of collective action only to the extent that they trust the structure to reciprocate their own efforts; otherwise these actors would free-ride on higher-level efforts to help solve these problems (thus cancelling out the effect of higher-level efforts) or oppose these efforts (Marshall 2009). Retaining governance structures that actors have self-organized, and minimizing restrictions on the autonomy of these structures, was seen as helping with the vertical problems of collective action since actors 'can be expected to place greater trust in units they create for themselves and in which they maintain collective-choice property rights' (Marshall 2008, 77). The potential for subsidiarity and the nesting principle to contribute towards realizing the environmental-citizenship-building aspirations of Australia's regional delivery model for NRM were recognized by Campbell (2016) when observing that the model had 'failed to capture the potential synergies inherent in what could have been one of the world's best examples of nested, multi-level systems of community-based governance of natural resources' (see also Ryan et al. 2010).

Self-organized structures that become nested in the process of developing more inclusive arrangements for environmental governance have been likened to the 'mediating structures' of civil society that the sociologists Berger and Neuhaus (1977, 3) identified as important for making members of modern society feel 'more "at home" in society, and the political order . . . more meaningful' (Marshall 2002; Bish 2014; Reeve, Marshall, and Musgrave 2002). Mediating structures are seen as fulfilling this role by retaining a capacity to present distinct 'private' and 'public' faces. They are claimed to protect individuals and their proximate groupings from the alienation of modern life, while strengthening the legitimacy of governments and other higher-level governance structures by helping them to connect with local perceptions, values and norms. They are thus seen as making it more possible to establish trust, reciprocity and cooperation up and down a governance arrangement by breaking into smaller steps what may otherwise be alienating social distances (Marshall 2005). This effect might be understood through an SDT lens as arising from inclusion of mediating structures within governance arrangements making it more likely that the arrangements will be perceived as supportive of individuals' autonomy.

9.4.2 Empirical Findings

Empirical evidence in respect of the foregoing claims made in the literature regarding the relationship between community-based polycentric governance and civic virtue (understood here as autonomous motivation to reciprocate higher-level contributions to collective action) remains limited, however. Cardenas, Stranlund, and Willis (2000) found from field experiments in rural Colombia that external control in solving local commons dilemmas led to inferior outcomes when (as is typically the case) the control is only modestly enforced, compared with allowing local community members to self-organize solutions to these dilemmas. The main reason for the inferior performance of external control was found to be its crowding out of group-regarding motivations associated with civic virtue.

Marshall, (2009) found from multiple regression of survey data from 821 farmers operating within 3 of the 56 regions serviced by Australia's regional delivery model for NRM (see Section 9.1.2) that farmers were more likely to practise reciprocity in their dealings with the model to the extent that their engagement with it was more localized. Reciprocity in this context involved an intention to increase adoption of the on-farm conservation practices promoted to them under the model when they trusted the model to support them in their adoption efforts. In two of the three regions, community engagement with the model occurred at the subregional level, whereas in the third region it occurred only at the regional level. It was proposed on the basis of this evidence that 'sub regional bodies have an advantage over regional bodies in motivating [reciprocity] from farmers because the former are better positioned to engage them sufficiently to turn around norms of free-riding or opposition entrenched by earlier paternalistic approaches to agri-environmental conservation' (Marshall 2009, 1507).

Referring subsequently to this research, Marshall (2011, 122) observed that it offers:

... some evidence ... for the proposition that the ability of a community-based approach to engage farmers in relationships of reciprocity ... tends to increase the more that responsibilities under the approach are devolved towards the local level. However, further evidence is needed for this proposition to be evaluated with reasonable confidence.

Other empirical evidence regarding the relationship between community-based polycentric governance and civic virtue comes from a study by Marshall, Hine, and East (2017) that was designed to test hypotheses deduced from SDT. The study sought to determine whether community-based, compared with government-centred, governance would increase citizens' support in the form of donations to a trust fund designed to support climate change adaptation. A total of 548 adults sampled from the Australian state of New South Wales (NSW) were randomly assigned to view one of two governance scenarios – government-centred and community-based. Each participant had been informed they would receive a supplementary payment of AUD$10 for participating in the study.

After briefly describing climate change threats, both scenarios advised that a trust fund had recently been established to increase the funds available for investing in the participant's region's capacities to adapt to climate change impacts.

In the government-centred scenario, the trust 'was established, and will be administered, by the regional office of the NSW Government agency responsible for helping communities adapt to climate change' (Marshall, Hine, and East 2017, 5). In the community-based scenario, the trust was established at:

a meeting between community representatives of voluntary community groups ... working on natural resource management issues in your region. The idea was further developed through a collaborative partnership between these community representatives and the regional office of the NSW Government agency responsible for helping communities adapt to climate change. The partners agreed that final decisions on how to invest the funds donated to the trust would be made by a committee comprised entirely of representatives from your regional community. (Marshall, Hine, and East 2017, 5)

Hence, the content of the two scenarios was identical, other than the description of the relative roles of government and community in establishing the trust fund and deciding how funds held in the trust would be invested.

Following the administration of the experimental treatment, participants answered questions regarding the degree to which governance
arrangements for the trust fund described in the scenario were perceived
as supportive of their community's autonomy, and about their personal
motivations for supporting such a trust. Finally, participants were asked
how much of their supplementary payment they would be willing to
donate to the trust fund, noting that they could keep what they chose
not to donate. Participants were informed following the study that the
scenarios were fictitious and they could keep all of their supplementary
payment, regardless of what they had agreed to donate.

Path analysis revealed that the community-based scenario yielded significantly higher levels of perceived autonomy support among the study's
participants. High levels of perceived autonomy support predicted higher
levels of autonomous motivation (or civic virtue) and lower levels of
amotivation. This motivational pattern predicted, in turn, significantly
greater willingness to donate to the trust fund. The conclusion from these
findings was that 'community-based governance may be an effective strategy for reducing crowding-out effects, and thereby strengthening citizenship, in institutional initiatives to facilitate climate change adaptation'
(Marshall, Hine, and East 2017, 7). Noting that the regional level was
chosen as the focus of both governance scenarios since it is a level at which
government-centred and community-based governance arrangements
have both operated in Australia, including under the NRM regional delivery model, it was suggested that future research could examine whether the
influence of community-based governance on civic virtue (and thereby
citizenship) depends on the spatial level at which individuals are able to
engage with this governance.

9.5 Conclusion and Suggestions for Further Research

Elinor Ostrom (2010, 665) closed her Nobel Prize acceptance address by
arguing that 'a core goal of public policy should be to facilitate the
development of institutions that bring out the best in humans. We need
to ask how polycentric institutions can help or hinder the innovativeness,
learning, adapting, trustworthiness, levels of cooperation of participants,
and the achievement of more effective, equitable, and sustainable outcomes
at multiple scales . . .'. In this chapter we have offered some answers to this
question, particularly in respect of the capacities and motivations of
citizens to contribute towards governance of collective action in conserving
nature and natural resources. In doing so, we have looked towards

scholarship from both the 'political theory' and 'policy analysis' traditions of the Bloomington School of Political Economy.

We find that polycentric governance does have potential to foster and sustain these capacities and motivations comprising environmental citizenship. We conclude also that the prospects for realizing this potential in any given context depend on how the governance is actually established and operated, which depends in turn on the metaconstitutional conditions pertaining to that context. The literature we have reviewed suggests that the potential for polycentric governance to strengthen and sustain environmental citizenship will be realized to the extent that this governance is established and operated in accordance with the subsidiarity principle and E. Ostrom's (1990) nesting principle; i.e. as a system of community-based governance. It suggests also that covenantal practices akin to those identified by V. Ostrom (1991) as central to the incremental development of American democracy may be important, more generally, for establishing and running such community-based systems of polycentric governance.

The evidence base from which these propositions have been derived remains patchy, however. Further empirical studies of the relationship between community-based governance and environmental citizenship are required to corroborate (or not) the few such evaluations completed to date. Although experimental evidence of the important role of face-to-face communication in enabling self-organized solutions to commons dilemmas is consistent with the identification of covenantal practices as integral to the evolution of American democracy, further research is needed to increase our understanding of the significance of such practices in diverse cultural and institutional settings, including within and between higher (including governmental and supranational) levels of governance.

Our understanding of the metaconstitutional conditions conducive to community-based governance (and its underpinning covenantal practices) in settings of environmental management, and of how to establish and sustain those conditions, is particularly thin. While the corrosive effects of political modernism on these conditions are clear, it is far less clear how these effects might be reversed in contemporary settings such that the prospects of establishing community based environmental governance, and in turn the environmental citizenship on which it depends, are made more favourable. There is a crucial role here for research that helps us to better understand the obstacles and opportunities in achieving such transitions in diverse settings. Specific research questions here include: (i) Are covenants (or functionally-equivalent understandings) universal or culturally specific? (ii) Is a norm of non-dominance jointly sufficient with covenant for well-functioning polycentric governance? (iii) Can entrepreneurial efforts to revive covenantal understandings improve the performance of polycentric governance in tackling environmental sustainability challenges? (iv) Beyond the empiricist concepts we use in positivist social science, what ways of knowing are appropriate for analysis of metaconstitutional concepts relating to metaphysics?

In this chapter, we particularly focused on the capacities and motivations of citizens in shaping polycentric governance. In contrast, Chapter 10 focuses on the challenges that citizens face when they aim to structure common affairs in the interests of overall societal welfare.

10

The Faustian Bargain

Power-Sharing, Constitutions, and the Practice of Polycentricity in Governance

Vlad Tarko, Edella Schlager, and Mark Lutter

10.1 Introduction

Polycentric governance arrangements often emerge in a bottom-up fashion. This is achieved by members of a society negotiating and agreeing upon a 'constitution'. Polycentric systems involve multiple, overlapping centres of decision-making, operating under formal and informal overarching rules, some of which the centres themselves may create and enforce (see Chapter 1 for more details). These overarching rules are 'constitutions' broadly understood. They spell out both how decision centres share power, often in pursuit of common ends, and exercise autonomous authority in their respective realms.

How do individuals and communities come together to form such larger-scale governance arrangements? A large part of the study of polycentric arrangements focuses on how quasi-independent decision centres can successfully address their coordination problems by crafting and enforcing good overarching rules (E. Ostrom 1990, 2005a, 2010; V. Ostrom 1991; V. Ostrom, E. Ostrom, Gardner, and Walker 1994). When communities succeed in preventing abuses of power and facilitating coordination, their constitutions maintain legitimacy, and credible commitments to follow and enforce the rules are preserved, making long-term productive interactions among members possible.

The process of constitution formation involves difficult trade-offs such as (i) devising governing arrangements sufficiently robust to act, but not so robust as to create unchecked power and (ii) creating credible commitments to existing rules, while also allowing adaptation of the rules to new challenges. In this chapter, we explore these challenges of constitution formation and power-sharing among centres of decision-making. We first introduce the concept of the 'Faustian' bargain, before addressing constitutive rules and explain how constitutive rules create the possibility of Faustian bargains. We then turn to the role of monitoring, conflict resolution, and sanctioning as means of building commitment to constitutions and how they may both provide for stability and flexibility. Finally, we illustrate different Faustian bargains through two cases of constitution-making: the New York City Watersheds, in which power-sharing occurs between the city government, counties, towns and villages, and the state of New York; and post-conflict situations, in which leaders of different ethnic groups come to agreement. Creating polycentric arrangements is challenging and cannot be taken for granted, but it is possible even under harsh conditions. We conclude with reflections on power-sharing and the possibility of polycentric governance.

10.2 The Challenges of the Faustian Bargain

Constitution-making involves a 'Faustian bargain' in which individuals and smaller communities give up some of their autonomy for the sake of the benefits brought by larger-scale societies. Transitioning from small-scale quasi-egalitarian societies towards a complex, but more hierarchical, political system makes possible collective action and the provision of public goods at much larger scales (Bednar 2009). This includes collective goods such as defence, establishing larger common markets, and basic infrastructure.

As defined, the concept of a Faustian bargain suggests a bottom-up process. Can the same happen from the top-down? Philosophical specula-tions aside, this has never happened, as large political units created in a top-down fashion have always been created by military force, and, as such, have failed to satisfy a self-governance ideal. The top-down creation of rules seems compatible to voluntary agreements only in relatively small-scale firms, organizations and clubs. As the scale gets large and if the rules are imposed from the top-down, it is highly unlikely that the top-down designers have the knowledge and/or the incentives to do things right (E. Ostrom 2005a; and see also Chapter 9). As a result, self-governing large-scale communities result from a bottom-up negotiating process, in which the smaller scale communities decide, via their representatives, to merge (along certain dimensions). In the process of such mergers, new higher-level institutional positions are created for the purpose of facilitating the large-scale organization. The largest scale example of such a process is the formation of the European Union, but as we illustrate later (Section 10.4), the same logic applies in a wider range of circumstances.

The fundamental challenge of any Faustian bargain is the following: in creating larger-scale governments, even via a self-governing negotiation process, oppression becomes a real possibility, particularly if poorly designed systems of political representation are created that give unchecked power to the rulers. The dilemma posed by the Faustian bargain is whether it is possible to reap the benefits of large-scale cooperation without unwittingly unleashing the forces of oppression and exploitation.

The classic solution to this dilemma, as developed by Montesquieu and *The Federalist*, is to have separation of powers and checks-and-balances, such that no single actor can have purely discretionary power over many others. The separation of powers is both between different types of institutions (executive, legislative, judiciary, civil society), and between different levels within a federal system. Federal systems are conventionally associated with quasi-hierarchical states and provinces, but Vincent Ostrom and others have challenged this view, and proposed instead a polycentric perspective (Bish 1999; V. Ostrom 1987, 1991; Bish 2014; Wagner 2005; see also Chapter 9). Rather than focusing exclusively on the analysis of the interactions between federal levels, they have shifted the attention to the governance options that a federal system provides to individuals, and to the fact that various public goods can be provided via a variety of arrangements between federal levels. This allows us to see more clearly how authority is shared among multiple centres of power that may cooperate to realize benefits that no single centre of power could realize alone, while checking one another's exercise of authority.

Another challenge involves maintaining long-term commitment to the constitution even as the circumstances that led to its creation change. The functioning of a constitution depends on credible commitments to monitoring, enforcement and sanctioning, and conflict resolution (North 1993; E. Ostrom 2005a). Otherwise, the rules stipulated in the constitution are merely rules-in-form. The commitments made under the constitution become credible when the outcomes of monitoring, enforcement/sanctioning, and conflict resolution are seen to support productive relations and limit opportunism. However, too much stability over the long term may lead to fragility if the governing arrangements established by the constitution become maladapted to new challenges. But allowing for ready change may also lead to instability as competing centres of authority may attempt to devise rules to benefit themselves at the expense of others. Thus, the challenge is to find a workable balance between stability and flexibility of the governing arrangements.

10.3 The Institutional Analysis of Political Power

The expansion of collective action (both geographically and in scope) by moving away from small-scale-quasi-unanimous decision-making to more extensive governing arrangements is made possible by the creation of representatives authorized to take decisions affecting an entire community. The use of constitutive rules by which the institutional reality of human societies is built (V. Ostrom 1980, 1997; Rust 2006; Searle 1995, 2003, 2005, 2010; Tomasello 2009), allows for the expansion of collective action. These are rules that establish *positions* or *social roles* (such as a 'representative') with specific rights and obligations, and which, under specific conditions, can be occupied by certain people, but not others. Such constitutive rules make possible complex patterns of authority and are the key to understanding both political power and the idea of rule of law. Furthermore, the process of institutional change is best understood through the lens of constitutive rules. Institutional changes can involve either a gradual reinterpretation of the rights and obligations defined by apparently stable constitutive rules, or a change in the formal structure of the constitutive rules. This roughly corresponds to Buchanan's distinction between constitutional moments (which fundamentally alter the constitutive rules themselves) and regular political activities (which operate within a given constitution) (Buchanan and Brennan 1985; Buchanan and Tullock 1962; Congleton 2014).

10.3.1 Constitutive Rules

The idea of constitutive rules recognises how institutions *enable* new types of behaviours (French 1967). For example, a game of chess does not exist absent of its rules – these rules enable the very existence of 'chess'. Similarly, constitutive rules are everywhere in the social realm. The nexus of contracts that defines positions in a firm or the constitution that defines a democratic state include constitutive rules. Institutions from marriage laws to election laws involve establishing networks of abstract institutional positions with rights and obligations, thus creating new social situations that would not exist in the absence of those constitutive rules.

Institutional economics usually defines 'institutions' in terms of *constraints*, or regulatory rules (Crawford and E. Ostrom 1995; North 1990). But constraints only allow us to analyse how pre-existing behaviours might be channelled into productive or unproductive directions. This is useful,

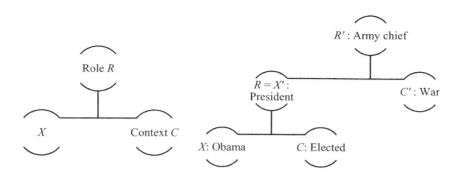

(a) General formula   **(b) Example of an institutional network**

Figure 10.1 Searle's role assignment formula and the creation of institutional networks: (a) General formula and (b) Example of an institutional network
Source: Searle 1995

and tools such as game theory allow us to analyse the consequences of alternative sets of constraints. But how does the set of possible behaviours come into existence? It is the concept of constitutive rules that allow us to explain how institutional arrangements enlarge the realm of possible human activities, and why people occupying different positions have different sets of options available to them.

Searle (1995, 2003, 2006, 2010) proposes that behind the bewildering complexity of human societies rests a single simple *role assignment formula,* which assigns an institutional function to people, things or animals (Rust 2009). As Searle (2006) put it, '[w]hat you discover when you go behind the surface phenomena of social reality is a relatively simple underlying logical structure even though the manifestations in actual social reality in political parties, social events, and economic transactions are immensely complicated'.

The role assignment formula (the 'constitutive rule') states that an item X is assigned the institutional role R in context C.[1] The key to social complexity is that the terms X and C can be defined in institutional terms themselves, and we can thus obtain highly complex recurrent formulae – i.e. a complex *network* of institutional roles (Figure 10.1). For example, the president (an institutional role) is also the commander of the army (a different role whose occupant is assigned depending on the first one). In

---

[1] There is some controversy as to whether this formula is indeed sufficient. Searle (2010) introduced some amendments in response to critics, but, for the sake of simplicity, it is sufficient here to stick to the original account (Searle 1995).

other words, the label 'army chief' is not attached directly to a flesh-and-blood person, it is attached to another label (the 'president'), and only indirectly to the person who has this other label.

As such, we can see *social order as a network of institutional roles, rather than of actual people*. People *inhabit* institutional roles and bring with them their personal preferences and their knowledge, thus affecting the specific ways in which the network operates and its concrete outcomes in terms of consumption, production and distribution, but social order still remains a network of *roles* and not of people (Lawson 2012). We know that this is so because, to a very large extent, any particular individual is replaceable – no one is necessary for the survival of the social order – while the undermining of certain constitutive rules (and the institutional roles defined by them) *can* cause a breakdown in social order.

The contexts are events that happen, but even aspects of the context and how it is understood depend on various institutional factors. For example, 'war' may mean that a foreign army crosses the border – and both 'border' and 'army' are institutional constructions (e.g. when armed members of a Mexican drug cartel cross the US border it does not count as 'Mexico started a war with United States' because of the way in which the 'army' is defined).[2]

The concept of constitutive rules applied to Elinor Ostrom's work on common-pool resources highlights the importance of a number of theoretical claims that she makes about self-governance (E. Ostrom 1990, 2005a), which apply to polycentric governance arrangements as well (Heikkila, Schlager, and Davis 2011; Schlager, Heikkila, and Case 2012). In particular, constitutive rules define the positions found in many of the design principles for long enduring self-governing arrangements (E. Ostrom 1990). These positions are occupied by resource users who bring their knowledge and experience to bear in designing governance rules (design principle two), monitoring compliance (design principle four), and resolving conflicts (design principle six). Thus, the design principles provide explanatory power not just because they capture key governing activities (rulemaking, monitoring, sanctioning), but also because resource users hold at least some of the positions, and these positions are linked. For instance, an irrigator may also be a monitor, and a representative to a governing board (Coward 1979; Tang 1992). It is

---

[2] Recent discussions about Russia's 'hybrid-wars' can be understood from this perspective as well.

these multiple, linked positions that are defined by constitutive rules that support self-governance.

10.3.2 The Faustian Bargain

V. Ostrom (1987, 140) has noted that '[a]ll systems of government *enable* a few to exercise extraordinary powers of government in relation to others' (emphasis added). This, in a nutshell, represents the Faustian bargain. Faustian bargains emerge as small-scale societies in which collective decisions are reached by quasi-consensus, grow and the scale of society increases. As such, the regular members of society give up their individual power to veto every collective decision for the sake of the benefits brought by the larger-scale coordination. This larger-scale coordination is mediated and made possible by representatives – who are given power thanks to the operation of constitutive rules. The 'Faustian bargain' refers to the bargain between the regular members of society and the representatives. It is 'Faustian' because of the risks it creates for the regular members of society. When representatives are given powers, they may abuse them. But it is a 'bargain' because the risk may be worth it. The benefits of large-scale coordination can be substantial (Buchanan and Tullock 1962, chapter15; V. Ostrom 1987, 97–101).

Careful attention must be given to the design of governing systems in which representatives exercise authority in relation to citizens. The delegation of authority to representatives must be sufficient to enable action, but not so robust as to permit abuse. For example, as showcased by *The Federalist*, constraining power was a concern embedded in the very design of political roles (V. Ostrom, 1987, 1991). As Vincent Ostrom has noted,

A government in a limited constitutional republic does not have the prerogative of defining its own authority. ... If governments were free to define their own authority, there would be no incentive for them to impose limits upon that exercise of authority. Furthermore, those who exercise governmental authority would, then, have incentives to use those prerogatives to their own advantage and to the disadvantage of those who oppose them. (V. Ostrom 1987, 62–63)

Dividing and limiting authority is the common prescription for addressing the dilemma presented by the Faustian bargain, but careful attention must be paid to the quality of political relationships (V. Ostrom 1997). Encouraging the creation of multiple centres of authority supports self-rule and the representation of many and diverse interests. However, multiple centres of authority must be provided with opportunities to productively take one another into account, otherwise the result is just fragmentation that fails to realize the potential coordinative benefits of polycentric governance.

This balance of authority and constraint is represented by the overarching rules that provide the context for the creation and functioning of polycentric governing arrangements. This balance is exhibited by the relations among centres of decision-making, in particular, how self-rule and shared-rule characterise such relations.

10.3.3 Self-Rule and Shared-Rule

Polycentric governing arrangements are a particular form of a Faustian bargain, intended to limit the abuse of authority while still allowing for collective action to provide shared benefits and solve shared problems among multiple centres of decision-making. Constitutions that enable the creation of polycentric governing arrangements pay attention to the quality of political relationships, allowing for self-rule and shared-rule simultaneously (Bednar 2009; Elazar 1987). Self-rule refers to centres of decision-making, whose identities, authorities, and autonomy are created by their own constitutions. Shared-rule supports the cooperation and coordination of centres of decision-making, while moderating and managing competition and conflict. Shared-rule is likewise dependent on constitutions that define the larger institutional context. Self-rule and shared-rule directly relate to the two challenges presented by the Faustian bargain, exclusion of interests and commitment to constitutional order while allowing for adaptation.

The creation of multiple centres of decision-making, or multiple sites for self-rule, provides opportunities for communities of interest to be organized and represented in political decision-making (Oakerson 1999; Schlager and Blomquist 2008). This occurs as citizens, drawing upon constitution-making authorities provided by the larger institutional context, devise governments, either special purpose or general purpose, to address shared problems, as we illustrate in the cases below (V. Ostrom 1987). As V. Ostrom (1987) recognizes, it is not possible to bound government jurisdictions in every instance so as to only or adequately include communities of interest. Nevertheless, creating multiple centres of decision-making increases the options for providing more responsive representation. In addition, the internal constitution of centres of decision-making allow for different combinations of interest representation in decision-making. As V. Ostrom (1987) illustrates in developing the logic of the US Constitution, different decision-making rules are used for different types of decisions. Crisis, such as an invasion by another country may be best addressed, at least initially, by a single decision-maker, the Commander-in-Chief of the Armed Forces, who is also the President. However, for solving other social problems, adopting legislation through simple majority may be sufficient (V. Ostrom 1987). Also, varying the constituencies of political representatives allows for different combinations of interests to be considered. Some representatives may be selected to represent all of the citizens of a jurisdiction, whereas other representatives are selected by district.

Allowing self-rule to flourish makes encouraging and supporting shared-rule critical. Shared-rule attends to a different set of political relationships. Shared-rule focuses on relations among centres of decision-making – managing conflict, supporting cooperation and coordination, guiding competition – all in the name of realizing the benefits of collective goods that individual centres of decision-making could not individually provide (Bednar 2009). As discussed, Bednar (2009) explains that productive relations among centres of decision-making are supported by providing safeguards that discourage shirking, limit opportunities for encroachment on one another's authorities, and limit the shifting of burdens from one jurisdiction to another. Each of these forms of opportunism undermines commitment to the larger constitutional order. Safeguards such as an independent judiciary for settling disputes, or transparent monitoring of actions and contributions, or shared decision-making venues populated by representatives of centres of decision-making, work to dissuade opportunism and encourage commitment to the constitutional order (Bednar 2009; Garrick, Schlager, and Villamayor-Tomás 2016). Furthermore, safeguards provide opportunities to make minor and major rule changes. Courts may reinterpret rules to better fit the existing setting, monitoring may uncover poorly designed rules that require revision, and decision-making venues may provide opportunities for rule innovation (Bednar 2009).

The political relationships that polycentric governance makes possible can counter the corrosive effects of exclusion of interests, while supporting compliance and commitment to the constitutions that make this type of governance possible. However, all artefacts reflect the skills and shortcomings of their artisans. If the artisans do not view each other and their artefacts as legitimate partners in governance, then self-rule and shared-rule are unlikely to be realized (Elazar 1987; V. Ostrom 1980).

10.3.4 The Concept of 'Rule of Law'

Supporting legitimacy of 'partners in governance' raises the concept of 'rule of law'. What do we mean by 'rule of law' societies (Buchanan and Congleton 1998; Hayek 1960; V. Ostrom 1987) and how does this relate to polycentric governance? Intuitively, a rule of law society is one in which there is 'neither domination nor discrimination' (to use Buchanan's famous quip). It is a society in which everyone is subjected to the same rules, the rules are not changed on a whim, and they are known in advance.

Besides such clarifications, the idea remains notoriously difficult to define more rigorously (Rajagopalan and Wagner 2013). The problem is that rules which deliberately create privileges and differential costs and benefits to special groups can be (and, in practice, often are) framed in a language that seems universal, and such a '[f]ailure to establish proper standards in legislation contributes to the general erosion of the rule of law' (V. Ostrom 1987, 212). But how are such 'standards' to be defined? If we look at *constitutive rules*, i.e. at how the roles are defined and at who can occupy them, we can, at least to some extent, overcome this important problem. Consider the following tentative proposal.

To understand what it means to have a society of laws, we need to look at the nature of the constitutive rules that create authority. At least at first glance, the following four basic criteria regarding the definition of political roles seem particularly relevant for assessing and evaluating whether a rule of law system is in place: (1) *Degree of free entry*: Who is eligible to occupy political roles? (2) *Predictability*: Are the rights and attributes of political roles invariant to changes of the particular flesh-and-blood person occupying them?[3] (3) *Degree of free exit*: How easy is it for those subjected to one authority to escape if they so desire? (4) *Degree of contestation*: How easy it is for those subjected to one authority to successfully challenge that authority when it over-reaches beyond its rights or fails to comply with its obligations?

First, if the constitutive rules define political roles with heavily restricted entry, then that is not a rule of law society. Although theoretically a dictator might uphold the rule of law, in practice this does not happen because of incentive-incompatibility. Absolutist monarchies are a typical example. Modern dictatorships may have free entry on paper, but in

---

[3] Interestingly, this is how children learn the concept of 'rules', by learning that *everyone* performing a particular role (e.g. in games played repeatedly) is subjected to the *same* rights and obligations (Tomasello 2009, 91–92).

practice they also have very strong entry restrictions to positions of power. Such restrictions of entry create an obvious separation between a dominant group and a group of subjects.

Second, even where entry is not restricted, if the rights and obligations associated with the role change significantly once a new person occupies it, we also do not have a rule of law society. In such a case, the rule of law society exists only on paper, mimicking the outer forms but lacking the substantive nature of an actual rule of law society. For example, the Indian constitution has changed so often since independence that the key institutional positions have lacked any long-term stability (Rajagopalan 2013).

Finally, the extent to which authority may be abused is a consequence of the constraints on exit and contestation (see also Chapter 3). If exit is very costly, for example because political units are so large that leaving involves prohibitive individual costs, the efficiency of Tiebout competition is diminished (Boettke, Coyne, and Leeson 2011; Howell-Moroney 2008; McPhail and Tarko 2017; Ostrom, Tiebout, and Warren 1961; Tiebout 1956). Alongside the possibility to complain and lobby for institutional changes ('voice'), the possibility of people simply leaving ('exit') badly governed jurisdictions creates constraints about how poor the performance of a government can get (Hirschman 1970). In the most obvious sense, this constraint manifests as diminished tax revenues, but they also touch upon other, most subtle factors, such as a loss of human capital ('brain-drain'). It is, indeed, not surprising that the most poorly governed countries also severely restrict the possibility of citizens emigrating.

10.3.5 The Interpretative Dynamic of Institutional Change

When the Supreme Court is interpreting the US Constitution, it is constantly creating a new *representation* of the roles, responsibilities, and rights, a representation that is adapted to whatever the new context is (e.g. the right to bear arms in light of new types of weapons). The point is that institutional reality is actually the set of institutional roles with their rights and obligations, which are then constantly reinterpreted as new contexts arise. This is what Searle (2010) means by 'institutional reality is maintained in its continued existence by representations'. All constitutions, laws and regulations can be seen as metaphors in constant need of interpretation.

Such constant reinterpretation creates obvious possible problems to the concept of rule of law, so some safeguards to reinterpretation are needed. Bednar (2009) develops a safeguards theory of federalism, but the safeguards may apply to polycentric governing arrangements more generally (Garrick, Schlager, and Villamayor-Tomás 2016). Safeguards are venues for holding actors accountable for their choices and actions. Those venues may include citizens voting for representatives and ballot initiatives or engaging in civil disobedience to protest the overreach of representatives. Political safeguards are mechanisms for public officials to coordinate their activities to respond to, as well as to express demands for change, such as political parties or associations of public officials, such as associations of mayors or governors. These safeguards may either constrain or penalize actions found to violate rules, or they may provide new interpretations of rules, or even confirm innovative actions not anticipated by rules.

This leads to the recognition of two qualitatively different types of institutional changes, mirroring Buchanan's distinction between changes within the rules (see Chapter 4) and changes of the rules (Buchanan and Brennan 1985; Buchanan and Tullock 1962; Congleton 2014; Lesson and Boettke 2009): major structural changes involve changes to the network of institutional roles itself, while relatively minor interpretative changes involve merely changes of their representations in terms of constraints. For instance, take the example of a parliamentary democracy where the president is also the chief of the army. When parliament limits the military budget, this creates constraints on the president acting in its function as army chief. By contrast, if, thanks to a constitutional change, the army is moved from under the authority of the president to that of a prime minister, a major institutional change has occurred.

To summarize, much of political phenomena can be understood by looking at the rules that establish who can occupy which role under which context. For example, immigration policies are all about the conditions under which foreigners can become 'visitors', 'residents', or 'citizens'. Institutional change involves either gradual reinterpretation of existing roles (i.e. gradual changes in their rights and obligations or in the rules for how to obtain them), or greater constitutive changes in the very structure of roles (i.e. involving the addition or elimination of certain roles).

10.4 Examples of Constitution-Making via Faustian Bargaining

10.4.1 New York City Watersheds Governing Arrangements

Constitution-making can occur at different scales, from the international to the local. It may result in the creation of general purpose and special purpose governments (Hooghe and Marks 2003); consequently, the process of constitution-making can include a wide variety of actors, from representatives of governments to non-profit organizations and citizens, all of whom will be subject to the new constitution. The diversity in type of governments, and in participants engaged in its creation, is illustrated by the New York City Watersheds governing arrangements.

Historically, New York City has sourced its potable water from upstream watersheds, such as the Delaware and the Catskills (Soll 2013). In order to develop the water and deliver it to the city, the state of New York granted extraordinary powers to the city, including the power of eminent domain by which the city could acquire land for dams, reservoirs, tunnels, and canals by a coercive process of purchasing the land, even if the landowner was unwilling to sell. In addition, the city used its power of eminent domain to condemn and acquire land for buffers so that economic activities, such as dairy farming, would not pollute its water sources (Soll 2013). Finally, the city was granted the authority to regulate activities, particularly all sorts of construction activities (road building, construction of housing, bridge building) that may negatively affect water quality. Before construction activities could commence, project owners would have to obtain permits from the city and those permits were conditioned on taking actions to minimize environmental impacts. Furthermore, the city deployed its own police force in the watershed to monitor for trespassing on its lands and to ensure that its regulations were followed (Hanlon 2015). This approach for realizing the requirements of New York City for potable water was very exclusive.

The towns, villages, and counties, not to mention private businesses and citizens found the role and activities of the city to be onerous. The authority granted to the city to protect its watersheds led to abuses of power, from the perspective of the citizens, towns and counties. They had few mechanisms for holding the city accountable and even fewer options for participating in decision-making that directly affected economic activities and recreational opportunities in the watersheds. Tensions and conflicts were high. Towns, counties, and non-profit organizations regularly turned to the courts, a form of safeguard, to challenge the city's actions, especially around the practice of eminent domain (Galusha 1999; Platt, Barten, and Pfeffer 2010).

It was in this context of conflict and tension that constitution-making occurred. In 1986, the US Environmental Protection Agency amended the Safe Drinking Water Act, requiring the treatment and filtration of potable water supplies prior to delivery for final consumption. Cities could avoid the considerable expense of building and operating treatment infrastructure if they could demonstrate that their water supplies met drinking-water standards and that they exercised sufficient control over their water sources to ensure that water-quality standards would continue to be met. The cost of filtration for a large water system (around 8 million customers) was estimated to be as high as $US 5 billion for constructing the infrastructure and tens of millions each year for operations and maintenance (New York City Independent Budget Office). The city and the state, wanting to avoid such expense, searched for alternatives.

The Governor of New York convinced the city and the watershed jurisdictions to attempt to devise a governing arrangement that would provide better protection for watershed quality, while addressing the long simmering grievances of the residents of the watersheds (Soll 2013). The result was the New York City Watersheds Memorandum of Agreement (MOA 1997), which is a constitution that created a polycentric governing arrangement. The city gave up its power of eminent domain and replaced it with a land acquisition program in which the city and the watershed towns and villages would jointly agree on areas in which the city would be allowed to solicit land for acquisition from willing sellers only (MOA 1997, Article). In addition, the city agreed to invest in environmentally sensitive economic development and infrastructure investment activities, such as wastewater treatment plants and septic systems (MOA 1997, Article). The economic development and infrastructure programmes were to be developed and implemented by the Catskills Watershed Corporation, a non-profit organization, whose board of directors are representatives of the City and watershed jurisdictions (MOA 1997, Article IV).

In addition to shared decision-making venues, this constitution also provides a conflict-resolution mechanism and credible enforcement mechanisms. The Watershed Protection and Partnership Council (WPPC) was created to both monitor compliance with the constitution and provide a means of resolving conflicts (MOA 1997, Article IV). If a jurisdiction disagreed with an action taken by another jurisdiction, a complaint could be filed with the WPPC, which would attempt to resolve the complaint. In addition, if the City failed to fund any of the economic development programmes, the watershed jurisdictions could petition the State to suspend the land acquisition program until payments resumed (MOA 1997, Article II). Conversely, if the watershed jurisdictions sued the City over land acquisitions under the new process, the City could suspend its funding of economic development activities (MOA 1997, Article IV).

The New York City Watersheds governing arrangement replaced a highly centralized and non-representative system with a polycentric arrangement composed of different centres of authority that represented the interests of the multiple jurisdictions. The governing arrangement has been in place for twenty years and has survived multiple threats (Hanlon 2015). While the constitution has not been amended in that time period, the governments have developed additional programmes, such as a riparian buffer system, to address new problems as they have arisen. The MOA revised the previous governing arrangement by sharing power among towns, counties, and New York City. It provided for collective benefits that they could not singly provide (e.g. high water quality and economic development investments) and it encouraged cooperation through multiple safeguards designed to detect and correct opportunism. The transformation of the original Faustian bargain, in which New York City exercised lightly checked authority, to one built on shared decision-making among the watershed jurisdictions and New York City, was made possible by changes in the larger institutional setting. That setting provided opportunities for the creation of a polycentric arrangement that allowed for robust, but limited, government.

10.4.2 Post-Conflict Situations

Some of the most difficult examples of constitution-making are those following conflict situations, especially those among different ethnic groups. A paradigmatic example is the establishment of relative peace in two regions of former Somalia: Somaliland (a region in north-western Somalia) and, to a lesser extent, Puntland (in northeast Somalia). After independence from Italy and Britain and unification in 1960, the country was ruled by a brutal dictator until 1991. After 1991, a civil war occurred and the country is still considered to be in a state of anarchy. The situation around the former capital, Mogadishu, is outside the scope of the present analysis, due to heavy outside involvement by the United States of America and United Nations. By contrast, Somaliland and Puntland, especially because they lack international recognition as independent states, have had to largely solve their problems endogenously.

After the war, Somaliland lay in ruins:

In Hargeysa [the future capital of Somaliland], a town of nearly 300,000 people, barely 10% of the structures remained intact, leaving only a vast field of blasted rubble strewn with explosives. ... Burco [the second largest city], to the east, had suffered roughly 70% destruction, and countless villages in the interior had been razed to the ground. Hospitals, schools, clinics and wells had all been destroyed, government offices ransacked, bridges blown up, and roads mined and made impassable. (War Torn Societies Project 2005, 24)

In this context, a series of inter-clan wars and peace agreements followed. All these agreements were organized by local clan leaders, rather than by international organizations. In February 1991, the Somali National Movement, a group made up of Isaaq clan members, tried to form an interim government for Somaliland, and in May 1991 clan elders from Isaaq, Harti, and Dir clans organized a peace conference in Burco. After three years of peace, the agreement failed in 1994 and all-out war lasted again until 1996. From October 1996 to February 1997 another peace conference was organized, with a formal end of hostilities declared. This peace has proved lasting. A referendum over a formal constitution was organized in 2001, establishing a democratic government (Bradbury 2008). Multi-party parliamentary elections and presidential elections have since been held, and international observers determined they were largely fair. The presidential vote in 2010 was delayed for two years, but then a peaceful transition of power occurred, with the ruling president voluntarily relinquishing power. Similarly, the 2015 presidential vote was also delayed by two years. A new president was elected, but he is from the same party as the previous one. Although Somaliland is still not an internationally recognized state, or perhaps *because* of it, it seems to have succeeded in creating a democratic society from the bottom-up. Moreover, this society is organized along polycentric lines, as an overarching set of rules was created, but without displacing the pre-existing lower-level rules.

A similar story occurred in Puntland, but somewhat less successfully (Mohamud and Nur 2007). After a period of war in 1991–93 between several military groups, the attempt to create a civilian government failed as one of the military leaders refused to step down. The Somali Salvation Democratic Front, which was fighting the United Somali Congress, organized a peace conference in 1994, but the different factions failed to reach agreement. However, local clan leaders were relatively more successful in establishing councils and settling disputes. Finally, in 1998, a local conference including participants from all Northeastern clans was held in Garowe and was successful in establishing a constitution and a government. However, in 2001 President Abdulahi Yusuf refused to step down from power, wanting another term, which sparked a new conflict with a part of the military. In 2003, a businessman managed to get the parties to stop hostilities, and Yusuf was succeeded by another president in 2004. Since then there were no more constitutional crises, and the country elected three different presidents. A new constitution was adopted in 2009 (and came into effect in 2012), instituting a multi-party democracy, alongside other reforms, including an expansion of the judicial system and stronger anti-terrorism policies.

Puntland is, on one hand, an example of a polycentric process in which the overarching rules that have facilitated conflict resolution during the conferences have been informal, rather than part of an existing written constitution. This is the case almost by definition in a post-conflict situation in which the pre-existing formal institutions have broken down. On the other hand, the first established constitution had important weaknesses as it failed to establish credible mechanisms for enforcing democratic results, but the resulting crisis seems to have generated enough impetus to fix the problem. It is still too early to tell whether other institutional weakness persist, but there is a clear change in the direction of a democratic system.

There are at least three important lessons to be learned from these cases. First, they both illustrate the difficulty of establishing a sustainable constitutional order. Second, they demonstrate that such an order can be established once all the parties affected are successfully brought together. Third, they remind us that governance is not merely a property of nation-states; it can be established, destroyed, rebuilt, and modified over many different spaces and peoples. The underlining rational-choice logic behind this kind of constitutional making is the fact that conflict is costly and all parties are able to recognise that they would be better off if they somehow succeeded in establishing a peaceful order (Hirschleifer 2001; Tullock 2005). Hence, all the parties have a strong vested interest in the constitution-making process, but whether the process succeeds depends on whether everyone's grievances and concerns are addressed. In other words, it depends on them forming together a polycentric governance system, rather than merely a fragmented version of polycentric governance, as a prerequisite of the constitutional-making process. These examples also showcase the very high stakes of the Faustian bargain. If the constitutional order does not properly guard against abuse, the peace will be fragile, as happened for a while in Puntland at tremendous cost to all the parties involved. Finally, this example also showcases that some of the key institutional roles, in this case the religious leaders organising the peace conferences, need not be entirely formal – they can be informal social roles underpinned by prestige and cultural norms.

10.5 Conclusion

The Faustian bargain emerges in any setting in which direct governance is replaced with some form of governance based on representatives, creating rulers and ruled. More complex governance allows for extensive collective action and the possibility of providing for collective goods that otherwise could not be realized. However, rulers may abuse their grants of authority. Wrestling with the Faustian bargain involves difficult trade-offs such as (i) devising governing arrangements sufficiently robust to act, but not so robust as to create unchecked power and (ii) creating credible commitments to existing rules, while also allowing adaptation of the rules to new challenges. In this chapter, we have explored these challenges of constitution formation and power-sharing among centres of decision-making. We examined the concept of constitutive rules, which establish *positions* or *social roles* (such as a 'representative') with specific rights and obligations, and makes possible constitutions that create complex patterns of authority. Constitutive rules make possible polycentric governing arrangements that allow for self-rule and shared-rule. For that to occur, however, monitoring, conflict resolution, and sanctioning mechanisms are necessary to support compliance with governing agreements and build commitment to constitutions. That commitment, in turn, allows for the possibility of revising constitutions in productive ways as circumstances change without falling back into exploitative relations. We illustrated different Faustian bargains through two cases of constitution-making: the New York City Watersheds governing arrangements, in which power-sharing occurs between the city government, counties, towns and villages, and the state of New York; and post-conflict situations, in which leaders of different ethnic groups come to agreement. These cases demonstrate the opportunities that productive relationships provide, but also the fragility of those relations, and the role of polycentric arrangements in creating robust forms of governance.

After Chapter 9 focused on the micro-level of analysis of individuals and this chapter focused on the challenges of structuring societal affairs through institutional choices and maintaining order in the context of ever-changing circumstances, in Chapter 11 we will address polycentric governance from a very different angle. We will leave behind our aim of providing greater conceptual and theoretical clarity to polycentric governance and inquiries about it. Instead we will focus on ways in which practitioners can use polycentric governance for inspiration about how to craft governance and what may be the tools to do so.

11

Practising Polycentric Governance

Bryan Bruns[1]

11.1 Introduction

Polycentric governance offers a perspective that emphasizes the potential for effective cooperation, conflict resolution, fruitful competition, and shared learning among multiple autonomous decision centres interacting with each other, such as:

- Federal governments with autonomous state governments and over-arching institutions;
- Local public economies composed of government agencies and specialized service providers in a metropolitan area;
- Nested natural resource management, as with multiple layers of water management organizations within irrigation systems and river basins; and
- Co-management between communities and agencies managing natural resources such as forests or fisheries.

The literature on polycentric governance and related ideas has emphasized practical principles, including the potential value of multiple centres and linkages across scales, empowering people to govern themselves, crafting institutions to fit specific situations, and sharing learning from diverse experiences and experiments. Table 11.1 summarizes these in a set of principles for practising polycentric governance.

The chapter begins with an example of polycentric practice in the development of land and water commons by communities in rural India,

[1] This work was partially supported by the CGIAR Research Program on Policies, Institutions, and Markets (PIM) led by the International Food Policy Research Institute (IFPRI). The opinions expressed here belong to the author, and do not necessarily reflect those of PIM, IFPRI, or CGIAR.

Table 11.1 *Principles for practising polycentric governance*

Organize at multiple scales. Do not assume that bigger is better, or that small is always beautiful. There are many alternatives to top-down hierarchies and institutional monocultures. Consider linking horizontally and across scales through federations, compacts, co-management agreements, and other overarching institutions for cooperation, regulation, conflict resolution, and competitive service provision. In exploring the scale and scope of how organizations could constitute institutions for cooperation and other fruitful interaction, consider not just government jurisdictions but also resource boundaries, the stakeholders involved, and 'problemsheds' around a particular issue.

Embrace self-governance. Accept and work with the necessary messiness, time-consuming processes, contestation, compromises, and trial-and-error of how self-governance with meaningful autonomy happens in practical politics among public and private actors. Acknowledge the importance of the consent of the governed, the distribution of power through checks-and-balances, and the challenges and opportunities these bring. Empower organizations to work together in solving problems. Enable institutional artisans to make agreements and put them into operation, for example through customary local governance practices, special districts, devolution of authority, contracts with service providers, court backing for binding agreements, and other mechanisms.

Customise solutions. Go beyond panaceas. Do not pursue or impose oversimplified standard solutions. There is no 'one best way' or unique set of 'best practices' that is ideal everywhere. Appreciate the benefits and complexity of institutional diversity and adaptation. Consider ways to increase flexibility, choice, and competition among alternative service providers. Analyse specific action situations to diagnose problems and identify opportunities. Encourage pragmatic innovation in crafting customized solutions.

Learn together. A core advantage that polycentric governance can offer is the opportunity to learn from multiple experiences, for example different communities, states, or other organizations trying different things to discover what may work and learning from each other as they proceed. Convene meetings, workshops, and other forums, as well as facilitating networks of communication, formal and informal that promote social learning.

---

including strengthening of community level governance and wider federations through processes that connect multiple communities, agencies, and programmes. Putting a polycentric perspective into practice can start with an assessment of existing polycentricity and participatory exploration of options for change, such as in the number of decision centres involved, their autonomy, and how they are linked. In crafting polycentric governance, institutional artisans can draw on a variety of mechanisms and design principles. Efforts to improve water governance in river and groundwater basins illustrate some of the opportunities and challenges for developing polycentric governance. The development of polycentric governance can be facilitated by institutional changes, including improving networks, sharing knowledge, and cultivating 'power with'.

11.2 Commoning Water: Polycentric Governance in Rajasthan

Rural communities in Rajasthan State in India face the challenges of governing shared surface and groundwater resources in the face of fluctuating monsoon rainfall. Technologies such as tube wells and pumps may help improve livelihoods, but risk leading to depletion of aquifers and degradation of land and water resources. The Foundation for Ecological Security (FES) works with communities to pursue a 'triple bottom line' of more inclusive and equitable governance, improved livelihoods, and environmental sustainability. Project activities help villagers to organize inclusive democratic institutions for managing land and water resources, understand the flows of surface and groundwater, claim or reclaim shared resources such as ponds and grazing land ('commoning'), increase surface and groundwater storage, and balance productive water use with renewable supplies (FES 2010, 2014).

A participatory planning process, including Participatory Rapid Appraisal (PRA) techniques, helps communities to assess their own resources and priorities, enhancing their capacity to cooperate with government programmes pro-actively as partners. This means engaging with programmes supported from outside as a way to pursue local goals, with deliberate selection and negotiation about when and how to cooperate with other organizations and programmes.

In this case, a key element of a polycentric strategy for change has been establishing inclusive governance institutions with universal membership at the 'habitation' level of small settlements. This strengthens organised, autonomous decision-making centres, in a way that is linked with a variety of other social actors and organizations. This is a key aspect of polycentricity, because habitations are the social villages of people who live close to each other and interact frequently, whereas the official 'revenue villages' are usually much larger and less tightly connected. Earlier FES work showed the limitations of focusing too narrowly on groups of resource users, such as forest user groups, particularly the risk of excluding poorer and more vulnerable people who may own little or no land, but who rely on common lands for fuel, food, fodder, and other resources. Organizing at the habitation level strengthens a centre of inclusive, democratic decision-making, which can then engage more effectively with other resource users, communities, agencies, and programmes.

This context contains multiple forms of polycentricity, with organizations ranging from households to settlements of various sizes through panchayats (sub-district level assemblies), districts and states, and multiple government units, including forest and water agencies. Activities go beyond individual communities to consider interaction with neighbouring communities that share land and water resources, such as ponds, aquifers, forests, and grazing land, as well as engaging with multiple levels of government jurisdictions and agencies involved in regulating land and water resources. Federations and other forums facilitate information-sharing, conflict resolution, and cooperation at multiple scales for forests and river basins.

11.3 Assessing Polycentricity in Governance

Stakeholder analysis and other techniques can explore the extent to which there are multiple actors involved in a situation, how they are connected, their converging or conflicting interests, and whether they already have a history of interacting with each other and are bound within larger sets of overarching rules. Stakeholder analysis may be relatively informal or more systematic, identifying those who are involved, their concerns, relationships, and how they might be engaged in making changes (Brugha and Varvasovszky 2000; Grimble and Wellard 1997; Prell, Hubacek, and Reed 2009; Reed et al. 2009; Sabatier et al. 2005; Varvasovszky and Brugha 2000). Participatory network mapping offers a practical and interesting way for stakeholder groups to visualize their connections (Hauck et al. 2015; Schiffer and Hauck 2010).

Conceptually, polycentricity may be analyzed in terms of the number of centres and how they are linked within social networks, including the extent of autonomy, mutual adjustment, cooperation, competition, conflict, and other interactions (Aligica and Tarko 2012; Lubell, Henry, and McCoy 2010). Systems may be tightly or loosely linked in networks and have power centralized or distributed, with polycentric systems typically having both strong linkages and distributed control (Cumming 2016). Polycentricity can be seen as a particularly interesting form of network governance (Carlsson and Sandström 2008; Jones, Hesterly, and Borgatti 1997), where many centres have substantial autonomy while being linked through overarching institutions.

Social network analysis (Borgatti, Everett, and Johnson 2013; Chaffin et al. 2016) offers tools for mapping and thinking about various patterns of linkage between individuals and organizations, and so holds considerable potential for a systematic understanding of the options for designing and modifying polycentric governance. From a social network perspective, diagnostic questions for assessing the extent of existing polycentricity and potential changes include asking:

- How are organizations and individuals connected, in terms of communication, influence, flows of funding and other resources, authority, and other links?
- What patterns do these linkages form, particularly in terms of the number of centres (nodes, clusters, etc.) and how these are connected?
- What do these patterns of linkages mean for awareness, voice, and ability to influence outcomes?
- What are the key linkages in terms of mutual adjustment (learning, cooperation, competition, conflict resolution, and so forth), and to what extent do these linkages allow or constrain autonomy? Are different centres tightly, moderately, or loosely connected?
- Are there major gaps or problems in the ways in which organizations are linked, particularly in terms of lack of overarching institutions, or lack of autonomy that could facilitate local adaptation, choice among service providers, learning, and performance improvements?

A polycentric perspective emphasizes the potential for self-governance, problem-solving arising from the initiative of people organizing themselves. An emphasis on self-governance involving multiple centres makes it particularly important to appreciate how those concerned with a problem or opportunity view their situation, their aspirations and priorities for change, and for them to take part in considering options and making decisions. Some particularly relevant approaches are part of what could be considered an 'appreciative turn' in applied social science, sharing a common concern with using participatory processes to understand what is good about the current situation, as a basis for those involved to consider potential improvements:

- PRA offers a philosophy and a variety of techniques through which people can use their own local knowledge to assess their situation and the available options for change, in ways that have been developed to be interesting, enjoyable, and empowering for those involved. PRA has been extensively applied in rural development, including situations where resources are shared between overlapping communities of users and as part of attempts to increase the involvement of communities in natural resources management, on their own or in co-management with government agencies (Chambers 1994). In the example discussed in Section 11.2, communities used PRA methods to map resources, assess trends, and consider options for change.

- SWOT analysis assesses strengths and opportunities, as well as weaknesses (problems) and threats (risks), providing a framework that tries to go beyond the tendency to only frame issues reactively in terms of problems, dangers, and deficiencies and instead to pay attention to capabilities and promising potentials.

- Appreciative inquiry (AI) asks people what they think is working well and how it could be made even better, emphasizing what they value and want more of. In contrast to a pre-occupation with problems, it concentrates on identifying positive options that are feasible and interesting for key stakeholders, including potential cooperation with other organizations (Cooperrider 2005; Mac Odell n.d.).

- Asset-based community development (Cunningham and Mathie 2002), and similar approaches also emphasize identifying the capacities that exist, and building on such strengths, often in the context of opportunities for partnering with external institutions.

- Positive deviance approaches emphasize looking at situations where things are 'going right' and exploring what might be learned to make things better elsewhere (Pascale, Sternin, and Sternin 2010).

- Albert Hirschman argued for the advantages of 'possibilism', building on what is already occurring and has been shown to be feasible in some cases, in ways that can harness the 'social energy' of citizen groups trying to better their lives, often in the context of working with other organizations (Ellerman 2006; Hirschman 1971, 1986; Lepenies 2008).

- While critical social science often emphasizes how social structures tend to serve existing interests and make change difficult, it also includes approaches that pay attention to the degree of autonomy, 'agency,' or 'room for manoeuvre', that various actors have. This may allow people to engage in initiatives and self-organize polycentrically. Meaningful and effective innovation may occur through using the opportunities that can be developed within existing structures of power (Gibson-Graham 2006).

- Citizens can be seen as 'co-creators' of their worlds, in how they implicitly and explicitly create, recreate, and transform ideas and institutions. (Boyte et al. 2014). Many approaches to improving people's capacity to act as citizens emphasize developing dialogue and deliberation among individuals and groups (NCDD 2017).

Assessment of existing polycentricity should include recognition of the extent to which various government agencies, and different units and levels within governments and their agencies, may have different interests and degrees of autonomy that would enable them to support or obstruct change. In practice, even situations that may appear hierarchical, such as within government or corporate bureaucracies, may contain many actors who have considerable discretion to help or hinder change. Rather than 'the state' as a unitary entity, governments at various levels are composed of a multiplicity of different agencies and interests. Courts and legislatures may offer a variety of forums and opportunities for action. Institutional diversity within governments enhances the possibility to construct coalitions and find venues to pursue particular goals.

The assessment of current polycentricity and the capabilities that may already exist provides a framework for thinking about what could be changed, and what changes may be most attractive and worthwhile for those involved.

- The number of centres could be expanded by establishing new ones, existing centres might be split up, or, alternatively, consolidated.
- The scale and scope of collective action could be changed to involve more centres, or fewer, bringing in more stakeholders, or focusing on a smaller coalition who may be ready to act.
- Inclusion of those who are left out or only weakly connected could help to promote better processes and outcomes.
- Interactions could be changed by activities to share information, or encourage cooperation, for example by convening meetings or providing funding for joint activities, as well as by constituting agreements about new overarching institutions that create rules, resolve conflicts, encourage competition, or organize collective efforts.
- There may be ways in which contestability among institutional alternatives can promote innovation and efficiency, for example competitive contracting in local public economies, or facilitating easier transfers of resources, movement of members between centres, or choices between service providers (exit options).
- Autonomy might be increased by devolving authority and money; or by reducing regulations, requirements for approval, or other

restrictions. Conversely, coordination, enforceable agreements, and conflict-resolution institutions may reduce autonomy, while helping to solve problems and achieve shared objectives.

11.4 Crafting Polycentric Governance

Citizens, including community leaders and government officials, act as public entrepreneurs and institutional artisans when they decide on ways to work together (V. Ostrom 1980). Institutional artisans may draw on a range of principles and mechanisms from many sources, including their own experience, public policy discussions, and research. The design of polycentric governance may benefit from frameworks such as institutional analysis and development (IAD) and social-ecological systems (Goodin 1996; E. Ostrom 2005a, 2009). However, while useful for analysts, such frameworks and associated methods often require more time to understand and apply than most participants have available. Those crafting new institutions usually take a more informal, improvisational, 'vernacular' approach to institutional artisanship, applying and modifying available patterns of organization. Rather than creating totally new institutions, the tendency is often to adapt existing institutions and organizations to new tasks, in a process of institutional bricolage, recombining familiar ideas and institutions in new ways (Cleaver 2012).

As an example of a trajectory for the development of polycentric governance, communication links for information-sharing could lead to informal collaboration, partnerships, cooperation in joint projects, and conflict resolution (Galaz et al. 2011). Existing institutional arrangements shape the potential for change, including restricting or expanding potential changes in polycentricity (DeCaro et al. 2017). A key question concerns the transaction costs of change, and whether the value of benefits and costs, and how they are distributed across stakeholders, make change attractive to those involved (Challen 2000; Coase 1990). Starting from the current situation, one can think about the 'adjacent possible' of feasible reforms (Kauffman 1995). Kauffman's idea of the adjacent possible draws on the analogy with chemical transformations in molecules: depending on the atomic properties and existing configurations, some changes require less energy and are easier to achieve. Other transformations may be much more difficult or dependent on special conditions.

On the one hand, a polycentric perspective can help expand the 'design space' of institutional options that are considered. Rather than assuming there is 'one best way', an ideal to be achieved, a single standardized solution or panacea, only one form of modernity, or just one form of polycentric governance, an open polycentric perspective can instead look at the space for institutional diversity, with multiple possible solutions, customized to match particular circumstances and needs (E. Ostrom, Janssen, and Anderies 2007). On the other hand, thinking about the adjacent possible may focus attention on more feasible nearby options that offer enough benefits, compared to the transaction costs of change, to attract initiative and support from stakeholders who can overcome obstacles to collective action.

There is sometimes a tendency to talk as if institutional changes can easily be deliberately designed, as if starting from scratch with a blank slate, or at least with great scope for making major changes. Closer study of institutional change suggests that most changes are highly constrained by history (path dependence), politics (contesting interests), and by the language (discourse) people use to think about and discuss their situation and the potential for change (Foucault 1984; North 1990; V. Ostrom 1997; Pierson 2000).Those crafting institutions make decisions, explicit and implicit, about what objectives to consider, including implications for equity, efficiency, sustainability and other characteristics of processes and outcomes. Efforts to institute polycentric reforms should be informed by an understanding of how differences in knowledge, power, wealth, and other characteristics may enhance or limit capabilities and the options for exploring and expanding the potential for improvement within or despite such conditions (Morrison et al. 2017). Concepts of citizenship and institutional artisanship are embedded in ideas and attitudes about who is entitled to have a voice in decisions, how people may be able to govern themselves and shape their shared lives, and how changes in ideas and attitudes sometimes have the potential to open up new possibilities.

Even when community leaders, government officials, legislators, corporate managers, and other institutional artisans consider proposals from academic analysts, recommendations are likely to require translation into simple, easily communicated messages that can survive the rough and tumble of political debate, and ideas often become transformed in the process. In translating changes in policy into practice, there are many opportunities for reinterpretation, contestation, and unintended consequences (Pressman and Wildavsky 1984). These provide additional illustrations of why policy changes, including efforts to improve polycentric governance, may be unlikely to go far if simply pushed from the top down. Instead change may be more successful if advanced by supportive policy coalitions, with negotiation and adjustment to respond to diverse interests, and continuing efforts by proponents that go well beyond just enacting legislation or having a new policy promulgated (Andrews 2013; Sabatier and Weible 2016).

Elinor Ostrom synthesized a set of design principles for robust governance of local commons (Cox, Arnold, and Villamayor-Tomás 2010; E. Ostrom 1990; Tarko 2017) including the use of nested organizational structures. A crucial insight leading to the design principles was that while local rules for resource governance were incredibly diverse, and had been customized to fit particular circumstances, there were nevertheless more general principles associated with long-enduring commons. The design principles do not offer a simple formula or checklist sufficient for success. However, they can be used to identify key questions to consider for institutional design of polycentric governance (E. Ostrom 2005a, 270–71). For practising polycentric governance at larger scales, some relevant questions and considerations for institutional design concern:

- *Boundaries.* Identifying how users from multiple communities could share or restrict access to resources, including situations where boundaries may be overlapping, ambiguous, or fuzzy.
- *Local fit.* Configuring rules to fit with conditions, including the movement of water, livestock, fish, air, or other mobile resources across wider areas that encompass multiple communities and governmental units.
- *Fairness of benefits and costs.* Understanding the potential gains and costs of changes in interaction across wider scales and multiple organizations; how costs and benefits are, or could be, distributed among different organizations and others affected, and whether potential gains are sufficient to offset higher transaction costs.
- *Representation.* How to choose representatives and keep them accountable within federations or other complex networks of relationships; how to ensure that large numbers of users are informed and able to participate
- *Accountability.* Monitoring resource use at wider scales, including impacts (externalities) affecting distant users, especially when impacts are not easily visible as part of self-monitoring by users during their everyday life.
- *Conflict resolution.* Finding low-cost and effective ways to resolve conflicts between communities, agencies, and other stakeholders.
- *Graduated sanctions.* How to get 'strangers' to efficiently comply with rules, particularly those less affected by local norms and social pressures.

- *Autonomy.* Whether and how government agencies and other power-ful interests may respect and empower local autonomy, or be open to sharing authority as part of co-management arrangements.
- *Nested enterprises.* Arranging nested or overlapping institutions, in terms of scale, types of linkages, conflict resolution mechanisms, and other considerations.

In institutional design, the concept of checks-and-balances involves distributing authority, 'using ambition against ambition' (Hamilton, Jay, and Madison 2009) so that those who are dissatisfied have recourse to voice their objections and contest actions that might harm their interests. While sometimes taken for granted, conventional institutional mechan-isms are part of an institutional heritage of ways to spread decision-making authority among multiple centres; these include specialized roles for an organization president, secretary, and treasurer; separation of executive, legislative, and judicial power; disclosure of information; and procedures for public deliberation. Such mechanisms may be particularly important for federations and other overarching institutions that link multiple deci-sion centres; and offer ways of arranging autonomy, mutual adjustment, and conflict resolution within a larger institutional framework. Similarly, good governance principles such as transparency and accountability increase the ability of those who are involved to monitor and engage. The sharing of information and decision-making processes may be able to take advantage of newer technologies such as mobile phones, the Internet, and remote sensing that affect monitoring, transparency and other principles. These may be particularly useful in polycentric contexts involving wide areas, multiple resources, complex interactions, and diverse networks of participants. Decision support systems can be designed to support a range of participants in polycentric systems (Zulkafli et al. 2017).

The composition of the board of a federation or other higher-level organizations often involves decisions about how various groups will be represented. It may incorporate decision rules designed to maintain the influence and autonomy of participating organizations, such as emphasiz-ing consensus or requiring supermajorities for some decisions. Conven-tional organizational design concerns, such as span of control, the optimal number of participants for effective meetings, and the use of committees and subcommittees, may be important considerations in designing effect-ive and efficient polycentric governance structures.

The discussion of the design of the United States Constitution contained in *The Federalist* papers offers a series of essays, by institutional artisans, about ways of arranging authority, including checks-and-balances, ways of distributing authority between national and state governments, and choices and trade-offs between faster versus more thorough processes for making decisions (Hamilton, Jay, and Madison 2009; V. Ostrom 2008b). There is sometimes a tendency to assume a simple choice between either unitary central rule, or independent local control. For thinking about polycentric governance, an example of an important but possibly non-intuitive concept is that of concurrent jurisdiction between federal and state governments, in which the federal government has direct jurisdiction over citizens for some matters, while other matters are left for the individual states (V. Ostrom 2008b). Concurrent jurisdiction offers an illustrative example of how overarching rules may be creatively arranged, including their associated tensions, debates, and changes over time.

The questions and mechanisms for crafting polycentricity discussed in this section illustrate some of the principles for polycentric practice outlined in the introduction. Polycentricity offers ideas about how to organize at multiple scales, linking different decision centres such as multiple communities and government agencies. Institutional artisans can work together to craft agreements, drawing on their knowledge and a shared heritage of examples and ideas. Principles for institutional design can identify important questions to ask, while institutional arrangements can be customized to fit specific conditions. Institutional artisans can engage in bricolage, recombining and adapting existing institutions in new ways, learning from the past and experience in other decision centres within polycentric systems.

Box 11.1 Vignette: Watersheds and problemsheds

Governance of river basins typically involves multiple communities, agencies, and uses of water, a multiplicity of organizations and issues, with shared and conflicting interests at multiple scales, and so is a promising area for application of polycentricity. In river basins, it has often proven possible to convene multi-stakeholder platforms to discuss issues, explore problems, and pursue improvements (Boelens et al. 1998; Lubell, Robins, and Wang 2014; Sabatier et al. 2005; Steins and Edwards 1998). There is a risk that such efforts may be ineffective, especially if driven more by outside interests than local initiative and may lead to time wasted on 'talk shops', agreements without substance, or plans that never get put into practice. There are important questions about who is included, and how to promote inclusion and equity. Nevertheless, even where there are strong conflicts, a process of continuing dialogue, including relevant fact-finding and exploration of options, has often turned out to be surprisingly effective in building shared understanding, consensus on ways to move forward, and practical efforts and results.

Efforts focused on addressing specific problems and conflicts may offer fertile opportunities for bringing together effective coalitions. Despite contentious debates about large dams, a variety of interesting results have been achieved through working to adjust releases from large reservoirs to better serve the needs of downstream habitats and water users. Such 'reservoir reoperation' often requires only minor costs in terms of energy income in comparison to the broader benefits downstream (Richter and Thomas 2007).

Groundwater basins in southern California face challenges including depletion and seawater intrusion. They offer an instructive example of polycentric governance where irrigation districts, urban water utilities and other specialized government agencies have cooperated, sometimes (but not always) successfully, to replenish aquifers and reverse seawater intrusion (Blomquist 1992). California's state government has not tried to take full control over local governance of surface or groundwater. Instead the state provided a legal framework that enabled water user organizations to be established and to work together, and supported research to better understand local conditions.

In California, groundwater disputes could be taken to court, for example to assert or protect rights to water (Blomquist 2009). Rather than a judge making a final decision, the judge instead could encourage and provide legal backing for a negotiated settlement agreement. An agreement to settle a dispute could thus constitute a new institution, with the legal authority to carry out tasks such as monitoring groundwater use, contracting for technical analysis and engineering design, pursuing funding, and carrying out works such as recharging aquifers, and monitoring and taking action against those who violate the agreement. Equity courts that could approve settlement agreements are an example of an enabling mechanism that facilitated the emergence of polycentric self-governance in some areas. More recently, California's 2014 Sustainable Groundwater Management Act provides a more specific legal framework, which still emphasizes local level groundwater governance within an overarching context of state-level rules (Conrad et al. 2018; Kiparsky et al. 2017).

Concepts concerning integrated water resources management (IWRM) (Global Water Partnership 2008) offer ideas seemingly quite compatible with polycentricity, including ways of incorporating the hydrological linkages of water within basins, competing uses, multiple government agencies and user organizations, and academic disciplines. The principles of IWRM explicitly include participation of stakeholders, and subsidiarity, putting decision-making at the lowest appropriate level. In theory IWRM is quite compatible with subsidiarity, participation, federated structures, and polycentric organization at multiple scales in river basins.

However, attempts to implement IWRM have often had limited impact (Biswas 2004; Schlager and Blomquist 2008). The ways in which water is linked within larger basins can become a justification for approaches that try to establish large-scale formal organization at the river basin level, pushed by national-level agencies, hierarchically arranged in terms of basins and levels of government jurisdiction. The principle of organization along the lines of basin hydraulic boundaries may also become an excuse to neglect or bypass key stakeholders, such as cities and their mayors, or provincial governors. A too-rigid emphasis on organizing water users solely along hydraulic lines of canals and catchments can fail to take advantage of the social capital of how people are already organised in villages, districts, cities, and associated patterns of settlement and political jurisdiction. Hydrologically based approaches to organization may also be used, or abused, to try to expand the authority of water agencies, while failing to build effective coalitions needed to enact and implement policy changes. In practice, IWRM efforts can end up emphasizing comprehensive formal planning mechanisms, reliant on expert analysis, and may miss opportunities for more modest self-organized problem-solving initiated by ad hoc coalitions of organizations, which would depend on lots of messy trial-and-error.

A polycentric perspective does not necessarily require rejecting the potential for management in accordance with resource boundaries, use of formal planning mechanisms, or forms of centralized control. It does raise questions about how to encourage problem-solving initiatives at appropriate scales, facilitating efforts by those involved, which may offer more feasible and appropriate pathways for change. This may involve looking at *problemsheds* (Kneese 1968) formed by those concerned with a particular issue, rather than only watersheds, and a more modest, pragmatic, or expedient approach to addressing priority opportunities (Lankford et al. 2007; Moriarty et al. 2010; Woodhouse and Muller 2017; World Bank 2003).

Comparative research on river basin governance in many countries indicates that polycentricity can contribute to better performance and better institutional adaptation, such as to climate change (Pahl-Wostl and Knieper 2014; Pahl-Wostl et al. 2012). Polycentricity makes a difference where there is both horizontal coordination and vertical distribution of power, in which lower level units have genuine autonomy, as well as overarching institutions in the form of coordination structures such as overall accepted rules. In practical terms, a pathway to polycentric governance requires paying attention to horizontal coordination, vertical distribution of power, and the development of overarching institutions.

11.5 Facilitating Polycentric Governance

A polycentric perspective tends to be particularly interested in ways in which people and organizations can act on their own initiative, self-organizing to cope with shared problems. Bringing together representatives of different water users and areas in a river basin has sometimes been an effective way to create agreement, even in the presence of many conflicting interests. For local natural resources management, a key intervention has often been to provide community organizers of some kind to facilitate collective action at the local level, and in some cases to also assist in the formation of higher-level federations. Examples include formation of water user federations at the secondary or scheme level, and forest user federations encompassing multiple villages, as well as wider forums at river basin, state/provincial, and national levels.

In his work as a consultant on the drafting of the natural resources article for the constitution of the State of Alaska, Vincent Ostrom declined to simply draft wording on his own as an expert. Instead, he chose to facilitate a process of common inquiry involving a series of discussions about draft language: within a subcommittee on natural resources; in the larger constitutional committee; through responses to drafts published in newspapers and sent to households; and at local meetings during a recess in the state's constitutional convention, (Allen 2014; Allen and Lutz 2009; V. Ostrom 2008b). This process of constitutional choice provided a way to explore a range of issues and seek language that would reflect the values and experience of Alaskans and fit with the complex characteristics of common and concurrent use of resources they sought to govern together. Those involved in writing the constitution acted as public entrepreneurs, drafting and redrafting institutional arrangements to serve the common good, with an outside expert acting only as one source of ideas, questions, and synthesis within the larger process of common inquiry.

A variety of techniques are available for helping people to get to know each other and learn to work together, including those developed in terms of facilitation, public participation, community engagement, dialogue and deliberation, and alternative dispute resolution. More specialized processes such as multi-stakeholder dialogue (Boelens et al. 1998; Edmunds and Wollenberg 2001; Focht and Trachtenberg 2005; Ratner and Smith 2014), may be particularly suitable for facilitating cooperation among diverse interests and organizations, but need due attention to differences among participants. Where adequate funding is available, it can be useful to hire specialized facilitators, especially in cases where there are severe and long-standing conflicts, or major differences in knowledge and power among participants. However, this does not mean that complicated methods are always essential or effective. Even in cases such as international negotiations, among highly skilled professionals with abundant resources, simple activities such as an informal 'walk in the woods' can play a crucial role in opening up solutions. Where participants are already familiar with workshop processes such as breakout groups and plenary reporting and discussions, a minimalist approach to facilitation may be sufficient (Weisbord and Janoff 2007).

Availability of information, and additional research may help to understand resource characteristics, especially where resource availability and dynamics are not easy to see and understand, such as for fisheries, groundwater, or water quality (Schlager 2005; Schlager, Blomquist, and Tang 1994). Understanding resource characteristics may be crucial in figuring out whether and how polycentric governance might be organised, such as whether the resource is highly localized or widely dispersed, fixed or mobile, rapidly renewable or vulnerable to degradation, easily observed or hard to understand without systematic analysis, very important (salient) for user livelihoods or not, and so forth. In multi-stakeholder processes, joint fact-finding can be important as a process, not only for forging personal connections, but also to build common knowledge and mutual understanding among those involved in trying to resolve disputes and craft cooperation for a river basin, forest, or other shared resources.

Academic disciplines, professional societies, and publications contribute to the exchange of ideas and creation of consensus within epistemic communities, such as among academics and experts, which help to define how problems are framed and what kind of solutions are considered (Haas 1993). Professional organizations and coalitions may also engage in deliberate setting of standards. Advocacy of new ideas, and relevant research, can help to shift understanding and agendas for action within epistemic communities and broader publics. Changes in professional networks and knowledge are themselves a polycentric process and may play a crucial role in changing ideas about polycentric governance, including for management of water and other natural resources.

A key argument for polycentricity is that it offers more opportunity for experimentation and learning, discovering useful new knowledge. Approaches that ostensibly decentralize, but impose standardized approaches, panaceas (E. Ostrom, Janssen, and Anderies 2007), and emphasize one-way top-down implementation, with extensive regulation and guidance (tutelage) thereby miss a major opportunity for learning and potential avenue to success. As an example of social learning, the fifty US states are sometimes referred to as 'laboratories for democracy'. Different states try out different approaches, see what happens, and then can learn from each other's experience. Similar opportunities for shared learning can be cultivated as an essential part of polycentricity.

Laws and policy may facilitate or impede the creation of polycentric governance. In many cases, an important way to 'develop' polycentric governance may well be to reduce regulation and top-down control, to leave more space for self-organization by citizens and their organizations. Beyond that are questions of what may be done, particularly by governments, to strengthen autonomy, promote fruitful interactions, and encourage development of overarching rules that make things better. There are multiple mechanisms through which governments can encourage self-organization (E. Ostrom 1990; Sarker 2013). Legislation can help empower polycentric governance if it enables associations and other organizations at different scales to obtain legal status, enter into binding contracts, protect their interests in court, and mobilize money and other resources, and to work together to create overarching institutions for cooperation, competition, and conflict resolution.

For natural resources governance, a key recommendation has often been to enable the creation of 'special districts', bodies with a degree of governmental authority, focused on a particular task. Special districts, such as irrigation districts, drainage districts, and so forth are essentially a form of local government authority concerned with a particular topic and organised along resource boundaries, rather than administrative jurisdictions such as districts and provinces. After being properly established, such an authority can have power to make and enforce rules concerning resource use, including requiring compulsory payment of fees and enforcing sanctions against those who violate rules. This contrasts with the risks of assuming that user groups for those sharing a natural resource can simply be organised using existing legislation for cooperatives or other voluntary associations, where people are free to join or leave as they wish. Instead, the ways in which each person's actions affect others mean that effective cooperation may depend on the ability to make enforceable rules about resource use, for example to exclude those who do not cooperate or contribute, and to credibly threaten to punish those whose actions harm others or damage the shared resource. Sometimes local social solidarity may suffice to overcome the lack of explicit legal authority, especially within small face-to-face communities. However, norms and informal sanctions become less effective as the scale and scope of governance become larger, and as people are less embedded in a web of overlapping social relationships. Special districts with legal authority can thus act as a crucial component of polycentric governance, able to cooperate among themselves and engage in co-management agreements with resource agencies.

As should be clear, polycentric governance goes beyond a one-dimensional concern with centralizing or decentralizing to look at a variety of options for horizontal (peer-to-peer), vertical (hierarchical), and diagonal (cross-scale) linkages and ways of arranging authority, including conflict resolution mechanisms and other specialized services. There may be many different opportunities for organizing at intermediate, 'meso' scales, and many ways in which such arrangements may be modified. In many cases, what is discussed in relation to the subsidiarity principle of organizing at the 'lowest possible level' may only be practicable if embedded within arrangements for wider scale linkages, including conflict resolution, recourse against local injustice, technical support, and regulation to protect broader interests, in other words, a polycentric network of institutional arrangements.

Power is often oversimplified into merely a matter of control and coercion, 'power over', while a polycentric perspective is very concerned with enabling the capacity for self-governance of communities and other organizations, 'power to' (power as freedom, capacity to act) (Sen 2000), and with the opportunities for making things better through cooperation, 'power with' (Follett 1951; V. Ostrom 1997). A polycentric perspective can aid in identifying the multiple opportunities that may exist for power-sharing, creating 'power with', capacity for constituting cooperation between organizations that can retain autonomy while becoming better able to coordinate their actions and resolve conflicts. On a more basic level, citizens can be considered, treated, and expected to act not simply as occasional voters and passive beneficiaries, but instead as people empowered to engage in improving their lives, co-producers and co-managers, active in constituting new arrangements for beneficial inter-action between autonomous organizations.

11.6 Conclusions: Practising Polycentric Governance

Polycentricity concerns not just a type of governance, but also a perspective on how organizations can interact. Polycentric governance offers a variety of alternatives to vertical hierarchies or flat decentralization. Practising polycentric governance focuses on the opportunities to organize governance arrangements that match the scale of particular problems and highlights the potential for action by those who are ready to work together in improving a situation. Polycentricity is made more effective by the ideas and attitudes of citizens who feel able to associate and act together to constitute new or improved organizations and inter-organizational arrangements.

For a particular situation, it is important to assess ways in which various aspects of polycentricity already exist, and how polycentricity may be created or modified. That involves looking at the stakeholders, the extent to which there are multiple centres for decision-making, what kinds of interaction exist between them, including how much (or how little) autonomy each has, and how these dimensions of governance might be changed to better fit a social situation and pursue the objectives of institutional artisans.

Research such as that reported in Part III of this book offers insights into different polycentric ways in which people organize themselves to govern water and other natural resources, and how such institutional arrangements perform. Such research can contribute to a better understanding of the options available for designing or improving polycentric governance structures, such as nested federations of user groups, co-management between resource users and government agencies, and contracting to provide specialized services in local public economies. There is much scope for better understanding the diversity of potential polycentric arrangements, how different institutional configurations may be related to resource characteristics and to performance outcomes, and how transformations in polycentric governance occur (Heikkila, Villamayor-Tomás, and Garrick 2018; Jordan et al. 2018).

Organization leaders, government officials, applied researchers, and others act as public entrepreneurs and institutional artisans as they engage in discussion and decisions at the constitutional level to establish or modify institutions for polycentric governance, and at the collective choice level in making specific rules, and then act operationally to put those rules into use. Artisanship often takes the form of institutional bricolage, creatively adapting and recombining existing institutions, including mechanisms that facilitate sharing power among multiple centres. The design of polycentric institutional arrangements is not a neutral technical exercise, but instead is inescapably political, part of larger processes of societal contestation over how power and benefits are created and distributed. In assessing institutional options, political feasibility is thus as important a constraint as technical feasibility. In contrast to the tendency to assume that solutions must be imposed through top-down control, a polycentric perspective highlights the potential for creating 'power with' through contestation, negotiation, and cooperation.

Polycentric governance may be promoted by providing information about polycentric possibilities, as this book does, and through policies and legislation that facilitate mutual adjustment and self-organization of overarching institutions for cooperation, shared learning, competitive improvement, and conflict resolution. More specific efforts may also be initiated to bring people together, to share information and experience and explore opportunities for fruitful interaction at wider scales, putting polycentric governance into practice.

Conclusions

Andreas Thiel, William A. Blomquist, and Dustin E. Garrick

Governing complexity has tended to produce complex governance. As stated in Chapter 1, across the world today we find 'social, political, economic, and cultural systems where there is no hierarchy holding the whole system together' and 'no single ultimate authority'. The absence of a hierarchy holding things together can lead observers to presume this equals disorganization or disintegration or even chaos, with accompanying disastrous consequences. We believe that presumption is often mistaken, but we also reject any presumption that complex, polycentric arrangements guarantee sound governance or assure efficiency, equity, reliability, and responsiveness.

We recommend analysing complex governance without prior expectations that it is sure to be chaotic and wasteful or a smoothly functioning order. Our claims about polycentric governance are as follows.

- It is ubiquitous and therefore worthy of serious attention from anyone who is interested in governance and policy.
- Polycentric arrangements exist and are widespread for understandable reasons.
- It is possible for polycentric arrangements to perform well, persist for long periods, and adapt.
- Whether they actually function well, persist, or adapt are empirical questions and the answers depend on myriad factors.

Governing Complexity has aimed to provide examples of the conceptual and empirical analysis of polycentric governance that can support future detailed research on its determinants, dynamics and performance. We have contended that polycentric governance is omnipresent, in water governance and beyond, and requires a mode of inquiry that builds on the Ostroms' work and extends and updates it.

Throughout this volume we have attempted to identify and describe many of those factors upon which the operation and performance of polycentric arrangements depend, and to share empirical examples of polycentric governance arrangements in practice. Such a review is necessarily incomplete, given the variety of polycentric arrangements and the contingencies that shape their successes and failures in particular times and locations. By their nature, polycentric governance arrangements are varied – perhaps endlessly so. In this book alone, we have shown that polycentric governance adopts a multitude of forms associated with different performances of governance. Therefore, we hope that this book, along with other scholars' recent contributions, mark the beginning of a broader research programme on polycentric governance.

The approach we advocate would require analysis of specific elements of polycentric governance to be embedded in a more comprehensive characterization that includes foundational considerations as well as particular empirical manifestations. Consistent with Cole (2013), Carlisle and Gruby (2017), Jordan et al. (2018), and Heikkila et al. (2018), we argue that such a more comprehensive characterization of the context in which governance relations operate could indeed contribute to an enhanced understanding of the elements of polycentric governance over time, if embedded into rigorous research designs of comparative institutional analysis. Furthermore, research on the foundations, operation, and performance of polycentric governance needs to invest in conceptual discussions of terms and definitions and ways of measuring.

Even then, in relation to performance, we cannot do much more than establish variation across cases and analyse that variation systematically. Over time, a research programme on polycentric governance may be able to pinpoint relationships that underpin patterns of performance. Such an analysis will need to take into account the role of timing and sequencing in polycentric governance. In other words, if research enables us to gather knowledge on pathways of development of polycentric governance that were considered socially beneficial, researchers and practitioners could probably act with greater understanding about whether a particular polycentric governance arrangement in a particular setting held promise for the future or not. An additional crucial question in this context is how to address external shocks.

Much of the literature on polycentric governance has focused on natural resources and especially water governance. In this book, we similarly drew on and added examples from this field. Still, notably and recently, vigorous discussions about the usefulness of the lens of polycentric governance have developed in relation to governance on the global and transnational levels. The consideration of climate governance, instigated by Elinor Ostrom herself, stands out in that regard (Jordan et al. 2018); likewise, work on cybersecurity (e.g. Shackelford 2014). Such work is highly welcome, as it demonstrates that addressing governance from a relational perspective couched in polycentric governance resonates with many fields and researchers. With this book, we have attempted to contribute to these developments by further detailing polycentric governance and describing approaches to its research, in hopes of supporting further theory-building in relation to clearly delineated empirical fields that are researched and conceptualized in detailed ways and thus can be shared across the growing community of researchers of governance. We expect that an ongoing research programme on polycentric governance, in regard to any empirical field, will need to follow a logic of iteration between deduction and induction for the purpose of theory-building on polycentric governance and that way disseminating experiences from a broad array of research and practice.

One of the largest challenges ahead, in our view, remains the issue of institutional change in polycentric governance (E. Ostrom 2011; Schmid 2004; North 1990). This topic arose in several chapters of this book (see, for example, Chapters 4 and 10), and no doubt it will need significant attention in the future with the perception of ever-faster changing socio-economic and biophysical environments taking hold (Adger et al. 2005; Fresco 2009). There is plenty of work to be done.

Finally, we want to come back to what has been an important background motivation of our work, but also of the Ostroms and others influenced by the Bloomington school. Although its full consideration was beyond the scope of what we could cover within the limits of this book, we refer to one of the normative and radical implications of polycentric governance: taking seriously the existence of systems of bottom-up self-organization (i.e. societies based on commoning) as alternative to more familiar ideas for societal order that emphasize either atomistic behaviour or central planning. To assess such claims, we need not only more rigorous understandings of the functioning and forms of polycentric governance as suggested in this book, but we also need deeper and collaborative engagement from political theory and philosophy, with the ideas and substantive findings derived from work on polycentric governance. Such work, which we could allude to only briefly in this book, remains as a future project that perhaps someone will want to take up.

We close with some thoughts about the relationship between the subject of polycentric governance and the position of researchers trying to make sense of it. There is a thin and permeable boundary between, on one hand, explaining why human beings may have chosen so often to create and maintain polycentric governance arrangements and, on the other hand, offering a normative argument in favour of polycentric governance. Nevertheless, the boundary exists. The two endeavours – explaining polycentric governance and promoting polycentric governance – are not the same. We have attempted to keep our focus on the former rather than the latter.

Everything about polycentric governance – the decision-making centres, the overarching rules within which they form and operate, the relationships and interactions they have with one another, the resulting manifestations of cooperation, competition, and conflict and conflict resolution, the initiation and direction of change – is created by human beings. As such, they can and do reflect the full ranges of human creativity and fallibility, and may be imbued with our most exalted or our most debased intentions. People can use polycentric governance arrangements to address problems successfully and improve their lives and environments. They can also use them to make matters worse, and even fail spectacularly. Nothing about polycentric governance ensures a happy ending.

We certainly understand and obviously have accepted the risk that our effort to make sense of the widespread use of polycentric governance arrangements may come across as a justification of them, or even as advocacy. To a considerable extent that risk is unavoidable: to articulate a rationale for the existence of some human-created artefact is bound to strike some readers as a defence of it. We maintain, nonetheless, that polycentric governance arrangements can be efficient or inefficient, just or unjust, cohesive and coordinated or disjointed and fragmented, and so on. In fact, any polycentric governance arrangement at any actual place and time will probably exhibit some mix of all of these attributes.

We also feel confident in stating that any actual polycentric governance arrangement can be critiqued and reformed. To the extent that an improved understanding of polycentric governance enhances the ability of human beings to make it better, that is something to which we all have been pleased to try to contribute.

References

Abbott, Kenneth W. 2012. The transnational regime complex for climate change. *Environment and Planning C-Government and Policy* 30 (4): 571–90. https://doi .org/10.1068/c11127.

Abe, Jacques, Bradford Brown, Emmanuel A. Ajao, and Stephen Donkor. 2016. Local to regional polycentric levels of governance of the Guinea Current Large Marine Ecosystem. *Environmental Development* 17: 287–95. https://doi.org/10.1016/ j.envdev.2015.06.006.

Acar, Muhittin, Chao Guo, and Kaifeng Yang. 2012. Accountability in voluntary partnerships: To whom and for what? *Public Organization Review* 12 (2): 157–74.

Acheson, J. M. 2003. *Capturing the Commons: Devising Institutions to Manage the Maine Lobster Industry*. Hanover, NH: University Press of New England.

Adger, W. Neil, Katrina Brown, and Emma L. Tompkins. 2005. The political economy of cross-scale networks in resource co-management. *Ecology and Society* 10 (2). https://doi.org/10.5751/ES-01465-100209.

Advisory Commission on Intergovernmental Relations. 1987. *The Organization of Local Public Economies*. Washington, DC: Advisory Commission on Intergovern- mental Relations.

Aligica, Paul D. 2003. Rethinking Governance Systems and Challenging Disciplinary Boundaries: Interview with Elinor Ostrom, from Rethinking Institutional Analy- sis: Interviews with Vincent and Elinor Ostrom, Commemorating a Lifetime of Achievement, George Mason University, Mercatus Center, November 7, 2003, 7–14. Reprinted in Aligica and Boettke 2009. *Challenging Institutional Analysis and Development: The Bloomington School*. New York: Routledge; and in Cole, Daniel H., and Michael D. McGinnis, eds. 2015. *Elinor Ostrom and the Blooming- ton School of Political Economy*. Lanham, MD: Lexington Books, 51–64.

2014. *Institutional Diversity and Political Economy: The Ostroms and Beyond*. Oxford University Press.

Aligica, Paul D., and Peter Boettke. 2009. *Challenging Institutional Analysis and Development: The Bloomington School*. New York: Routledge.

Aligica, Paul D., and F. Sabetti, eds. 2014a. *Choice, Rules and Collective Action: The Ostroms on the Study of Institutions and Governance*. Colchester, UK: ECPR Press.

2014b. Introduction: The Ostroms' research program for the study of institutions and governance: Theoretical and epistemic foundations. In Paul D. Aligica and F. Sabetti, eds., *Choice, Rules and Collective Action: The Ostroms on the Study of Institutions and Governance*. Colchester, UK: ECPR Press, 1–19.

Aligica, Paul D., and Vlad Tarko. 2012. Polycentricity: From Polanyi to Ostrom, and beyond. *Governance – An International Journal of Policy Administration and Institutions* 25 (2): 237–62. https://doi.org/10.1111/j.1468-0491.2011.01550.x.

2013. Co-production, polycentricity, and value heterogeneity: The Ostroms' public choice institutionalism revisited. *American Political Science Review* 107 (4): 726–41. https://doi.org/10.1017/S0003055413000427.

Allen, Barbara. 2014. *Vincent Ostrom and the Alaska Constitution in Ostroms the Movie*. https://vimeo.com/channels/ostromsthemovie/84354523.

Allen, Barbara, and Donald Lutz. 2009. Experience guides theory: Discovering the political theory of a compound republic. In Filippo Sabetti, Barbara Allen, and Mark Sproule-Jones, eds., *The Practice of Constitutional Development: Vincent Ostrom's Quest to Understand Human Affairs*. Lanham, MD: Lexington Books, 73–104.

Anderies, John M., and Marco A. Janssen. 2013. Robustness of social-ecological systems: Implications for public policy. *Policy Studies Journal* 41 (3): 513–36.

Anderies, John M., Marco A. Janssen, and Elinor Ostrom. 2004. A framework to analyze the robustness of social-ecological systems from an institutional perspective. *Ecology and Society* 9 (1).

Andersson, Krister P., and Elinor Ostrom. 2008. Analyzing decentralized resource regimes from a polycentric perspective. *Policy Sciences* 41 (1): 71–93. https://doi.org/10.1007/s11077-007-9055-6.

Andrews, Matt. 2013. *The Limits of Institutional Reform in Development: Changing Rules for Realistic Solutions*. Cambridge: Cambridge University Press.

Aoki, Masahiko. 2001. *Toward a Comparative Institutional Analysis*. Cambridge, MA: MIT Press.

Aranda-Martín, José Francisco. 2009. Irrigation and water policies in Aragon. In A., K. Biswas, C. Tortajada, and R. Izquierdo, eds., *Water Management in 2020 and Beyond*, 213–35. Springer.

Arnold, Gwen, and Holahan Robert. 2014. The federalism of fracking: How the locus of policy-making authority affects civic engagement. *The Journal of Federalism* 44 (2): 344–68.

Arnold, Gwen, Nguyen Long Le Anh, and Madeline Gottlieb. 2017. Social networks and policy entrepreneurship: How relationships shape municipal decision making about high-volume hydraulic fracturing. *Policy Studies Journal* 45 (3): 414–41.

Arthur, W. Brian. 1994. *Increasing Returns and Path Dependence in the Economy*. Ann Arbor: University of Michigan Press. www.jstor.org/stable/10.3998/mpub.10029.

Axelrod, Robert, and Michael D. Cohen. 2000. *Harnessing Complexity: Organizational Implications of a Scientific Frontier*. Riverside, New York: Free Press.

Baldwin, Elizabeth, Camille Washington-Ottombre, Jampel Dell'Angelo, Daniel Cole, and Tom Evans. 2016. Polycentric governance and irrigation reform in Kenya. *Governance* 29 (2): 207–25. https://doi.org/10.1111/gove.12160.

Ban, Natalie C., Vanessa M. Adams, Glenn R. Almany, Stephen Ban, Josh E. Cinner, Laurence J. McCook, Morena Mills, Robert L. Pressey, and Alan White. 2011. Designing, implementing and managing marine protected areas: Emerging trends and opportunities for coral reef nations. *Journal of Experimental Marine Biology and Ecology* 408 (1–2, SI): 21–31. https://doi.org/10.1016/j.jembe.2011.07.023.

Bardhan, Pranab, and Dayton-Johnson, Jeff. 2002. Unequal irrigators heterogeneity and commons management in large-scale multivariate research. In Elinor Ostrom, ed., *The Drama of the Commons.* Washington, DC: National Academy Press, 87–112.

Basurto, Xavier. 2013. Linking multi-level governance to local common-pool resource theory using fuzzy-set qualitative comparative analysis: Insights from twenty years of biodiversity conservation in Costa Rica. *Global Environmental Change* 23 (3): 573–87. https://doi.org/10.1016/j.gloenvcha.2013.02.011.

Basurto, Xavier, and Elinor Ostrom. 2009. Beyond the tragedy of the Commons. *Economia delle fonti di energia e dell'ambiente* (1): 35–60.

Beach, D. (2016). It's all about mechanisms – What process-tracing case studies should be tracing. *New Political Economy*, 21(5): 463–72.

Beach, D., and R. B. Pedersen, (2016). Selecting appropriate cases when tracing causal mechanisms. *Sociological Methods & Research* 47(4): 837–71. https://doi.org/10.1177/0049124115622510

Becker, Gert, Dave Huitema, and Jeroen C. J. H. Aerts. 2015. Prescriptions for adaptive comanagement: The case of flood management in the German Rhine basin. *Ecology and Society* 20 (3). https://doi.org/10.5751/ES-07562-200301.

Bednar, Jenna. 2009. *The Robust Federation: Principles of Design: Political Economy of Institutions and Decisions.* Cambridge. New York: Cambridge University Press.

Bednar, Jena. 2011. The political science of federalism. *Annual Review of Law and Social Science* 7: 269–88.

Bendor, Jonathan B. 1985. *Parallel Systems: Redundancy in Government.* Berkeley, CA: University of California Press.

Bennett, A., and C. Elman. (2006). Complex causal relations and case study methods: The example of path dependence. *Political Analysis* 14(3): 250–67.

Benson, David, Animesh K. Gain, and Josselin J. Rouillard. 2015. Water governance in a comparative perspective: From IWRM to a 'Nexus' approach? *Water Alternatives* 8 (1): 756–73.

Berardo, Ramiro, and Mark Lubell. 2016. Understanding what shapes a polycentric governance system. *Public Administration Review* 76 (5): 738–51. https://doi.org/10.1111/puar.12532.

Berardo, Ramiro, and J. T. Scholz. 2010. Self-organizing policy networks: Risk, partner selection, and cooperation in estuaries. *American Journal of Political Science* 54 (3): 632–49. www.scopus.com/inward/record.url?eid=2-s2.0-77954255825&partnerID=40&md5=04a8bf211ac39eee3961d75675609dc4.

Berbel, Julio, Carlos Gutiérrez-Martín, Juan A. Rodríguez-Díaz, Emilio Camacho, and Pilar Montesinos. 2015. Literature review on rebound effect of water saving measures and analysis of a Spanish case study. *Water Resources Management* 29 (3): 663–78.

Berger, P. L., and R. J. Neuhaus. 1977. *To Empower People: The Role of Mediating Structures in Public Policy.* Washington, D.C.: American Enterprise Institute.

Berkes, Fikret. 2005. Why keep a community-based focus in times of global interactions? *Topics in Arctic Social Sciences* 5: 33–43.

Berkes, Fikret. 2006. From community-based resource management to complex systems: The scale issue and marine commons. *Ecology and Society* 11 (1). https://doi.org/10.5751/ES-01431-110145.

2007. Community-based conservation in a globalized world. 104 (39): 15188–93.

2017. Environmental governance for the Anthropocene? Social-ecological systems, resilience and collaborative learning. *Sustainability* 9:1232. https://doi.org/10.3390/su9071232.

Beyer, Jürgen. 2011. Pfadabkehr: Die Internationalisierung des deutschen Unternehmenskontroll-und Rechnungslegungssystems. In Thomas M. J. Möllers, ed., *Internationalisierung von Standards*, 145–74.

Bidwell, R. D., and C. M. Ryan. 2006. Collaborative partnership design: The implications of organizational affiliation for watershed partnerships. *Society and Natural Resources* 19 (9): 827–43.

Biggs, Reinette, Maja Schlüter, and Michael L. Schoon, eds., 2015. *Principles for Building Resilience: Sustaining Ecosystem Services in Social-Ecological Systems.* Cambridge: Cambridge University Press.

Bish, Robert. 1999. Federalist Theory and Polycentricity: Learning from Local Governments. In Donald P. Racheter, and Richard E. Wagner, eds., *Limiting Leviathan*. Cheltenham, UK; Northampton, MA, USA: Edward Elgar.

2014. Vincent Ostrom's contribution to political economy. *Publius: The Journal of Federalism* 44 (2): 227–48.

Biswas, A. K. 2004. Integrated water resources management: A reassessment. *Water International* 29 (2): 248–56. https://doi. 10.1080/02508060408691775.

Blomquist, William. 1992. *Dividing the Waters: Governing Groundwater in Southern California*. San Francisco, CA: ICS Press.

2009. Crafting Water Constitutions in California. In *The Practice of Constitutional Development: Vincent Ostrom's Quest to Understand Human Affairs*. Lanham, MD: Lexington Books, 105.

BOE. 2005. Real Decreto-ley 15/2005, de 16 de diciembre, de medidas urgentes para la regulación de las transacciones de derechos al aprovechamiento de agua.

Boelens, Rutgerd, Axel Dourojeanni, Alfredo Duran, and Paul Hoogendam. 1998. Water rights and watersheds: Managing multiple water uses and strengthening stakeholder platforms. In Rutgerd Boelens and Gloria Davila, eds., *Searching for Equity: Conceptions of Justice and Equity in Peasant Irrigation*. Assen, the Netherlands: Van Gorcum.

Boelens, Rutgerd, and Gloria Davila, eds. 1998. *Searching for Equity: Conceptions of Justice and Equity in Peasant Irrigation*. Assen, the Netherlands: Van Gorcum.

Boelens, Rutgerd, Jaime Hoogesteger, and Michiel Baud. 2015. Water reform governmentality in Ecuador: Neoliberalism, centralization, and the restraining of polycentric authority and community rule-making. *Geoforum* 64: 281–91. https://doi.org/10.1016/j.geoforum.2013.07.005.

Boelens, Rutgerd, Margreet Zwarteveen, and Dik Roth. 2005. *Legal Complexity in the Analysis of Water Rights and Water Resources Management*. New Brunswick, NJ: Rutgers University Press.

Boettke, Peter J., and Christopher J. Coyne. 2005. Methodological individualism, spontaneous order and the research program of the Workshop in Political Theory and Policy Analysis. *Journal of Economic Behavior & Organization* 57 (2): 145–58. https://doi.org/10.1016/j.jebo.2004.06.012.

Boettke, Peter J., Christopher J. Coyne, and Peter T. Leeson. 2011. Quaimarket Failure. *Public Choice* 149 (1/2): 209–24.

Boettke, Peter J., and Paul D. Aligica. 2009. *Challenging Institutional Analysis and Development*. Abingdon, UK; New York: Routledge.

Borgatti, Stephen P., Martin G. Everett, and Jeffrey C. Johnson. 2013. *Analyzing Social Networks*. London: SAGE Publications Limited.

Boyte, Harry, Stephen Elkin, Peter Levine, Jane Mansbridge, Elinor Ostrom, Karol Soltan, and Rogers Smith. 2014. The new civic politics: Civic theory and practice for the future. *The Good Society* 23 (2): 206–11.

Bromley, Daniel W. 1989. *Economic Interests and Institutions: The Conceptual Foundations of Public Policy*. New York, NY: Basil Blackwell.

1991. *Environment and Economy: Property Rights and Public Policy*. Oxford: Blackwell.

2006. *Sufficient Reason: Volitional Pragmatism and the Meaning of Economic Institutions*. Princeton, NJ: Princeton University Press. www.loc.gov/catdir/enhancements/fy0734/2005017807-b.html.

2008. Volitional pragmatism. *Ecological Economics* 68: 1–13.

2012. Environmental governance as stochastic belief updating: Crafting rules to live by. *Ecology and Society* 17 (3). https://doi.org/10.5751/ES-04774-170314.

Brugha, Ruairi, and Zsuzsa Varvasovszky. 2000. Stakeholder analysis: A review. *Health Policy and Planning* 15 (3): 239–46.

Brunner, Ronald D. 2002. Problems of governance. In Ronald D. Brunner, Christine H. Colburn, Chritsina M. Cromley, and Roberta A. Klein, eds., *Finding Common Ground: Governance and Natural Resources in the American West*. New Haven, CT: Yale University Press, 1–47.

Bryson, John, Alessandro Sancino, John Benington, and Eva Sorensen (2017) Towards a multi-actor theory of public value co-creation. *Public Management Review* 19 (5): 640–54.

Buchanan, James M., and Geoffrey Brennan. 1985. *The Reason of Rules*. Cambridge, UK, New York: Cambridge University Press.

Buchanan, James M., and Gordon Tullock. 1962. *The Calculus of Consent. Collected Works of James M. Buchanan*. 3 vols. Ann Arbour, MI : University of Michigan Press.

Buchanan, James M., and Roger D. Congleton. 1998. *Politics by Principle, Not Interest: Towards Nondiscriminatory Democracy*. Cambridge, New York: Cambridge University Press.

Buthe, T. (2012). Taking temporality seriously: Modeling history and the use of narratives as evidence. *American Political Science Review*, 96(3): 481–93.

Buytaert, Wouter, Art Dewulf, Bert de Bievre, Julian Clark, and David M. Hannah. 2016. Citizen science for water resources management: Toward polycentric modeling and governance? *Journal of Water Resources Planning and Management* 142 (4): 1–4.

Byron, N. 2011. What can the Murray-Darling Basin Plan achieve? Will it be enough? In D. Connell, and R. Q. Grafton, eds., *Basin Futures: Water Reform in the Murray-Darling Basin*. Canberra: ANU E Press, 385–98.

Campbell, A. 2016. Two steps forward, one step back: The ongoing failure to capture synergies in natural resource management (Australia). In M. D. Young, and C. Esau, eds., *Transformational Change in Environmental and Natural Resource Management: Guidelines for Policy Excellence*. New York: Routledge, 80–94.

Capano, Giliberto. 2009. Understanding policy change as an epistemological and theoretical problem. *Journal of Comparative Policy Analysis: Research and Practice* 11 (1): 7–31. https://doi.org/10.1080/13876980802648284.

Cardenas, J. C., J. K. Stranlund, and C. Willis. 2000. Local environmental control and institutional crowding out. *World Development* 28(10): 1719–33.

Carlisle, Keith, and Rebecca L. Gruby. 2017. Polycentric systems of governance: A theoretical model for the commons. *Policy Studies Journal* 10 (2): 629. https://doi.org/10.1111/psj.12212.

Carlsson, L., and A. Sandström. 2008. Network governance of the commons. *International Journal of the Commons* 2 (1): 33–54.

Cash, D. W. 2000. Distributed assessment systems: An emerging paradigm of research, assessment and decision-making for environmental change. *Global Environmental Change-Human and Policy Dimensions* 10 (4): 241–44.

Cash, David, W., Adger, W. Neil, Fikret Birkes, Po Garden, Louis Lebel, Per Olsson, Lowell Pritchard, and Oran Young. 2006. Scale and cross-scale dynamics: Governance and information in a multi-level world. *Ecology & Society* 11 (2).

CESA. 2012. *Informe socioeconómico de la década 2001-2010 en Aragón*. Zaragoza: Consejo Económico y Social de Aragón.

Chaffin, B. C., A. S. Garmestani, H. Gosnell, and R. K. Craig. 2016. Institutional networks and adaptive water governance in the Klamath River Basin, USA. *Environmental Science & Policy* 57: 112–21. https://doi.org/10.1016/j.envsci .2015.11.008.

Challen, Ray. 2000. *Institutions Transaction Cost and Environmental Policy: Institutional Reform for Water Resources*. Aldershot, UK: Edward Elgar.

Chambers, R. 1994. Participatory rural appraisal (PRA): Analysis of experience. *World Development* 22 (9): 1253–68.

Chen, X., F. Lupi, G. He, and J. Liu. 2009. Linking social norms to efficient conservation investment in payments for ecosystem services. *Proceedings of the National Academy of Sciences* 106 (28): 11812–17.

Chirkov, V. I, R. M Ryan, and K. M Sheldon, eds. 2011. *Human Autonomy in Cross-Cultural Contexts: Perspectives on the Psychology of Agency, Freedom and Well-Being*. Dordrecht: Springer.

Christin, Thomas, and Simon Hug. 2012. Federalism, the geographic location of groups, and conflict. *Conflict Management and Peace Science* 29 (1): 93–122.

Cleaver, Frances. 2002. Reinventing institutions: Bricolage and the social embeddedness of natural resource management. *The European Journal of Development Research* 14 (2): 11–30. https://doi.org/10.1080/714000425.

    2012. *Development through Bricolage: Rethinking Institutions for Natural Resource Management*. 1st edn. New York: Routledge.

Coase, R. H. 1990. *The Firm, the Market and the Law*. Chicago IL: University of Chicago Press.

Cochrane, Cathy, ed., 2017. *State of the Sound*. Washington DC: Puget Sound Partnership.

Cole, Daniel H. 2011. From global to polycentric climate governance. *Climate Law* 2(3): 395–413.

2013. The varieties of comparative institutional analysis. *Wisconsin Law Review* 2013: 383–409.

2015. Advantages of a polycentric approach to climate change policy. *Nature Climate Change* 5 (2): 114–18. https://doi.org/10.1038/NCLIMATE2490.

Cole, Daniel H., and Michael D. McGinnis, eds. 2014. *Elinor Ostrom and the Bloomington School of Political Economy, Volume 1: Polycentricity in Public Administration and Political Science.* Lanham, MD: Lexington Books.

eds. 2015. *Elinor Ostrom and the Bloomington School of Political Economy.* Lanham, MD: Lexington Books.

Colorado Supreme Court. 2016. No. 15SC667. City of Longmont v. Colo. Oil and Gas Ass'n Preemption—Inalienable Rights Provision.

Columbia Basin Water Transactions Programme (CBWTP). 2017. 2016 Annual Report. Portland, OR: CBWTP.

Congleton, Roger D. 2014. The contractarian constitutional political economy of James Buchanan. *Constitutional Political Economy* 25 (1): 39–67.

Conrad, E., T. Moran, M. DuPraw, D. Ceppos, J. Martinez, and W. Blomquist. 2018. Diverse stakeholders create collaborative, multilevel basin governance for groundwater sustainability. *California Agriculture* 72 (1): 44–53.

Cooperrider, David L. 2005. *Appreciative Inquiry: A Positive Revolution in Change.* 1st edn. San Francisco, CA: Berrett-Koehler.

Copes, P. 1986. A critical review of the individual quota as a device in fisheries management. *Land Economics* 62(3): 278–91.

Cosens, Barbara, Matthew McKinney, Richard Paisley, and Aaron T. Wolf. 2018. Reconciliation of development and ecosystems: the ecology of governance in the International Columbia River Basin. *Regional Environmental Change* 18(6): 1679–92. doi: 10.1007/s10113-018-1355-1.

Council of Australian Governments. 2000. Our vital resource: A National Action Plan for Salinity and Water Quality.

Coward, Walter Jr. E. 1979. Principles of social organisation in an indegenous irrigation system. *Human Organisation* 38 (1): 29–36.

Cox, Michael, Gwen Arnold, and Sergio Villamayor Tomás. 2010. A review of design principles for community-based natural resource management. *Ecology & Society* 15 (4).

Crawford, Sue, and Elinor Ostrom. 1995. A grammer of institutions. *American Political Science Review* 89 (3): 582–600.

Cumming, Graeme S. 2016. Heterarchies: Reconciling networks and hierarchies. *Trends in Ecology & Evolution* 31 (8): 622–32.

Cunningham, Gord, and Alison Mathie. 2002. Asset-based community development: An overview. *Coady International Institute.* http://www.synergos.org/knowledge/02/abcdoverview.htm (1 of 5)9/10/2009 2:25:00 PM Retrieved February 4, 2009.

Curtis, A., H. Ross, G. R. Marshall, C. Baldwin, J. Cavaye, C. Freeman, A. Carr, and G. J. Syme. 2014. The great experiment with devolved NRM governance: Lessons from community engagement in Australia and New Zealand since the 1980s. *Australasian Journal of Environmental Management* 21 (2): 175–99.

Davenport, Coral. (2016). Obama Fracking Rule Is Struck Down by Court. *The New York Times*, 22 June 2016. Retrieved from www.nytimes.com/2016/06/23/us/politics/hydraulic-fracturing-interior-department-regulations.html

Davis, Charles. 2012. The politics of 'fracking': Regulating natural gas drilling practices in Colorado and Texas. *Review of Policy Research* 29 (2): 177–91.

DeCaro, Daniel, Brian Chaffin, Edella Schlager, Ahjond Garmestani, and J. B. Ruhl. 2017. Legal and institutional foundations of adaptive environmental governance. *Ecology and Society* 22 (1).

DeCaro, Daniel A., and Michael K. Stokes. 2013. Public participation and institutional fit: A social–psychological perspective. *Ecology and Society* 18 (4). https://doi.org/10.5751/ES-05837-180440.

Deci, E. L. 1971. Effects of externally mediated rewards on intrinsic motivation. *Journal of Personality and Social Psychology* 18 (1): 105–15.

1975. *Intrinsic Motivation*. New York: Plenum Press.

Dietz, T., Elinor Ostrom, and P. C. Stern. 2003. The struggle to govern the commons. *Science* 302 (5652): 1907–12.

Dobson, A. 2007. Environmental citizenship: Towards sustainable development. *Sustainable Development* 15 (4): 276–85.

Dobson, A., and D. Bell. 2005. *Environmental Citizenship*. Cambridge MA: MIT Press.

Dorsch, Marcel J., and Christian Flachsland. 2017. A polycentric approach to global climate governance. *Global Environmental Politics* 17 (2): 45–64. https://doi.org/10.1162/GLEP_a_00400.

Edmunds, David, and Eva Wollenberg. 2001. A strategic approach to multi-stakeholder negotiations. *Development and Change* 32: 231–53.

Ekstrom, Julia A., and Oran R. Young. 2009. Evaluating functional fit between a set of institutions and an ecosystem. *Ecology and Society* 14 (2).

Elazar, Daniel. 1987. *Exploring Federalism*. Tuscaloosa, AL: University Press of Alabama.

1998. *Covenant and Civil Society: The Constitutional Matrix of Modern Democracy*. New Brunswick, NJ: Transaction Publishers.

Elkin, Stephen L. 1988. Political institutions and political practice. In Edward B. Portis and Michael B. Levy, eds., *Handbook of Political Theory and Policy Science*. New York: Greenwood Press, 111–25.

Ellerman, D. 2006. *Helping People Help Themselves: From the World Bank to an Alternative Philosophy of Development Assistance*. Ann Arbour, MI: University of Michigan Press.

Embid, Antonio 2013. La crisis del sistema concesional y la aparición de fórmulas complementarias para la asignación de recursos hídricos. Algunas reflexiones sobre los mercados de derechos de uso del Agua. In *XVIII Jornadas de Derechos de Aguas: Usos de aguas, Concesiones, Autorizaciones y Mercados de Aguas*. Zaragoza.

Emerson, K., P. J. Orr, D. L. Keyes, and K. M. McKnight. 2009. Environmental conflict resolution: Evaluating performance outcomes and contributing factors. *Conflict Resolution Quarterly* 27 (1): 27–64.

Engle, N. L., Lemos, M.C., 2010. Unpacking governance: Building adaptive capacity to climate change of river basins in Brazil. *Global Environmental Change* 20(1): 4–13.

Falconer, Katherine. 2002. Developing cooperative approaches to agri-environmental policy: A transaction cost perspective on farmer participation in voluntary schemes. In Konrad Hagedorn, ed., *Environmental Co-Operation and Institutional*

Change: Theories and Policies for European Agriculture. Cheltenham, UK: Edward Elgar.

Falk, Armin, and Urs Fischbacher. 2001. *A Theory of Reciprocity.* Discussion paper series. Industrial organization / CEPR 3014. London: CEPR.

Falleti, T. G., and Lynch, J. (2008). From process to mechanism: Varieties of disaggregation. *Qualitative Sociology* 31(4): 333–39.

Feiock, R. C. 2013. The Institutional Collective Action Framework. *Policy Studies Journal* 41 (3): 397–425.

FES. 2010. *Social and Institutional Aspects: FES Source Book*: FES.

2014. Evolving Concepts for Assisting Villages in Governing Landscapes. FES.

Focht, Will, and Zev Trachtenberg. 2005. A trust-based guide to stakeholder participation. In Paul A. Sabatier, Will Focht, Mark Lubell, Zev Trachtenberg, Arnold Vedlitz, and Marty Matlock, eds., *Swimming Upstream: Collaborative Approaches to Watershed Management*: Cambridge, MA: MIT Press, 85–135.

Folke, Carl. 2006. Resilience: The emergence of a perspective for social-ecological systems analyses. *Global Environmental Change* 16: 253–67.

Folke, Carl, Jr Lowell Pritchard, Fikret Berkes, Johan Colding, and Uno Svedin. 2007. The problem of fit between ecosystems and institutions: Ten years later. *Ecology and Society* 12 (1).

Folke, Carl, Thomas Hahn, Per Olsson, and Jon Norberg. 2005. Adaptive governance of social-ecological systems. *Annual Review of Environment and Resources* 30 (1): 441–73. https://doi.org/10.1146/annurev.energy.30.050504.144511.

Follett, Mary Parker [1924] 1951 *Creative Experience.* New York. Peter Smith.

Foucault, M. 1984. *The Foucault Reader.* New York: Pantheon Books.

Frack Tracker. 2018. Fracking Bans and Moratoria in New York State. www.fractracker.org/map/us/new-york/moratoria/.

French, Stanely G. 1967. Kant's constitutive-regulative distinction. *The Monist* 51 (4): 623–39.

Fresco, Louise O. 2009. Challenges for food system adaptation today and tomorrow. *Environmental Science and Policy* 12 (4): 378–85. https://doi.org/10.1016/j.envsci.2008.11.001.

Frey, B. S. 1997. *Not Just for the Money: An Economic Theory of Personal Motivation.* Brookfield, USA: Edward Elgar.

2012. Crowding out and crowding in of intrinsic preferences. In E. Brousseau, T. Dedeurwaerdere, and B. Siebenhüner, eds., *Reflexive Governance for Global Public Goods.* Cambridge, MA: MIT Press 75–83.

Frey, B. S., and R. Jegen. 2001. Motivation crowding theory: A survey of empirical evidence. *Journal of Economic Surveys* 15: 589–611.

Fritsch, Michael. 2014. *Marktversagen und Wirtschaftspolitik: Mikroökonomische Grundlagen staatlichen Handelns.* 9., vollst. überarb. Aufl. Vahlens Handbücher der Wirtschafts- und Sozialwissenschaften. München: Vahlen.

Galaz, Victor, Beatrice Crona, Henrik Österblom, Per Olsson, and Carl Folke. 2012. Polycentric systems and interacting planetary boundaries — Emerging governance of climate change–ocean acidification–marine biodiversity. *Ecological Economics* 81:21–32. https://doi.org/10.1016/j.ecolecon.2011.11.012.

Galusha, Diane. 1999. *Liquid Assests: A History of New York City's Water System.* Fleishmanns, New York: Purple Mountain Press.

Garmestani, Ahjond S., and Melinda Harm Benson. 2013. A framework for resilience-based governance of social-ecological systems. *Ecology & Society* 18 (1). https://doi.org/10.5751/ES-05180-180109.

Garrick, Dustin. 2015. *Water Allocation in Rivers under Pressure: Water Trading, Transaction Costs and Transboundary Governance in the Western US and Australia.* Cheltenham, UK: Edward Elgar.

Garrick, Dustin, and Bruce Aylward. 2012. Transaction costs and institutional performance in market-based environmental water allocation. *Land Economics* 88 (3): 536–60.

Garrick, Dustin, Edella Schlager, and Sergio Villamayor-Tomás. 2016. Governing an international transboundary river: Opportunism, safeguards, and drought adaptation in the Rio Grande. *Publius: The Journal of Federalism* 46 (2): 170–98.

Garrick, Dustin, and Erin O'Donnell. 2016. Exploring private roles in environmental watering in Australia and the US. In *Protecting the environment, privately*, 203–231. Singapore: World Scientific.

Garrick, D., Siebentritt, M. A., Aylward, B., Bauer, C. J., and Purkey, A. (2009). Water markets and freshwater ecosystem services: Policy reform and implementation in the Columbia and Murray-Darling Basins. *Ecological Economics*, 69(2): 366–79.

Garrick, Dustin, Stuart M. Whitten, and Anthea Coggan. 2013. Understanding the evolution and performance of water markets and allocation policy: A transaction costs analysis framework. *Ecological Economics* 88: 195–205. https://doi.org/10.1016/j.ecolecon.2012.12.010.

Garrido, Alberto. 2007. Water markets design and evidence from experimental economics. *Environmental and Resource Economics* 38 (3): 311–30.

Garrido, Alberto, and M Ramón Llamas. 2009. Water management in Spain: An example of changing paradigms. In A. Dinar and J. Albiac, eds., *Policy and Strategic Behaviour in Water Resource Management*. London: Earthscan. 125–46.

Gibson, Clark, Elinor Ostrom, and Ahn T. K. 2000. The concept of scale and the human dimensions of global change. *Ecological Economics* 32: 217–39.

Gibson-Graham, Julie Katherine. 2006. *A Postcapitalist Politics*. Minneapolis, MN: University of Minnesota Press.

Giffinger, Rudolf, and Johannes Suitner. 2014. Polycentric metropolitan development: From structural assessment to processual dimensions. *European Planning Studies* 1–18. https://doi.org/10.1080/09654313.2014.905007.

Giordano, Mark, and Tushaar Shah. 2014. From IWRM back to integrated water resources management. *International Journal of Water Resources Development* 30 (3): 364–76. https://doi.org/10.1080/07900627.2013.851521.

Glick, D., K. Ray, and T. Wood. 2016. Fractured, Part V: Trouble in Triple Creek. *The Colorado Independent*, 2 November 2016. www.coloradoindependent.com/162050/fractured-triple-creek-extraction-oil-and-gas.

Global Water Partnership. 2008. *Integrated Water Resources Management*. www.gwptoolbox.org/index.php?option=com_content&view=article&id=8&Itemid=3.

Golten, Ryan, Tabor Ward, and Kathryn Mutz. 2016. Stakeholder Assessment: Colorado Oil and Gas Development. Insights from the Field. Toward an Understanding of Industry-Community MOUs. www.oilandgasbmps.org/docs/CO189_MOU_Stakeholder_Assessment_2016.pdf

Goodin, Robert E. 1996. *The Theory of Institutional Design*. Cambridge UK; New York, NY, USA: Cambridge University Press.

Grimble, Robin, and Kate Wellard. 1997. Stakeholder methodologies in natural resource management: A review of principles, contexts, experiences and opportunities. *Agricultural Systems* 55 (2): 173–93.

Gruby, Rebecca L., and Xavier Basurto. 2014. Multi-level governance for large marine commons: Politics and polycentricity in Palau's protected area network. *Environmental Science & Policy* 36: 48–60. https://doi.org/10.1016/j.envsci.2013.08.001.

Grzymala-Busse, Anna. 2011. Time will tell? Temporality and the analysis of causal mechanisms and processes. *Comparative Political Studies* 44 (9): 1267–97. https://doi.org/10.1177/0010414010390653.

Gupta, Joyeeta, Catrien Termeer, Judith Klostermann, Sander Meijerink, Margo van den Brink, Pieter Jong, Sibout Nooteboom, and Emmy Bergsma. 2010. The adaptive capacity wheel: A method to assess the inherent characteristics of institutions to enable the adaptive capacity of society. *Environmental Science & Policy* 13 (6): 459–71. https://doi.org/10.1016/j.envsci.2010.05.006.

Haas, Peter M. 1993. Epistemic communities and the dynamics of international environmental co-operations. In Volker Rittberger, and Peter Mayer, eds., *Regime Theory and International Relations*. Oxford: Clarendon Press, 168–201.

Hagedorn, Konrad, ed. 2002. *Environmental Co-Operation and Institutional Change: Theories and Policies for European Agriculture. New Horizons in Environmental Economics*. Cheltenham UK: Edward Elgar.

  2008. Particular requirements for institutional analysis in nature-related sectors. *European Review of Agricultural Economics* 35 (4): 357–84.

  2015. Can the concept of integrative and segregative institutions contribute to the framing of institutions of sustainability? *Sustainability* 7 (1): 584–611. https://doi.org/10.3390/su7010584.

Hakim, D. 2012. Shift by Cuomo on Gas Drilling Prompts Both Anger and Praise. *New York Times*, 30 September 2012.

Hamilton, Alexander, John Jay, and James Madison. 2009. *The Federalist Papers*. www.gutenberg.org/files/1404/1404-h/1404-h.htm.

Hanlon, Jeffery Wyatt. 2015. Maintaining Robust Resource Governance: Mechanisms of Formal Institutional Change in a Federal Bargain. Electronic Dissertation, University of Arizona. http://hdl.handle.net/10150/577203.

Hardin, G. 1968. The tragedy of the commons. *Science* 162 (December 13): 1243–48.

Hardy, Scott D., and Tomas M. Koontz. 2008. Reducing nonpoint source pollution through collaboration: Policies and programs across the US states. *Environmental Management* 41 (3): 301–10.

Hauck, Jennifer, Christian Stein, Eva Schiffer, and Marie Vandewalle. 2015. Seeing the forest and the trees: Facilitating participatory network planning in environmental governance. *Global Environmental Change* 35: 400–10.

Hayek, Friedrich A. 1960. *The Constitutional of Liberty*. Chicago IL: University of Chicago Press.

Heater, D. B. (2004). *Citizenship: The Civic Ideal in World History, Politics and Education*. Manchester UK: Manchester University Press.

Heikkila, Tanya, and Christopher M. Weible. 2015. A Summary Report of a 2015 Survey of the Politics of Oil and Gas Development Using Hydraulic Fracturing in Colorado. www.ucdenver.edu/academics/colleges/SPA/researchandoutreach/SPA %20Institute/Centres/WOPPR/WOPPRresearch/natgasdev/Documents/CO% 20Stakeholder%20Report%202015%207-24-15.pdf.

— 2016. Contours of coalition politics on hydraulic fracturing within the United States of America. In Christopher M. Weible, Tanya Heikkila, K. Ingold, and Fischer M., eds., *Policy Debates on Hydraulic Fracturing*. New York: Palgrave Macmillan. 29–52.

— 2017. Unpacking the intensity of policy conflict: A study of Colorado's oil and gas subsystem. *Policy Sciences* 50 (2): 179–93.

— 2018. A semiautomated approach to analyzing polycentric governance. *Environmental Policy and Governance* 28(4): 308–18.

Heikkila, Tanya, Christopher M. Weible, and Jonathan J. Pierce. 2014. Exploring the policy narratives and politics of hydraulic fracturing in New York. In M. D. Jones, E. A. Shanahan, and M. K. McBeth, eds., *The Science of Stories*. New York: Palgrave Macmillan, 185–205.

Heikkila, Tanya, and Edella Schlager. 2012. Addressing the issues: The choice of environmental conflict-resolution venues in the United States. *American Journal of Political Science* 56 (4): 774–86.

Heikkila, Tanya, Edella Schlager, and Mark W. Davis. 2011. The role of cross-scale institutional linkages in common pool resource management: Assessing interstate river compacts. *Policy Studies Journal* 39 (1): 121–45.

Heikkila, Tanya, Jonathan J. Pierce, Samuel Gallahar, Jennifer Kagan Deserai, A. Crow, and Christopher M. Weible. 2014. Understanding a period of policy change: The case of hydraulic fracturing disclosure policy in Colorado. *Review of Policy Research* 31 (2): 65–87.

Heikkila, Tanya, Sergio Villamayor-Tomás, and Dustin Garrick. 2018. Bringing polycentric systems into focus for environmental governance. *Environmental Policy and Governance* 28 (4): 207–318.

Henry, A. D., Mark Lubell, and Michael McCoy. 2011. Belief systems and social capital as drivers of policy network structure: The case of California regional planning. *Journal of Public Administration Research and Theory* 21 (3): 419–44.

Hernandez Garcia, Alberto. 2014. Modernizacion de regadios, situacion actual y retos de futuro. *iagua*.

Hernández-Mora, Nuria, and Leandro Del Moral. 2015. Developing markets for water reallocation: Revisiting the experience of Spanish water mercantilización. *Geoforum* 62: 143–55.

Hernández-Mora, Nuria, and Lucia De Stefano. 2013. Los mercados informales de aguas en España: una primera aproximación. *ponencia presentada en las XVIII Jornadas de Derecho de Aguas Concesiones, autorizaciones y mercados de aguas, Zaragoza*.

Hirschleifer, Jack. 2001. *The Dark Side of the Force: Economic Foundations of Conflict Theory*. Cambridge, UK; New York: Cambridge University Press.

Hirschman, Albert O. 1970. *Exit, Voice, and Loyalty: Responses to Decline in Firms, Organizations, and States*. Cambridge, MA: Harvard University Press.

1971. Introduction: Political economics and possibilism. *A Bias for Hope: Essays on Development and Latin America.* New Haven, CT: Yale University Press.

1986. In defense of possibilism. In *Albert O. Hirschman, ed., Rival Views of Market Society and Other Recent Essays.* Cambridge, MA: Harvard University Press. 171–75.

Hodgson, Geoffrey M. 2004. *The Evolution of Institutional Economics.* New York: Routledge.

2010. Darwinian coevolution of organizations and the environment. *Ecological Economics* 69 (4): 700–06. https://doi.org/10.1016/j.ecolecon.2008.06.016.

Hooghe, Liesbet, and Gary Marks. 2003. Unraveling the central state, but how? Types of multi-level governance. *American Political Science Review* 97 (02): 233–43.

Horne, A., and E. O'Donnell. 2014. Decision making roles and responsibility for environmental water in the Murray-Darling Basin. *Australian Journal of Water Resources* 18 (2): 118–32.

Howell-Moroney, Michael. 2008. The Tiebout hypothesis 50 years later: Lessons and lingering challenges for metropolitan governance in the 21st century. *Public Administration Review* 68 (1): 97–109.

Huitema, Dave, Erik Mostert, Wouter Egas, Sabine Moellenkamp, Claudia Pahl-Wostl, and Resul Yalcin. 2009. Adaptive water governance: Assessing the institutional prescriptions of adaptive (co-)management from a governance perspective and defining a research agenda. *Ecology and Society* 14 (1).

Huntjens, Patrick, Claudia Pahl-Wostl, Benoit Rihoux, Maja Schlüter, Zsuzsanna Flachner, Susana Neto, Romana Koskova, Chris Dickens, and Isah Nabide Kiti. 2011. Adaptive water management and policy learning in a changing climate: a formal comparative analysis of eight water management regimes in Europe, Africa and Asia. *Environmental Policy and Governance* 21 (3): 145–63. https://doi.org/10.1002/eet.571.

Innes, Judith E., and David E. Booher. 2010. *Planning with Complexity: An Introduction to Collaborative Rationality for Public Policy.* New York: Routledge.

Ison, R., C. Blackmore, and B. L. Iaquinto. 2013. Towards systemic and adaptive governance: exploring the revealing and concealing aspects of contemporary social-learning metaphors. *Ecological Economics*, 87, 34–42.

Jensen, Olivia, and Xun Wu. 2016. Embracing uncertainty in policy-making: The case of the water sector. *Policy and Society* 35 (2): 115–23. https://doi.org/10.1016/j.polsoc.2016.07.002.

Jones, Candace, William S. Hesterly, and Stephen P. Borgatti. 1997. A general theory of network governance: Exchange conditions and social mechanisms. *Academy of Management Review* 22 (4): 911–45.

Jordan, Andrew, and Dave Huitema. 2014. Policy innovation in a changing climate: Sources, patterns and effects. *Global Environmental Change-Human and Policy Dimensions* 29: 387–94. https://doi.org/10.1016/j.gloenvcha.2014.09.005.

Jordan, Andrew J., Dave Huitema, Harro van Asselt, and Johanna Forster. 2018. *Governing Climate Change.* Cambridge University Press.

Jordan, Andrew J., Dave Huitema, Mikael Hildén, Harro van Asselt, Tim J. Rayner, Jonas J. Schoenefeld, Jale Tosun, Johanna Forster, and Elin L. Boasson. 2015.

Emergence of polycentric climate governance and its future prospects. *Nature Climate Change* 5 (11): 977–82. https://doi.org/10.1038/NCLIMATE2725.

Jupille, J., J. T. Checkel, and J. A. Caporaso. 2003. Integrating institutions: Rationalism, constructivism and the study of the European Union. *Comparative Political Studies* 36 (1/2): 7–40.

Kaplan, Thomas. 2014. Citing health risks, Cuomo bans fracking in New York state. *New York Times*, 17 December 2014.

Kauffman, Stuart. 1995. *At Home in the Universe: The Search for Laws of Self-Organization and Complexity*. Oxford University Press.

Kauffman, Stuart, and Simon Levin. 1987. Towards a general theory of adaptive walks on rugged landscapes. *Journal of theoretical Biology* 128 (1): 11–45.

Keast, Robyn, Myrna, P., Kerry Brown Mandell, and Geoffrey Woolcock. 2004. Network structures: Working differently and changing expectations. *Public Administration Review* 64 (3): 363–71.

Kendy, Eloise, Bruce Aylward, Laura S. Ziemer, Brian D. Richter, Bonnie G. Colby, Theodore E. Grantham, Leslie Sanchez, Will B. Dicharry, Emily M. Powell, and Season Martin. 2018. Water transactions for streamflow restoration, water supply reliability, and rural economic vitality in the western United States. *JAWRA Journal of the American Water Resources Association* 54 (2): 487–504.

Kerber, Heide. 2017. Marine Litter and the Commons: How Can Effective Governance Be Established? Biennial conference of the International Association for the Study of the Commons, July 10. Utrecht, the Netherlands.

Kerr, John. 2007. Watershed management: Lessons from common property theory. *International Journal of the Commons* 1 (1): 89–109.

Kiser, Larry L., and E. Ostrom. 1982. The three worlds of action: A metatheoretical synthesis of institutional approaches. In E. Ostrom, ed., *Strategies of Political Inquiry*. Beverly Hills, CA: SAGE Publications Limited, 179–222.

Kiparsky, Michael, Anita Milman, Dave Owen, and Andrew T. Fisher. 2017. The importance of institutional design for distributed local-level governance of groundwater: The case of California's Sustainable Groundwater Management Act. *Water* 9 (10): 755.

Kneese, Allen V. 1968. The problem shed as a unit for environmental control. *Archives of Environmental Health: An International Journal* 16 (1): 124–27.

Knieper, Christian, and Claudia Pahl-Wostl. 2016. A comparative analysis of water governance, water management, and environmental performance in river basins. *Water Resources Management* 30 (7): 2161–77. https://doi.org/10.1007/s11269-016-1276-z.

Knight, Jack. 1992. *Institutions and Social Conflict*. Cambridge: Cambridge University Press.

Koehler, Brandi, and Tomas M. Koontz. 2008. Citizen participation in collaborative watershed partnerships. *Environmental Management* 41 (2): 143–54. https://doi.org/10.1007/s00267-007-9040-z.

Konisky, David M. 2007. Regulatory competition and environmental enforcement: Is there a race to the bottom? *American Journal of Political Science* 51 (4): 853–72. https://doi.org/10.1111/j.1540-5907.2007.00285.x.

Koontz, Tomas M. 2004. *Collaborative Environmental Management: What Roles for Government?* Washington, DC: Resources for the Future.

2014. Social learning in collaborative watershed planning: The importance of process control and efficacy. *Journal of Environmental Planning and Management* 57 (10): 1572–93.

Koontz, Tomas M., and Craig Thomas. 2006. What do we know and need to know about the environmental outcomes of collaborative management? *Public Administration Review* 66 (6): 111–21.

2016. The Role of Science in Collaborative Environmental Management: Top Down and Bottom Up Efforts. Paper presented at Midwest Political Science Association annual meeting, April 8–10, Chicago.

Use of science in collaborative environmental management: Evidence from local watershed partnerships in the Puget Sound. *Environmental Science and Policy* 88: 17–23.

Koontz, Tomas M., Divya Gupta, Pranietha Mudliar, and Pranay Ranjan. 2015. Adaptive institutions in social-ecological systems governance: A synthesis framework. *Environmental Science & Policy* 53. https://doi.org/10.1016/j.envsci.2015.01.003.

Koontz, Tomas M., and Jens Newig. 2014. From planning to implementation: Top down and bottom up approaches for collaborative watershed management. *Policy Studies Journal* 42 (3): 416–42.

Koontz, Tomas M., JoAnn Carmin, Toddi A. Steelman, Craig Thomas, Katrina Smith Korfmacher, and Moseley Cassandra. 2004. *Collaborative Environmental Management: What Roles for Government?* Washington, D.C. Resources for the Future Press.

Koontz, Tomas M., and Sucharita Sen. 2013. Community responses to government defunding of watershed projects: A comparative study in India and the USA. *Environmental Management* 51 (3): 571–85.

Korfmacher, Katrina Smith. 1998. Invisible successes, visible failures: Paradoxes of ecosystem management in the Albemarle-Pamlico estuarine study. *Coastal Management* 26: 191–211.

Korhonen, J., and T. P. Seager. 2008. Beyond eco-efficiency: A resilience perspective. *Business Strategy and Management* 17 (7): 411–19.

Landau, Martin. 1969. Redundancy, rationality, and the problem of duplication and overlap. *Public Administration Review* 29 (4): 346. https://doi.org/10.2307/973247.

1973. Federalism, redundancy, and system reliability. *The Journal of Federalism* 3 (2): 173–96.

Lankford, Bruce, and Nick Hepworth. 2010. The cathedral and the bazaar: Monocentric and polycentric river basin management. *Water Alternatives* 3 (1): 82–101.

Lankford, Bruce A., Douglas J. Merrey, Julien Cour, and Nick Hepworth. 2007. *From Integrated to Expedient: An Adaptive Framework for River Basin Management in Developing Countries*. Colombo, Sri Lanka: International Water Management Institute.

Lawson, Tony. 2012. Ontology and the study of social reality: Emergence, organisation, community, power, social relations, corporations, artefacts and money. *Cambridge Journal of Economics* 36 (2): 345–85.

Leach, William D., and Neil W. Pelkey. 2001. Making watershed partnerships work: A review of the empirical literature. *Journal of Water Resources Planning and Management* 127 (6): 378–85. https://doi.org/10.1061/(ASCE)0733-9496(2001)127:6(378).

Lecina, S., D. Isidoro, E. Playán, and R. Aragüés. 2010. Irrigation modernization and water conservation in Spain: The case of Riegos del Alto Aragón. *Agricultural Water Management* 97 (10): 1663–75.

Lepenies, Philipp H. 2008. Possibilism: An approach to problem-solving derived from the life and work of Albert O. Hirschman. *Development and Change* 39 (3): 437–59.

Lesson, Peter T., and Peter J. Boettke. 2009. Two-tiered entrepreneurship and economic development. *International Review of Law and Economics* 29 (3): 252–59.

Levi, Margaret (2009) Reconsiderations of rational choice in comparative and historical analysis. In Lichbach, M. I., and Zuckerman, A. S., eds., (2007). *Comparative Politics: Rationality, Culture and Structure*. Cambridge, UK: Cambridge University Press.

Levi, Simon, ed. 2009. *The Princeton Guide to Ecology*. Princeton, NJ: Princeton University Press.

Levin, S. A. 1998. Ecosystems and the biosphere as complex adaptive systems. *Ecosystems* 1 (5): 431–36. www.scopus.com/inward/record.url?eid=2-s2.0-0000519269&partnerID=40&md5=3204204de11c8d57f167763bbcf73105.

Lieberman, Evan S. 2011. The perils of polycentric governance of infectious disease in South Africa. *Social Science & Medicine (1982)* 73 (5): 676–84. https://doi.org/10.1016/j.socscimed.2011.06.012.

Lin, J. Y. 1989. An economic theory of institutional change: Induced and imposed change. *Cato Journal* 9 (1): 1–33.

LIO 1. 2016. *Memo: A Proposal to Restructure*.

Loehman, Edna T, and Sasha Charney. 2011. Further down the road to sustainable environmental flows: Funding, management activities and governance for six western US states. *Water International* 36 (7): 873–93.

Low, Bobbi, E. Ostrom, and James Wilson. 2003. Redundancy and diversity: Do they influence optimal management? In Fikret Berkes, Johan Colding, and Carl Folke, eds., *Navigating Social-Ecological Systems: Building Resilience for Complexity and Change*. New York: Cambridge University Press, 83–114.

Lubell, Mark. 2004. Collaborative environmental institutions: All talk and no action? *Journal of Policy Analysis and Management* 23 (3): 549–73. https://doi.org/10.1002/pam.20026.

 2013. Governing institutional complexity: The ecology of games framework. *Policy Studies Journal* 41 (3): 537–59. https://doi.org/10.1111/psj.12028.

Lubell, Mark, A. D. Henry, and Mike McCoy. 2010. Collaborative Institutions in an ecology of games. *American Journal of Political Science* 54 (2): 287–300.

Lubell, Mark, Garry Robins, and Peng Wang. 2014. Network structure and institutional complexity in an ecology of water management games. *Ecology and Society* 19 (4).

Lurie, S., and M. Hibbard. 2008. Community-based natural resource management: Ideals and realities in Oregon watershed councils. *Society and Natural Resources: An International Journal* 21 (5): 430–40.

Mac Odell. *Appreciative Planning and Action: Mission Statement*. www.macodell.com/page-Appreciative-Planning.

Malik, A. 2013. Reconciliation between Muslims and Christians: Collective action, norm entrepreneurship, and 'A Common Word between Us'. *Journal of Religious Ethics* 41 (3): 457–73.

2017. Polycentricity and cultural diversity. In F. Sabetti, and D. Castiglione, eds., *Political Theory, Policy Analysis and Institutional Creativity: Extending the Work of the Bloomington School.* Lanham, MD: Lexington Books, 107–28

2018. *Polycentricity, Islam, and Development: Potentials and Challenges in Pakistan.* Lanham, MD: Lexington Books.

Margerum, Richard D. 2011. *Beyond Consensus: Improving Collaboration to Solve Complex Public Problems.* Cambridge, MA: MIT Press.

Marsh, David. 1992. *Policy Networks in British Government.* Oxford: Clarendon Press. www.gbv.de/dms/bowker/toc/9780198278528.pdf.

Marshall, G. R. 2002. Institutionalising cost sharing for catchment management: Lessons from land and water management planning in Australia. *Water, Science and Technology* 45 (11): 101–11.

2005. *Economics for Collaborative Environmental Management: Renegotiating the Commons.* London: Earthscan.

2008. Nesting, subsidiarity, and community-based environmental governance beyond the local level. *International Journal of the Commons* 2 (1): 75–97.

2009. Polycentricity, reciprocity, and farmer adoption of conservation practices under community-based governance. *Ecological Economics* 68 (5): 1507–20.

2010. Governance for a surprising world. In S. Cork, ed., *Resilience and Transformation: Preparing Australia for Uncertain Futures.* Melbourne: CSIRO Publishing, 49–57.

2011. What 'community' means for farmer adoption of conservation practices. In D. J. Pannell, and F. M. Vanclay, eds., *Changing Land Management: Adoption of New Practices by Rural Landholders.* Melbourne: CSIRO Publishing, 107–27.

2015. Polycentricity, subsidiarity and adaptive efficiency. A paper presented to the international workshop on polycentricity, Ostrom Workshop in Political Theory and Policy Analysis, Indiana University, Bloomington, Indiana USA, 14–17 December.

2017. Cost-effective environmental water for NSW wetlands and rivers. Final report to the NSW Environmental Trust. Armidale: University of New England.

Marshall, G. R., and D. M. Stafford Smith. 2010. Natural resources governance for the drylands of the Murray-Darling Basin. *The Rangeland Journal* 32 (3): 267–82.

Marshall, Graham R., D. W. Hine, and M. J. East. 2017. Can community-based governance strengthen citizenship in support of climate change adaptation? Testing insights from self-determination theory. *Environmental Science and Policy* 72: 1–9. https://doi.org/10.1016/j.environsci.2017.02.010.

Marshall, Graham R., Michael J. Coleman, Brian M. Sindel, Ian J. Reeve, and Peter J. Berney. 2016. Collective action in invasive species control, and prospects for community-based governance: The case of serrated tussock (Nassella trichotoma) in New South Wales, Australia. *Land Use Policy* 56: 100–11. https://doi.org/10.1016/j.landusepol.2016.04.028.

McCord, Paul, Jampel Dell'Angelo, Elizabeth Baldwin, and Tom Evans. 2016. Polycentric transformation in Kenyan water governance: A dynamic analysis of institutional and social-ecological change. *Policy Studies Journal.* https://doi.org/10.1111/psj.12168.

McCoy, Amy L., S. Rankin Holmes, and Brett A. Boisjolie. 2018. Flow restoration in the Columbia River Basin: An evaluation of a flow restoration accounting framework. *Environmental management* 61 (3): 506–19.

McGinnis, Michael. 1999a. *Polycentric Governance and Development*. Ann Arbor, MI: University of Michigan Press.

1999b. *Polycentricity and Local Public Economies: Readings from the Workshop in Political Theory and Policy Analysis*. Ann Arbor, MI: University of Michigan Press.

2000. *Polycentric Games and Institutions*. Ann Arbor, MI: University of Michigan Press.

2005a. Beyond individualism and spontaneity: Comments on Peter Boettke and Christopher Coyne. *Journal of Economic Behavior & Organization* 57 (2): 167–72. https://doi.org/10.1016/j.jebo.2004.06.014.

McGinnis, Michael D. 2005b. Costs and Challenges of Polycentric Governance. Workshop on Analyzing Problems of Polycentric Governance in the Growing EU, Berlin, June 16.

2011a. An introduction to IAD and the language of the Ostrom workshop: A simple guide to a complex framework. *Policy Studies Journal* 39 (1): 169–83. https://doi.org/10.1111/j.1541-0072.2010.00401.x.

2011b. Networks of adjacent action situations in polycentric governance. *Policy Studies Journal* 39 (1): 51–78.

2015. Elinor Ostrom: Politics as problem-solving in polycentric settings. In Cole, Daniel H., and Michael D. McGinnis, eds. 2015. *Elinor Ostrom and the Bloomington School of Political Economy*. Lanham, MD: Lexington Books, 281–306.

2016. Polycentric Governance in Theory and Practice: Dimensions of Aspiration and Practical Limitations. Paper presented at Ostrom Workshop, Indiana University, Bloomington.

McGinnis, Michael D., and Elinor Ostrom. 2012. Reflections on Vincent Ostrom, public administration, and polycentricity. *Public Administration Review* 72 (1): 15–25. https://doi.org/10.1111/j.1540-6210.2011.02488.x.

McPhail, Edward, and Vlad Tarko. 2017. The evolution of governance structures in a polycentric system. In Morris Altman, ed., *Handbook of Behavioral Economics and Smart Decision-Making: Rational Decision-Making within the Bounds of Reason*. Cheltenham, UK; Northampton, MA, USA: Edward Elgar, 290–313.

Milman, Anita, and Christopher A. Scott. 2010. Beneath the surface: Intranational institutions and management of the United States—Mexico transboundary Santa Cruz aquifer. *Environment and Planning C: Government and Policy* 28 (3) 528–51.

Milward, H. B., K. G. Provan, and B. A. Else. 1993. What does the hollow state look like? In B. Bozeman ed., *Public Management: The State of the Art*. San Francisco, CA: Jossey-Bass, 309–32.

MIMA. 2001. Real Decreto Legislativo 1/2001, de 20 de julio, por el que se aprueba el texto refundido de la Ley de Aguas. Ed, Boletín Oficial del Estado. Madrid: BOE.

MOA. 21 January 1997. *New York City Watershed Memorandum of Agreement*.

Mohamud, Abdirahman Mohamed, and Amina Abdulkadir M Nur. 2007. The Puntland Experience: A Bottom up Approach to Peace and State Building. Garowe, Puntland: Interpeace and the Puntland Development Research Center (chapter in forthcoming publication).

Moriarty, Patrick, Charles Batchelor, Peter Laban, and Hazem Fahmy. 2010. Developing a practical approach to light IWRM in the Middle East. *Water Alternatives* 3 (1): 122–36.

Morrison, Tiffany H., W. Neil Adger, Katrina Brown, Maria Carmen Lemos, Dave Huitema, and Terry P. Hughes. 2017. Mitigation and adaptation in polycentric systems: sources of power in the pursuit of collective goals. *Wiley Interdisciplinary Reviews: Climate Change* 8 (5).

Moschitz, Heidrun. 2009. Moving on-European organic farming movements between political action and self-reflection. *International Journal of Agricultural Resources, Governance and Ecology* 8 (5–6): 371–87.

Moss, Timothy. 2012. Spatial fit, from panacea to practice: Implementing the EU water framework directive. *Ecology and Society* 17 (3): 2.

Mueller, Dennis C. 2003. *Public Choice III*. Cambridge: Cambridge University Press. www.gbv.de/dms/bowker/toc/9780521815468.pdf.

Muro, Melanie, and P. Jeffrey. 2012. Time to talk? How the structure of dialog processes shape stakeholder learning in participatory water resources management. *Ecology and Society* 17 (1).

Myint, Tun. 2012. *Governing International Rivers: Polycentric Politics in the Mekong and the Rhine*. Cheltenham: Edward Elgar Publications.

Nagendra, Harini, and Elinor Ostrom. 2012. Polycentric governance of multifunctional forested landscapes. *International Journal of the Commons* 6 (2): 104–33.

NCDD. 2017. *NCDD Resource Center. National Conference on Dialogue and Deliberation.* http://ncdd.org/rc/

New York City Independent Budget Office. The Impact of Catskill/Delaware Filtration on Residential Water and Sewer Charges in New York City. www.ibo.nyc.ny.us/iboreports/waterreport.pdf.

Newig, Jens, Daniel Schulz, and Nicolas W. Jager. 2016. Disentangling puzzles of spatial scales and participation in environmental governance – the case of governance re-scaling through the European Water Framework Directive. *Environmental Management* 58 (6): 998–1014. https://doi.org/10.1007/s00267-016-0753-8.

Niskanen, William A. 1994. *Bureaucracy and Public Economics*. Aldershot, Hants, UK: Brookfield, VT, USA: Edward Elgar.

Norberg, Jon, and Graeme S. Cumming. 2008. *Complexity Theory for a Sustainable Future*. New York: Columbia University Press.

North, Douglass Cecil. 1990. *Institutions, Institutional Change and Economic Performance*. Cambridge: Cambridge University Press.

 1993. Institutions and credible commitment. *Journal of Institutional and Theoretical Economics* 149 (1): 11–23.

 1994. *Institutional Change: A Framework of Analysis Economic History*. Accessed: 10 October 10 2007. http://ideas.repec.org/p/wpa/wuwpeh/9412001.html#provider.

 2005. *Understanding the Process of Institutional Change*. Princeton, New Jersey: Princeton University Press.

O'Donnell, E., and D. Garrick. 2017. Defining success: A multi-criteria approach to guide evaluation and investment. In A. Horne, M. Stewardson, A. Webb, B. Richter, and M. Acreman., eds., *Water for the Environment*. Amsterdam: Elsevier, 625–45.

Oakerson, Ronald J. 1999. *Governing Local Public Economies: Creating the Civic Metropolis.* Oakland, CA: ICS Press.

Oakerson, Ronald, and Roger B. Parks. 1988. Citizen voice and public entrepreneurship: The organisational dynamic of a complex metropolitan county. *Publius: The Journal of Federalism* 18 (4): 91–112.

2011. The study of local public economies: Multi-organizational, multi-level institutional analysis and development. *Policy Studies Journal* 39 (1): 147–67. https://doi.org/10.1111/j.1541-0072.2010.00400.x.

Obinger, Herbert. 2015. Funktionalismus. In Georg Wenzelburger, and Reimut Zohlnhöfer, eds., *Handbuch Policy-Forschung.* Springer VS Handbuch. Wiesbaden: Springer VS, 35–54.

Olson, Mancur. 1965. *The Logic of Collective Action.* Cambridge, MA: Harvard University Press.

1994. *The Logic of Collective Action: Public Goods and the Theory of Groups.* Harvard University Press 1971, Reprinted.

Ostrom, Elinor. 1983. A public service industry approach to the study of local government structure and performance. *Policy and Politics* 11 (3): 313–41. https://doi.org/10.1332/030557383782628599.

1986. Multiorganizational arrangements and coordination: an application of institutional analysis. In F. X Kaufmann, Giandomenico Majone, and V. Ostrom, eds., *Guidance, Control, and Evaluation in the Public Sector.* Berlin: De Gruyter, 495–510.

1990. *Governing the Commons: The Evolution of Institutions for Collective Action.* Cambridge: Cambridge University Press.

1998. A behavioral approach to the rational choice theory of collective action. *American Political Science Review* 92 (1): 1–22.

1999. Polycentricity, complexity, and the commons. *The Good Society* 9 (2): 37–41.

2000. Crowding out citizenship. *Scandinavian Political Studies* 23 (1): 3–15.

2001. Vulnerability and Polycentric Governance Systems. *Newsletter of the International Human Dimensions Program on Global Environmental Change* 3: 2.

2002. *The Drama of the Commons.* Washington, DC: National Academies Press.

2005a. *Understanding Institutional Diversity.* Princeton: Princeton University Press.

2005b. Policies that crowd out reciprocity and collective action. In H. Gintis, S. Bowles, R. Boyd, and E. Fehr, eds., *Moral Sentiments and Material Interests: The Foundations of Cooperation in Economic Life.* Cambridge, MA: MIT Press, 253–75.

2007. Collective action theory. In Carles Boix, and Susan C. Stokes, eds., *The Oxford Handbook of Comparative Politics.* Oxford; New York: Oxford University Press.

2009. A general framework for analyzing sustainability of social-ecological systems. *Science* 325 (5939): 419–22. https://doi.org/10.1126/science.1172133.

2010. Beyond markets and states: Polycentric governance of complex economic systems. *American Economic Review* 100 (3): 641–72.

2011. Background on the institutional analysis and development framework. *Policy Stud Journal* 39 (1): 7–27. https://doi.org/10.1111/j.1541-0072.2010.00394.x.

2012. Nested externalities and polycentric institutions: Must we wait for global solutions to climate change before taking actions at other scales ? *Economic theory* 49 (2): 353–69.

2014a. A frequently overlooked precondition of democracy: citizens knowledgable about and engaged in collective action. In Cole, Daniel H., and Michael D. McGinnis, eds. 2014. *Elinor Ostrom and the Bloomington School of Political Economy, Volume 1: Polycentricity in Public Administration and Political Science*: Lanham, MD: Lexington Books, 337–52.

2014b. Developing a method for analyzing institutional change. In Cole, Daniel H., and Michael D. McGinnis, eds. 2014. *Elinor Ostrom and the Bloomington School of Political Economy, Volume 1: Polycentricity in Public Administration and Political Science*: Lanham, MD: Lexington Books. 281–316.

Ostrom, Elinor, Larry Schroeder, and Susan Wynne. 1993. Polycentric institutional arrangements. In E. Ostrom, L. Schroeder, and S. Wynne, eds., *Institutional Incentives and Sustainable Development* Boulder, CO: Westview Press, 107–123.

Ostrom, Elinor, Marco A. Janssen, and John M. Anderies. 2007. Introduction: Going beyond panaceas. *Proceedings of the National Academy of Sciences* 104 (39): 1517615176-8.

Ostrom, Elinor, Roy Gardner, and Jimmy Walker. 1994. *Rules, Games and Common-Pool Resources*. Ann Arbor: The University of Michigan Press.

Ostrom, Elinor, and Xavier Basurto. 2011. Crafting analytical tools to study institutional change. *Journal of Institutional Economics* 7 (03): 317–43. https://doi.org/10.1017/S1744137410000305.

Ostrom, Vincent. 1962. The water economy and its organization. *Natural Resources Journal* 2 (4): 55–73.

1972. *Polycentricity*. Paper presented at Annual Meeting of the American Political Science Association.

1980. Artisanship and Artifact. *Public Administration Review* 40 (4): 309–17.

1987. *The Political Theory of Compound Republic: Designing the American Experiment*, 3rd ed. Lanham, MD: Lexington Books.

1991a. *The Meaning of American Federalism: Constituting a Self-Governing Society*. San Francisco, CA: Institute for Contemporary Studies Press.

1991b. Polycentricity: The structural basis of self-governing systems. In *The Meaning of American Federalism: Constituting a Self-Governing Society*. San Francisco, CA: Institute for Contemporary Studies Press. 223–48.

1997. *The Meaning of Democracy and the Vulnerability of Democracies. A Response to Tocqueville's Challenge*. Ann Arbor: The University of Michigan Press.

1999a. Polycentricity (Part 1). In McGinnis, Michael. 1999. *Polycentricity and Local Public Economies: Readings from the Workshop in Political Theory and Policy Analysis*. Ann Arbor, MI: University of Michigan Press, 52–74.

1999b. Polycentricity (Part 2). In McGinnis, Michael. 1999. *Polycentricity and Local Public Economies: Readings from the Workshop in Political Theory and Policy Analysis*. Ann Arbor, MI: University of Michigan Press, 119–38.

2008a. *The Intellectual Crisis in American Public Administration*. 3rd edn. Tuscaloosa, USA: University of Alabama Press.

2008b. *The Political Theory of a Compound Republic: Designing the American Experiment*. Lanham, MD: Lexington Books.

2015. Executive leadership, authority relationships, and public entrepreneurship. In Cole, Daniel H., and Michael D. McGinnis, eds. 2015. *Elinor Ostrom and the Bloomington School of Political Economy*. Lanham, MD: Lexington Books, 217–32.

Ostrom, Vincent, Charles M. Tiebout, and Robert Warren. 1961. The organization of government in metropolitan areas: A theoretical inquiry. *American Political Science Review* 55 (4): 831–42.

Ostrom, Vincent, and Elinor Ostrom. 1999. Public goods and public choices. In McGinnis, Michael. 1999. *Polycentricity and Local Public Economies: Readings from the Workshop in Political Theory and Policy Analysis*. Ann Arbor, MI: University of Michigan Press, 75–106.

Paavola, Jouni. 2007. Institutions and Environmental Governance: A Reconceptualization. *Ecological Economics* 63 (1): 93–103.

Pacheco-Vega, Raúl. 2012. *Governing Wastewater: A Cross-Regional Analysis within the Lerma-Chapala River Basin in Mexico*. Canadian Association of Latin American and Caribbean Studies (CALACS) 2012 (May 18th–20th, 2012. Kelowna, BC, Canada)

2013. *Polycentric Water Governance in Mexico: Beyond the Governing-by-River-Basin-Council Model*: 1–30. Paper presented in the 2013 Meeting of the Latin American Studies Association Meeting. Washington, D.C. 29 May–June 1 2013.

Pahl-Wostl, Claudia. 2009. A conceptual framework for analysing adaptive capacity and multi-level learning processes in resource governance regimes. *Global Environmental Change-Human and Policy Dimensions* 19 (3): 354–65.

2015. *Water Governance in the Face of Global Change: From Understanding to Transformation*: Springer.

Pahl-Wostl, Claudia, Angela Arthington, Janos Bogardi, Stuart E. Bunn, Holger Hoff, Louis Lebel, Elena Nikitina, M. Palmer, L. N. Poff, K. Richards, and M. Schlüter M. 2013. Environmental flows and water governance: Managing sustainable water uses. *Current Opinion in Environmental Sustainability* 5 (3–4): 341–51.

Pahl-Wostl, Claudia, and Christian Knieper. 2014. The capacity of water governance to deal with the climate change adaptation challenge: Using fuzzy set qualitative comparative analysis to distinguish between polycentric, fragmented and centralized regimes. *Global Environmental Change* 29: 139–54. https://doi.org/10.1016/j.gloenvcha.2014.09.003.

Pahl-Wostl, Claudia, and Hare, M., 2004. Processes of social learning in integrated resources management. *Journal of Community and Applied Social Psychology* 14, 193–206.

Pahl-Wostl, Claudia, Louis Lebel, Christian Knieper, and Elena Nikitina. 2012. From applying panaceas to mastering complexity: Toward adaptive water governance in river basins. *Environmental Science & Policy* 23: 24–34.

Palomo-Hierro, Sara, José A Gómez-Limón, and Laura Riesgo. 2015. Water markets in Spain: performance and challenges. *Water* 7 (2): 652–78.

Parks, Roger B., and Ronald J. Oakerson. 2000. Regionalism, localism, and metropolitan governance: Suggestions from the research program on local public economies. *State & Local Government Review* 32 (3): 169–79.

Pascale, Richard, Jerry Sternin, and Monique Sternin. 2010. *The Power of Positive Deviance: How Unlikely Innovators Solve the World's Toughest Problems*: Brighton, MA: Harvard Press Business Review.

Pelletier, L. G., D. Baxter, and V. Huta. 2011. Personal autonomy and environmental sustainability. In Chirkov, V. I., R. M. Ryan, and K. M. Sheldon, eds. 2011. *Human Autonomy in Cross-Cultural Contexts: Perspectives on the Psychology of Agency, Freedom and Well-Being*. Dordrecht: Springer, 257–77.

Perez Picazo, Maria Teresa, and Guy Lemeunier. 2000. Formation et mise en cause du modèle de gestion hydraulique espagnol de 1780 a 2000. *Economies et Sociétés* no. Hors-Série:85.

Peters, B. Guy. 2015. *Pursuing Horizontal Management: The Politics of Public Sector Coordination*. Lawrence, KS: University Press of Kansas.

Peters, B. Guy, and Jon Pierre. 2004. Multi-level governance and democracy: A Faustian bargain? In Ian Bache, and Matthew V. Flinders, eds., *Multi-Level Governance*. Oxford; New York: Oxford University Press, 75–89.

Pierce, Jonathan J., Jennifer Kagan, Tanya Heikkila, Christopher M. Weible, and Samuel Gallahar. 2013. *A Summary Report of Perceptions of the Politics and Regulation of Hydraulic Fracturing in Colorado*. Denver, CO: University of Colorado.

Pierson, Paul. 2000. The limits of design: Explaining institutional origins and change. *Governance* 13 (4): 475–99. https://doi.org/10.1111/0952-1895.00142.

Platt, R. H., P. K. Barten, and M. J. Pfeffer. 2010. A full, clean glass? Managing New York City's watershed. *Environment: Science and Policy for Sustainable Development* 42 (5): 8–20.

Polanyi, Karl. 1953. *Semantics of General Economic History (Revised)*. New York: Colombia University Press.

Polanyi, Michael. 1951. *The Logic of Liberty*. Chicago, IL: University of Chicago Press. 1964. *Science, Faith, and Society*. Chicago, IL: University of Chicago Press.

Postel, Sandra, and Stephen Carpenter. 1997. Freshwater ecosystem services. In Daily, Gretchen C., ed., *Nature's Services: Societal Dependence on Natural Ecosystems*. Washington DC: Island Press, 195–214.

Poteete, A. R., M. A. Janssen, and E. Ostrom. 2010. *Working Together: Collective Action, the Commons, and Multiple Methods in Practice*. Princeton: Princeton University Press.

Poussard, H. (ed.) 1992. Community Landcare to test government policies and programs. In *Proceedings of the seventh International Soil Conservation conference: People protecting their land*. Sydney, Australia, April 10, 1992.

Prell, Christina, Klaus Hubacek, and Mark Reed. 2009. Stakeholder analysis and social network analysis in natural resource management. *Society and Natural Resources* 22 (6): 501–18.

Pressman, Jeffrey L., and Aaron B. Wildavsky. 1984. *Implementation: How Great Expectations in Washington are Dashed in Oakland: Or Why It's Amazing that Federal Programs Work at All, This Being a Saga of the Economic Development Administration as Told by Two Sympathetic Observers Who Seek to Build Morals on a Foundation of Ruined Hopes*. California: University of California Press.

Prokopy, Linda Stalker, Nathan Mullendore, Kathryn Brasier, and Kristin Floress. 2014. A typology of catalyst events for collaborative watershed management in the United States. *Society & Natural Resources* 27 (11): 1177–91. https://doi.org/10.1080/08941920.2014.918230.

Puget Sound Partnership. 2014. Briefing Memo: LIO Organization History. Puget Sound Partnership, Tacoma, Washington DC.

2016. *Puget Sound Partnership Understanding of the Value of Local Integrating Organizations Regarding LIO Ecosystem Recovery Plans.*

2017. State of the Sound 2017. Olympia, Washington. November 2017. www.psp.wa.gov/so

Purdy, J. M. 2012. A framework for assessing power in collaborative governance processes. *Public Administration Review* 72 (3): 409–17.

Quiggin, J. 2011. Why the guide to the proposed basin plan failed, and what can be done to fix it. In J. Quiggin, T. Mallawaarachchi, and S. Chambers, eds., *Water Policy Reform: Lessons in Sustainability from the Murray-Darling Basin.* Cheltenham, UK: Edward Elgar.

Rada, J. 2007. Managing Garfield County's Air Quality: 2008 Air Monitoring Proposal. *Garfield County.*

Rajagopalan, Shruti. 2013. Economic Analysis of Amendments to the Indian Constitution. Economics Department, George Mason University. http://hdl.handle.net/1920/8223.

Rajagopalan, Shruti, and Richard E Wagner. 2013. Constitutional craftsmanship and the rule of law. *Constitutional Political Economy* 24 (4): 295–309.

Rast, J. (2012). Why history (still) matters: Time and temporality in urban political analysis. *Urban Affairs Review* 48 (1): 3–36. https://doi.org/10.1177/1078087411418178

Ratner, Blake D., and William E. Smith. 2014. Collaborating for Resilience: A Practitioner's Guide. Manual. *Collaborating for Resilience.*

Rayner, Tim, and Andrew Jordan. 2013. The European Union: The polycentric climate policy leader? *WIREs Climate Change* 4 (2): 75–90. https://doi.org/10.1002/wcc.205.

Reed, Mark S., Anil Graves, Norman Dandy, Helena Posthumus, Klaus Hubacek, Joe Morris, Christina Prell, Claire H. Quinn, and Lindsay C. Stringer. 2009. Who's in and why? A typology of stakeholder analysis methods for natural resource management. *Journal of Environmental Management* 90 (5): 1933–49.

Reeve, I., G. R. Marshall, and W. Musgrave. 2002. Resource Governance and Integrated Catchment Management. Issues Paper no. 2 for Murray-Darling Basin Commission project MP2004.

Regional Implementation Working Group of the NRM Ministerial Council. 2005. Regional delivery of natural resource management - Moving forward. NRM Ministerial Council, Canberra.

Richter, Brian D., and Gregory A. Thomas. 2007. Restoring environmental flows by modifying dam operations. *Ecology and Society* 12 (1): 12.

Rinfret, Sara, Jeffrey Cook, and Michelle Pautz. 2014. Understanding state rulemaking processes: Developing fracking rules in Colorado, New York, and Ohio. *Review of Policy Research* 31 (2): 88–104.

Rixen, T., & Viola, L. A. (2015). Putting path dependence in its place: Toward a taxonomy of institutional change. *Journal of Theoretical Politics* 27(2): 301–23.

Rodriguez, C. 2014. Negotiating conflict through federalism: Institutional and popular perspectives. *Yale Law Journal* 124: 2094.

Roe, Emery, and Paul R. Schulman. 2008. *High Reliability Management: Operating on the Edge*. (High Reliability and Crisis Management). Stanford, CA. Stanford Business Books, an imprint of Stanford University Press.

Rust, Joshua. 2006. *John Searle and the Construction of Social Reality*. London: Continuum.

Ryan, C. M., and J. S. Klug. 2005. Collaborative watershed planning in Washington State: Implementing the Watershed Planning Act. *Journal of Environmental Planning and Management* 48 (4): 491–506.

Ryan, R. M., and E. L. Deci. 2011. A self-determination theory perspective on social, institutional, cultural, and economic supports for autonomy and their importance for well-being. In Chirkov, V. I., R. M. Ryan, and K. M. Sheldon, eds. 2011. *Human Autonomy in Cross-Cultural Contexts: Perspectives on the Psychology of Agency, Freedom and Well-Being*. Dordrecht: Springer, 45–64.

Ryan, S., K. Broderick, Y. Sneddon, and K. Andrews. 2010. Australia's NRM governance system: Foundations and principles for meeting future challenges. Australian Regional NRM Chairs, Canberra

Sabatier, Paul A., and Christopher M. Weible. 2016. The advocacy coalition framework: Innovations and clarifications. In P. A. Sabatier, ed., *Theories of the Policy Process*, 2nd edn., New York: Routledge, 189–217.

Sabatier, Paul A., Will Focht, Mark Lubell, Zev Trachtenberg, Arnold Vedlitz, and Marty Matlock. 2005. *Swimming Upstream: Collaborative Approaches to Watershed Management*: Cambridge, MA: MIT Press.

Sabetti, Filippo, Barbara Allen, and Mark Sproule-Jones. 2009. *The Practice of Constitutional Development: Vincent Ostrom's Quest to Understand Human Affairs*. Lanham, MD: Lexington Books.

Sabetti, Filippo, and Dario Castiglione, eds. 2017. *Institutional Diversity in Self-Governing Societies: The Bloomington School and Beyond*. Lanham, MD: Lexington Books.

Salter, Alexander William, and Vlad Tarko. 2017. Polycentric banking and macroeconomic stability. *Business and Politics* 19 (02): 365–95. https://doi.org/10.1017/bap.2016.10.

Sarker, Ashutosh. 2013. The role of state-reinforced self-governance in averting the tragedy of the irrigation commons in Japan. *Public Administration* 91(3): 727–43.

Sayles, Jesse S., and Jacopo A. Baggio. 2017. Social-ecological network analysis of scale mismatches in estuary watershed restoration. *Proceedings of the National Academy of Sciences of the United States of America* 114 (10): E1776–E1785. https://doi.org/10.1073/pnas.1604405114.

Schafer, Josephine Gatti. 2016. Mandates to coordinate: The case of the Southern Nevada Public Lands Management Act. *Public Performance & Management Review* 40 (1): 23–47. https://doi.org/10.1080/15309576.2016.1177555.

Schiffer, Eva, and Jennifer Hauck. 2010. Net-Map: Collecting social network data and facilitating network learning through participatory influence network mapping. *Field Methods* 22 (3): 231–49.

Schlager, Edella. 2005. Getting the relationships right in water property rights. In Bryan Bruns, Claudia Ringler, and Ruth Meinzen-Dick, eds., *Water Rights Reform: Lessons for Institutional Design*. Washington DC: IFPRI, 27–54.

Schlager, Edella, Tanya Heikkila, and Carl Case. 2012. The costs of compliance with interstate agreements: lessons from water compacts in the Western United States. *Publius: The Journal of Federalism* 42 (3): 494–515.

Schlager, Edella, and William Blomquist. 2008. *Embracing Watershed Politics*. Boulder, CO: University Press Colorado.

Schlager, Edella, William Blomquist, and Shui Yan Tang. 1994. Mobile flows storage and self-organized institutions for governing common-pool resources. *Land Economics* 70 (3): 294–317.

Schlüter, Achim. 2001. *Institutioneller Wandel und Transformation: Restitution, Transformation und Privatisierung in der tschechischen Landwirtschaft*. Aachen: Shaker.

Schmid, Alfred Allan. 2004. *Conflict and Cooperation: Institutional and Behavioral Economics*. Malden, MA: Blackwell. www.loc.gov/catdir/toc/ecip048/2003018398.html.

Schneider, Mark. 1989. Intercity competition and the size of the local public work force. *Public Choice* 63 (3): 253–65.

Scott, Tyler A. 2016. Analyzing policy networks using valued exponential random graph models: do government-sponsored collaborative groups enhance organizational networks? *Policy Studies Journal* 44 (2): 215–44.

Scott, Tyler A., and Craig Thomas. 2015. Do Collaborative Groups Enhance Interorganizational Networks? *Policy Studies Journal* 38 (4): 654–83.

Searle, John. 1995. *The Construction of Social Reality*. New York: Free Press.

2003. Social ontology and political power. In F. F. Schmitt, ed., *Socializing Metaphysics: The Nature of Social Reality*. Oxford: Rowman & Littlefield, 195–210

2005. What is an Institution? *Journal of Institutional Economics* 1 (1): 1–22.

2006. Social ontology: Some principles. *Anthropological Theory* 6 (1): 12–29.

2010. *Making the Social World: The Structure of Human Civilization*. New York: Oxford University Press.

Sen, Amartya. 2000. *Development as Freedom*: New York: Anchor Books.

Shaffer, Austin, Skylar Zilliox, and Jessica Smith. 2014. Memoranda of understanding and the social license to operate in Colorado's unconventional energy industry: A study of citizen complaints. *Journal of Energy and Natural Resources Law*, 1–42.

Shackelford, Scott. 2014. *Managing Cyber Attacks in International Law, Business, and Relations: In Search of Cyber Peace*. New York: Cambridge University Press.

Shivakumar, S. 2005. *The Constitution of Development: Crafting Capabilities for Self-Governance*. New York: Palgrave Macmillan.

da Silveira, André R., and Keith S. Richards. 2013. The link between polycentrism and adaptive capacity in river basin governance systems: Insights from the River Rhine and the Zhujiang (Pearl River) Basin. *Annals of the Association of American Geographers* 103 (2): 319–29. https://doi.org/10.1080/00045608.2013.754687

Simonelli, Jeanne. 2014. Home rule and natural gas development in New York: Civil fracking rights. *Journal of Political Ecology* 21 (1): 258–78.

Smaldino, P. E., and M. Lubell. 2011. An institutional mechanism for assortment in an ecology of games. *PLoS ONE* 6 (8). www.scopus.com/inward/record.url?eid=2-s2.0-79961158100&partnerID=40&md5=37d2a30be789640853ea7a500b3c4422.

Snohomish Camano. 2015. *ECO Net Quarterly Meeting Notes.*

Soll, David. 2013. *Empire of Water: An Environmental and Political History of the New York City Water Supply.* Ithaca, New York: Cornell University Press.

Sovacool, Benjamin K. 2011. An international comparison of four polycentric approaches to climate and energy governance. *Energy Policy* 39 (6): 3832–44. https://doi.org/10.1016/j.enpol.2011.04.014.

Spreng, Connor P., Benjamin K. Sovacool, and Daniel Spreng. 2016. All hands on deck: Polycentric governance for climate change insurance. *Climatic Change* 139 (2): 129–40. https://doi.org/10.1007/s10584-016-1777-z.

Sproule-Jones, Mark, Barbara Allen, Filippo Sabetti, Stephan Kuhnert, Brian Loveman, Anas Malik, Michael D. McGinnis, Tun Myint, Vincent Ostrom, and Jamie Thomson. 2008. *The Struggle to Constitute and Sustain Productive Orders: Vincent Ostrom's Quest to Understand Human Affairs.* Lanham, MD: Lexington Books. http://site.ebrary.com/lib/alltitles/docDetail.action?docID=10774665.

Steins, Nathalie A., and Victoria M. Edwards. 1998. Platforms for Collective Action in Multiple-Use CPRs. Paper presented at Crossing Boundaries, the seventh annual conference of the International Association for the Study of Common Property.

Susskind, Larry, and J. L. Cruikshank. 1987. *Breaking the Impasse: Consensual Approaches to Resolving Public Disputes.* New York: Basic Books.

Sydow, Jörg, Georg Schreyögg, and Jochen Koch. 2009. Organizational path dependence: Opening the black box. *Academy of Management Review* 34 (4): 689–709.

Tam-Kim, Yong, Pakping Uravian, and Bruns Chalad, eds. 2003. *The Emergence of Polycentric Water Governance in Northern Thailand (Revised)* 1. Oxford University Press.

Tang, Shui Yan. 1992. *Institutions and Collective Action: Self-Governance in Irrigation.* San Francisco, CA: ICS Press.

Tarko, Vlad. 2017. *Elinor Ostrom: An Intellectual Biography.* London, New York: Rowman & Littlefield International.

Tarlock, A. Dan. 2001. The future of prior appropriation in the new west. *Natural Resources Journal* 41 (4):769–93.

Theesfeld, Insa. 2005. *A Common Pool Resource in Transition: Determinants of Institutional Change for Bulgaria's Postsocialist Irrigation Sector.* Aachen: Shaker Verlag. www.gbv.de/dms/bsz/toc/bsz120714744inh.pdf.

Thelen, Kathleen. 2000. Timing and temporality in the analysis of institutional evolution and change. *Studies in American Political Development* 14(1), 101–108. https://doi.org/10.1017/S0898588X00213035.

———. 2003. How institutions evolve – insights from comparative historical analysis. In J. Mahoney, and D. Rueschemeyer, eds., *Comparative Historical Analysis in the Social Sciences.* Cambridge, MA: Cambridge University Press, 208–40.

Thiel, Andreas. 2010a. Institutions shaping coastal ecosystems: The Algarve case. *Coastal Management* 38: 2, 144–64. https://doi.org/10.1080/08920751003605027.

———. 2010b. Constructing a strategic, national resource: European policies and the up-scaling of water services in the Algarve, Portugal. *Environmental Management* 46 (1): 44–59. https://doi.org/10.1007/s00267-010-9498-y.

———. 2012. *Developing Institutional Economics for the Analysis of Social-Ecological Systems.* Berlin: Humboldt-Universität zu Berlin.

2014. Rescaling of resource governance as institutional change: Explaining the transformation of water governance in Southern Spain. *Environmental Policy and Governance* 24(4). https://doi.org/10.1002/eet.1644.

2015. Constitutional state structure and scalar re-organization of natural resource governance: The transformation of polycentric water governance in Spain, Portugal and Germany. *Land Use Policy* 45: 176–88. https://doi.org/10.1016/j.landusepol.2015.01.012.

2016. *The Polycentricity Approach and the Research Challenges Confronting Environmental Governance: THESys Discussion Paper No. 2016-1.* Berlin.

2017. The scope of polycentric governance analysis and resulting challenges. *Journal of Self-Governance and Management Economics* 5 (3): 52–82.

Thiel, Andreas, and Christine Moser. 2018. Toward comparative institutional analysis of polycentric social-ecological systems governance. *Environmental Policy and Governance* 28 (4): 269–83. https://doi.org/10.1002/eet.1814.

Thiel, Andreas, Christian Schleyer, Jochen Hinkel, Maja Schlüter, Konrad Hagedorn, Sandy Bisaro, Ihtiyor Bobojonov, and Ahmad Hamidov. 2016. Transferring Williamson's discriminating alignment to the analysis of environmental governance of social-ecological interdependence. *Ecological Economics* 128: 159–68. https://doi.org/10.1016/j.ecolecon.2016.04.018.

Thiel, Andreas, Farhad Mukhtarov, and Dimitrios Zikos. 2015. Crafting or designing? Science and politics for purposeful institutional change in Social–Ecological Systems. *Environmental Science & Policy* 53: 81–86. https://doi.org/10.1016/j.envsci.2015.07.018.

Thiel, Andreas, and Mukhtarov, Farhad. 2018. Institutional design for adaptive governance of natural resource governance: How do we cater for context and agency? In Terry Marsden, ed., *The SAGE Handbook of Nature*, 1st edn. London: Sage Publications, 143–60.

Thomas, Craig W. 2002. *Bureaucratic Landscapes: Interagency Cooperation and the Preservation of Biodiversity.* Cambridge, Mass: MIT Press.

Tiebout, Charles M. 1956. A pure theory of local expenditures. *Journal of Political Economy* 64 (5): 416–24.

Tocqueville, A. de. 2003. *Democracy in America.* Washington, DC: Regnery Publishing.

Tomasello, Michael. 2009. *Why We Cooperate.* Cambridge, MA: MIT Press.

Toonen, Theo A. J. 1983. Administrative plurality in a unitary state: The analysis of public organizational pluralism. *Policy & Politics* 11: (3) 247–71.

Trampusch, Christine, and Bruno Palier. 2016. Between X and Y: How process tracing contributes to opening the black box of causality. *New Political Economy* 21 (5): 437–54. https://doi.org/10.1080/13563467.2015.1134465.

Tsebelis, George. 2002. *Veto Players: How Political Institutions Work.* New York, Princeton: Russell Sage Foundation; Princeton University Press. www.jstor.org/stable/10.2307/j.ctt7rvv7.

Tullock, Gordon. 2005. *The Social Dilemma: Of Autocracy, Revolution, Coup d'Etat, and War.* Indianapolis: Liberty Fund.

Tullock, Gordon, Arthur Seldon, and Gordon L. Brady. 2002. *Government Failure: A Primer in Public Choice.* Washington, DC: Cato Institute.

U.S. Energy Information Administration. 2018. Colorado State Profile and Energy Estimates: Profile Analysis. *US Energy Information Administration.*

Ulibarri, Nicola. 2015. Collaboration in federal hydropower licensing: Impacts on process, outputs, and outcomes. *Public Performance and Management Review* 38 (4): 578–606.

United States Advisory Commission on Intergovernmental Relations. 1987. The Organization of Local Public Economies. Report A-109.

Van Riper, C. J., A. Thiel, M. Penker, M. Braito, A. C. Landon, and J. M. Thomsen 2018 Incorporating multi-level values into the social-ecological systems framework. *Ecology and Society* 23 (3): 25.

van Zeben, Josephine A. W. 2013. Research Agenda for a Polycentric European Union. Working Paper Series W13–13.

Vanberg, Viktor, and Wolfgang Kerber. 1994. Institutional competition among jurisdictions: An evolutionary approach. *Constitutional Political Economy* 5 (2): 193–219. https://doi.org/10.1007/BF02393147.

Varvasovszky, Zsuzsa, and Ruair Brugha. 2000. How to do (or not to do) ... A stakeholder analysis. *Health Policy and Planning* 15 (3): 338–45.

Vatn, A. 2002. Multifunctional agriculture: Some consequences for international trade regimes. *European Review of Agricultural Economics* 29 (3): 309–27.

2005. *Institutions and the Environment.* Cheltenham: Edward Elgar.

Villamayor-Tomás, Sergio. 2014a. Adaptive irrigation management in drought contexts: Institutional robustness and cooperation in the Riegos del Alto Aragon project (Spain). In Anik Bhaduri, Janos Boardi, Jan Leentvar, and Sina Marx, eds., *The Global Water System in the Anthropocene.* New York: Springer, 197–215.

2014b. Cooperation in common property regimes under extreme drought conditions: Empirical evidence from the use of pooled transferable quotas in Spanish irrigation systems. *Ecological Economics* 107: 482–93. doi: http://dx.doi.org/10.1016/j.ecolecon.2014.09.005

2018. Polycentricity in the water-energy nexus: A comparison of polycentric governance traits and implications for adaptive capacity of water user associations in Spain. *Environmental Policy and Governance* 28: 252–68.

Vousden, David. 2016. Local to regional polycentric governance approaches within the Agulhas and Somali current large marine ecosystems. *Environmental Development* 17:277–86. https://doi.org/10.1016/j.envdev.2015.07.008.

Wagner, Richard E. 2005. Self-governance, polycentrism, and federalism: Recurring themes in Vincent Ostrom's Scholarly Oeuvre. *Journal of Economic Behaviour & Organization* 57 (2): 173–88.

Walker, B. H. 1992. Biodiversity and ecological redundancy. *Conservation Biology* 6 (1): 18–23.

Walt, G., Shiffman, J., Schneider, H., Murray, S. F., Brugha, R., & Gilson, L. (2008). 'Doing' health policy analysis: Methodological and conceptual reflections and challenges. *Health Policy and Planning* 23(5): 308–17.

War Torn Societies Project. 2005. *Rebuilding Somaliland: Issues and Possibilities.* Lawrenceville, N J: Red Sea Press.

Washington State Dept of Ecology. (n.d.) Watershed plan archive. https://ecology.wa.gov/Water-Shorelines/Water-supply/Streamflow-restoration/Watershed-plan-archive (accessed 4/8/2018)

Wegerich, K. 2007. Against the conventional wisdom: Why sector reallocation of water and multi-stakeholder platforms do not take place in Uzbekistan. Multi-stakeholder platforms for integrated water management. In J. Warner, ed., *Multi-Stakeholder Platforms for Integrated Water Management*. Bodmin, UK: Ashgate, 235–44.

Weible, Christopher M., and Tanya Heikkila. 2016. Comparing the politics of hydraulic fracturing in New York, Colorado, and Texas. *Review of Policy Research* 33 (3): 232–50.

2017. Policy conflict framework. *Policy Sciences* 50 (1): 23–40.

Weisbord, M. R., and S. Janoff. 2007. *Don't Just Do Something Stand There! Ten Principles for Leading Meetings that Matter*. Oakland, CA: Berrett-Koehler Publishers.

Weller, M., and S. Wolff. 2005. *Autonomy, Self-Governance and Conflict Resolution: Innovative Approaches to Institutional Design in Divided Societies*. New York: Routledge.

Wheeler, S. A., D. H. MacDonald, and P. Boxall. 2017. Water policy debate in Australia: Understanding the tenets of stakeholders' social trust. *Land Use Policy* (63): 246–54.

Wibbels, Erik. 2005. *Federalism and the Market: Intergovernmental Conflict and Economic Reform in the Developing World*. New York: Cambridge University Press.

Williamson, Oliver E. 1985. *The Economic Institutions of Capitalism*. New York, NY: Free Press.

1991. Comparative economic organization: The analysis of discrete structural alternatives. *Administrative Science Quarterly* 36: 269–96.

Wolf, J., K. Brown, and K. Conway. 2009. Ecological citizenship and climate change: Perceptions and practice. *Environmental Politics* 18 (4): 503–21.

Woodhouse, P., and M. Muller. 2017. Water governance – an historical perspective on current debates. *World Development* 92: 225–41. https://doi.org/10.1016/j.worlddev.2016.11.014.

World Bank. 2003. World Bank Water Resources Sector Strategy: Strategic Directions for World Bank Engagement. Washington, DC: World Bank.

Yaffee, S. L., and J. M. Wondolleck. 2003. Collaborative ecosystem planning processes in the United States: Evolution and challenges. *Environments* 31 (2): 59–72.

Young, Oran Reed. 2002. *The Institutional Dimensions of Environmental Change: Fit, Interplay, and Scale*. Cambridge, MA; London: MIT Press.

Zulkafli, Zed, Katya Perez, Claudia Vitolo, Wouter Buytaert, Timothy Karpouzoglou, Art Dewulf, Bert de Bievre, Julian Clark, David M. Hannah, and Simrita Shaheed. 2017. User-driven design of decision support systems for polycentric environmental resources management. *Environmental Modelling & Software* 88: 58–73.

Index